MAKING THE
Common Core Standards Work

D1521797

CORWIN
A SAGE Company

MAKING THE
Common Core Standards Work

Using Professional Development to Build World-Class Schools

ROBERT J. MANLEY • RICHARD J. HAWKINS

Foreword by DAN DOMENECH

CORWIN
A SAGE Company

CORWIN
A SAGE Company

FOR INFORMATION

Corwin
A SAGE Company
2455 Teller Road
Thousand Oaks, California 91320
(800) 233-9936
www.corwin.com

SAGE Publications Ltd.
1 Oliver's Yard
55 City Road
London, EC1Y 1SP
United Kingdom

SAGE Publications India Pvt. Ltd.
B 1/I 1 Mohan Cooperative Industrial Area
Mathura Road, New Delhi 110 044
India

SAGE Publications Asia-Pacific Pte. Ltd.
3 Church Street
#10-04 Samsung Hub
Singapore 049483

Acquisitions Editor: Arnis Burvikovs
Associate Editor: Desirée A. Bartlett
Editorial Assistant: Kim Greenberg
Production Editor: Veronica Stapleton
Copy Editor: Pam Schroeder
Typesetter: Hurix Systems Pvt. Ltd
Proofreader: Dennis W. Webb
Indexer: Jean Casalegno
Cover Designer: Michael Dubowe
Permissions Editor: Karen Ehrmann

Printed in the United States of America

Library of Congress Cataloging-in-Publication Data

A catalog record of this book is available from the Library of Congress.

9781452258577

This book is printed on acid-free paper.

Certified Chain of Custody
SUSTAINABLE FORESTRY INITIATIVE
Promoting Sustainable Forestry
www.sfiprogram.org
SFI-01268

SFI label applies to text stock

12 13 14 15 16 10 9 8 7 6 5 4 3 2 1

Contents

Dedication

We would like to thank Kay Manley and Sue Hawkins for their love, support, and infinite patience throughout the process of writing this book.

Bob dedicates this book to Kathryn and his children, Michael and Linda Schechter Manley, and their children, Zachary, Heather, Ethan, and Tyler and to Patrick and Barbara Harrison Manley, and their children, Jillian and Ryan. They and their cohorts are the future of our nation and our global society. We spent many hours in this labor of love in hopes that we could make a difference in the lives of teachers and students. We learned school leaders and teachers need the same caring, loving, and demanding family that children need. Much of what we propose in this book relies upon trust in each other as professionals who see our own fallibility and vulnerability as we try to improve learning for all children.

Rich dedicates this book to his wife Sue, his daughter Jacqui, son Bob and his lovely wife Jess, and my beautiful, bright, and loving grandchildren Jack, Camryn, and Jamison. The truth be told, having grandchildren just entering or about to enter our public schools was a very real motivator for writing this book. We hope this book reveals new pathways for educational leaders and teachers in the United States to succeed where others have failed. We hope they defy gravity and inertia and use the Common Core State Standards (CCSS) as an opportunity to discuss and challenge all of the political hyperbole and the preconceived notions about education that our nation holds. We hope that they integrate the common core standards into their daily lessons and develop world-class schools systemically. Our nation and grandkids are depending upon you!

Foreword

The United States of America are not united when it comes to education. We have 50 states with 50 sets of standards for their educational systems. Admittedly, the Constitution of our great country placed the obligation for the development and administration of public schools on the backs of the states. Consequently, our 50 states have fiercely guarded that prerogative in the past and, until recently, fought off attempts by our federal government to interfere in education matters.

It was Lyndon Johnson who, in 1965, shepherded the passage of the Elementary and Secondary Education Act (ESEA) through Congress, signaling the first large-scale incursion of the federal government into education. Under the civil rights banner, ESEA attempted to equalize the playing field for the children of poverty. Federal dollars would flow to school districts with large concentrations of poor children to ensure that they would have an equal opportunity to receive a quality education. For more than 30 years, school district accountability for the funds received was restricted to reports about how federal funds were spent. The districts and schools receiving federal dollars had annual reports to file with the Department of Education (DOE). With the reauthorization of ESEA, popularly known as No Child Left Behind, the federal role expanded to include all schools. Today, every public school in America must make Adequate Yearly Progress on state exams and evaluate teachers according to student performance on state and local tests.

In recent years, the specter of global competition has extended to education with international academic competitions that do not flatter the performance of American students. By comparison to countries like Finland, Singapore, and most recently Shanghai (not a country, by the way, but a Chinese province), our students do not fare well. We can debate whether the comparisons with much smaller countries and a province are fair. At some point, we must recognize that our students participating in the Program for International Student Assessment (PISA) and Trends in International Mathematics and Science Study (TIMSS) learn in 50 states with 50 different standards. It seems obvious that we would be better off if we, like the countries we compete with, had one set of national standards. Thus, the dilemma—our states do not want the federal government imposing a set of standards, yet in addition to international competitions, there are many reasons why our schools would benefit from national standards.

The National Governors Association (NGA) and the Council of Chief State School Officers (CCSSO) have been the prime movers of the common core standards, an attempt to get all 50 states to agree to a national standard for K–12 education and not one imposed by the federal government. To help expedite the process, the U.S. DOE has awarded two grants for the development of instruments that would assess student progress toward the common core standards. A number of states have adopted the standards, and many school districts are now grappling with the task of developing curriculum and instructional materials and strategies for the classroom. It is precisely at this point that Bob Manley and Rich Hawkins have authored *Making the Common Core Standards Work* because they want America's schools to be world-class learning centers.

America is great. Its education system is part of that greatness. But, as Manley and Hawkins point out in this book, the measure of our greatness is changing because the world is changing. Educators have a part to play: School leaders and teachers must adapt to the new standards or fade away. The authors clearly argue why we must choose the former. They hit many topics, beginning with what the CCSS are and why they are important. They show us why we must give our children the tools to excel by elevating and transforming what we consider as the high standards of today into the basic standards of tomorrow.

Manley and Hawkins provide a model for implementing the standards. I particularly appreciate their approach of using inquiry to promote dialogue. Throughout the process, they remain mindful of what may already exist in each school district so as not to recreate the wheel. They also provide valuable data and target specific grades and subject matters as they focus on common core implementation and its impact on curriculum and school management and culture.

The authors acknowledge the current attacks on public education, and I agree with their point that vilifying teachers and administrators is neither the answer nor likely to facilitate change. Yes, budgets are tight. Yes, funding is limited. Tenure, performance measures, and benefit packages are key issues in the new millennium, along with student performance. But, there is one fact that is consistently ignored: America's public schools today are the best that they have ever been.

Scores on the National Assessment of Educational Progress for fourth and eighth grade reading and math are the highest they have ever been. Graduation rates are the highest they have ever been, while the dropout rate is the lowest. College enrollment is at an all-time high, while high school courses are the most rigorous ever. While our students' performance on the TIMSS are not as high as we would want them to be, they have improved with every administration and are above the international average. According to the most recent Gallop Poll, parents' satisfaction with the schools their children attend is the highest ever. Yet, are we satisfied with average performance? Can American schools raise student learning to competitive world standards? Yes, we can.

We are the best that we have ever been, but we are not as good as we want to be, particularly when it comes to the education of our African American and Latino students that comprise the bulk of the population in the dropout factories of America. The CCSS could pave the way for a brighter future for American education, and Bob Manley and Rich Hawkins provide us with the practical strategies to get us there.

—Dan Domenech

Executive Director

American Association of School Administrators

Preface

This book examines the rationale for CCSS and provides readers with the means to use them to transform their schools into world-class educational institutions. We write as proponents of CCSS who recognize many of the limitations of a common core, not the least of which is that the common core is the lowest common level of performance to which teachers and school leaders should aspire. The purpose of the CCSS and their inherent strengths and weaknesses need discussion and debate. Those who will implement the CCSS must understand their strengths and weaknesses.

We recognize that teachers, especially new and aspiring teachers, need to have a rationale and a purpose for their work with students in the CCSS. If teachers are to innovate and adapt to the learners in their classes, they must deeply understand the purpose of the common core.

We provide school leaders with a practical guide to implement the CCSS. We write in a way so that teachers and school leaders can see clearly how they must work together to implement the common core standards and prepare students to function beyond the limits of the common core standards.

In our effort to share a rationale and vision for the CCSS, we first help school leaders and teachers to understand why America needs common core standards and more rigorous curricula and how it is possible to have almost all of our students prepared to compete in a global economy. We distinguish common core standards from local curriculum and performance expectations. In our design for more effective schools, we see the CCSS as the framework for teacher and school leader development, innovation, and continuous improvement.

We provide a thorough discussion of the merger of local language arts and math curricula with the CCSS. We infuse into the discussion science and social studies curricular designs and efforts by teachers to meet the writing and comprehension expectations that high-performing nations achieve with many of their students.

We discuss challenges that school leaders and teachers face as they try to make the CCSS work in their schools. In this effort, we focus on practical methods that teachers who employ formative assessments use to guide instruction and have almost all of their students achieve mastery of their lessons. In addition, we discuss the leadership challenge to all educators, and we offer practical pathways to success.

Diversity of ethnicity, wealth, languages, schools, and culture pose exceptional challenges in the United States. We provide a winning view of diversity and multicultural issues in our schools. We show how teachers and school leaders can experience diversity as a strength and resource within their schools. We try to show how multiculturalism can become a barrier or a resource for exceptional learning in our schools. We encourage teachers and school leaders to innovate by understanding deeply the CCSS and using the common core as a "melody line" from which they can improvise to create great "jazz" and accomplished learners.

Finally, we provide a tried-and-true method to improve a school in the detailed outline that we share about joint intervention teams (JITs). We give school boards, principals, teachers, and parents a blueprint to construct their own self-renewing schools. We show them how to collaborate and discover their own pathways for children to explore and to master skills for future productive citizenship. We offer liberating principles that take school leaders and teachers beyond the common core standards, and we show them the mental models necessary for freedom and the pursuit of happiness far beyond the limits of public education policy. The simplistic legislative acts that federal and state agencies initiate to monitor schools and that state governments provide to test students and evaluate teachers only matter if we permit them to restrict our performance in our schools. We want all educators to view the CCSS and state measurements of student achievements as springboards from which they launch their gymnastic gyrations into a mastery ballet of student and teacher synchronized learning.

We hope that this book will help our readers master the intricacies of the CCSS and free them from restrictive mental models and efforts to teach to tests. We believe that our book can enable school leaders and teachers to collaborate in new ways. We believe that educators who adopt our approach to the CCSS will see themselves as the true innovators and the guiding hands that set children free to be lifelong learners.

Acknowledgments

Bob and I wish to acknowledge the thousands of dedicated and talented educators with whom we have worked or taught over the years that get up every morning and, despite the mounting challenges they face, joyfully and professionally do everything in their power to make the lives of children better in every way. We have learned from every one of them. Their thirst for continuous learning and efforts to improve their knowledge and practice are nothing short of inspirational. They give us hope that, in spite of America's misguided educational policy makers in Washington, D.C., and state houses across our land, school leaders and their faculties will continue to focus on teaching and learning and building upon children's strengths. The people we admire the most know that test prep is not a curriculum and that failure does not motivate children. They learn from error when errors are pathways to learning.

Our deepest thanks and gratitude to Arnis Burvikovs, Kimberly Greenberg, and Pam Schroeder of Corwin for their unfailing support, expertise, and guidance through the process of bringing this book to fruition.

We wish to express our sincere appreciation to our colleague, Dan Domenech, Executive Director of the American Association of School Administrators, for his wisdom, advice, and the insights he offers in the Foreword to this book.

We acknowledge our reliance and the NGA and CCSSO for giving all of us who write about the common core access to the entire document.

Publisher's Acknowledgments

Corwin would like to thank the following individuals for taking the time to provide their editorial insight:

Charlotte R. Bihm
Instructional Specialist
St. Landry Parish School Board
Opelousas, LA

William Richard Hall, Jr.
Principal
R. C. Longan Elementary School
Henrico, VA

Martin J. Hudacs
Superintendent
Solanco School District
Quarryville, PA

Virginia Kelsen, PhD
Principal
Rancho Cucamonga High School
Rancho Cucamonga, CA

Tanna Nicely
Assistant Principal
Dogwood Elementary
Knoxville, TN

Lyne Ssebikindu
Assistant Principal
Crump Elementary School
Memphis, TN

About the Authors

Dr. Robert J. Manley graduated from Iona College with a BA in Spanish Language Arts and minors in Philosophy and Education. He completed his MA degree in the Humanities at Hofstra University and his Professional Diploma and Doctor of Philosophy degrees in Educational Administration at St. John's University. He taught Spanish language skills and served as an instructor in a New York State Model Humanities program at West Babylon High School. For 21 years, he served in a variety of administrative positions including Assistant Principal at Babylon Jr./Sr. High School, Principal in Plainedge School District, and Assistant Superintendent for Curriculum and Instruction and Superintendent of Schools in West Babylon, New York. He served as President of the Board of Directors for the Suffolk County Library System and the Suffolk County Organization to Promote Education. Currently, he is Professor of Educational Administration and Leadership in the Doctoral Program at Dowling College, New York.

In the last six years, he has presented peer-reviewed papers at the Sixth Annual Conference on Social Issues at Oxford University, England; the World Association for Case Research and Application in Mannheim, Germany, and Lucerne, Switzerland; and the Eastern Educational Research Association in Hilton Head, South Carolina, and Clearwater, Florida. In addition, he presented workshops on School Board Governance practices at the New York State School Boards Annual Convention and at the National School Boards Conference. On January 8, 2009, he presented "Systems That

Work for Students in Higher Education" as Keynote Speaker at the International Symposium for Quality in Higher Education at Shri M.D., Shah Mahila College of Arts and Commerce, Mumbai, India. In January 2011, his paper titled "Indian, Mexican and USA Management Students Interpret Moral Leadership for a Global Economy" was awarded Best Paper for Management at the International Business and Economy Conference at Universidad Panamericana, Guadalajara, Mexico. He is the coauthor with Richard Hawkins of a book on school reform titled *Designing School Systems for All Students: A Toolbox to Fix America's Schools.*

 **Dr. Richard J. Hawkins** graduated from Hofstra University with his BS in Music Education. He completed his MS in Education and Professional Diploma in Education Leadership at Long Island University. Rich received his doctorate in Educational Administration at Dowling College. He began his teaching career in the William Floyd School District as an instrumental music teacher and later became District Coordinator of Music and Art. After his department was recognized as the Outstanding Music Program in the country by the Music Educators National Conference, Rich moved to district office as the Assistant Superintendent for Elementary Education and Personnel. Schools under his supervision received designation as New York State (NYS) Schools of Excellence and U.S. DOE Blue Ribbon Schools. Rich served as Superintendent of the William Floyd School District for almost 12 years. He has served as President of the Suffolk County School Superintendents Association (SCSSA) and held various roles with the New York State Council of School Superintendents (NYSCOSS). Currently, he is Director of Contract Services for the College of St. Rose, Albany, NY.

Since retiring from William Floyd, Rich served as an Adjunct Associate Professor in the Advanced Certificate and EdD programs in Educational Leadership at Dowling College. He also is an instructor in the Educational Leadership program at the College of Saint Rose in Albany, NY. In addition, Rich taught full time at the College of St. Elizabeth as Assistant Professor in their EdD and

Master's programs. In 2006, Rich formed Hawkins and Associates: Organizational Learning Consultants to help leaders and their organizations reach their goals and aspirations. Over the last nine years, he has had peer-reviewed papers presented at the World Association for Case Research and Application in Lucerne, Switzerland, and Mannheim, Germany; the Eastern Educational Research Association in Hilton Head, South Carolina; and in the *Long Island Education Review*. Rich has made numerous presentations to the NYS School Boards Association, NYSCOSS, and SCSSA. He has presented at Hofstra University's Social Emotional Literacy Conference and Dowling College's Annual Practical Research Symposium. He was also a Keynote Presenter at the U.S. DOE Safe School/Healthier Students Conference, Tysons Corner, VA.

He is the coauthor with Robert Manley of a book on school reform titled *Designing School Systems for All Students: A Toolbox to Fix America's Schools*.

Introduction

Why American Schools Must Move Toward Common Core State Standards

THE WORLD IS FLAT

Thomas Friedman's (2005) best seller *The World Is Flat* caused spirited conversations throughout the United States. Many pundits asked if America was declining. Could India and China surpass America and be the economic global leaders of the 21st century? Has America lost its innovative engineering and scientific drive? Is the age of America over?

Well, the truth is the death of America has been announced prematurely. The future of the United States remains closely entwined with the future of its educational institutions. Since September 11, 2001, it is clear that the world has changed—or flattened out—dramatically. Decisions made in countries thousands of miles away affect everything from the cost of gasoline to the quality of air that residents breathe. Policy decisions always cause a reaction—some intended and some unintended. In the 21st century, reactions can be worldwide, and in a digital economy, information travels at the speed of light.

In 2008, an economic meltdown that seemed to begin in the United States expanded globally. Each new day brought bad news from another region of the world. Major U.S. financial institutions like Merrill Lynch and Lehman Brothers, once thought indestructible, collapsed. Many others had to be bailed out across the globe, and taxpayers were assigned large debts for untold sums of money that generations to come would have to pay. The United States had to borrow money from China. China had to bail out the U.S. Federal Treasury so that the U. S. federal government could bail out the

U.S. banks that caused an unprecedented home mortgage failure that almost destroyed the American economy (Stiglitz, 2010). The average American could not comprehend the global economic exchange. Too many competing forces and too many veiled interest groups were aligned in opposition to one another for simple judgments about what would or would not bring the world out of its declining economies, mounting national debt in Europe and North America, and the ever-expanding loss of jobs. The years 2006 to 2012 have been aptly described as the Great Recession, when the value of property and goods declined worldwide and significant levels of unemployment befell many countries. Conflict was inevitable in this time of change. New global and restructured national economies were bound to emerge from this global debate about financial solvency, robotic and commoditized work, and future opportunities for the youth of the world.

At the local community level, Americans now grapple with a new world reality that they find difficult to interpret and in which they can barely envision new roles for themselves, much less new jobs.

Tsunamis in the Far East literally sent ripples throughout the world. Nuclear meltdowns in Japan caused legitimate concerns about radiation on the West Coast of America. The costs, economically and socially, of wars in Iraq and Afghanistan were impossible to measure without sophisticated software and access to enormous amounts of privileged information. The Arab Spring, European restructured debt, and individual losses of economic well-being and slowing economies in China, India, and Brazil make the second decade of the 21st century more challenging than the first.

In North Africa, dictatorial governments were overthrown by students using Facebook and Twitter. A new day dawned; the future seemed less predictable, and the implications for everyone were just beginning to be understood. Most Americans recognized that they were members of a global community who shared many of the aspirations and hopes that people of every faith, culture, and community shared: a pursuit of liberty, dignity and happiness.

The United States is no longer calling all the shots on the world stage. Our military and economic might in the 21st century reaches only as far as our partners with whom we share common understandings and perceived mutual benefits. Small events in less populated countries influence how people and nations perform on the world stage. In the United States, one critical and local issue will control the future of our economy—the quality of our public schools.

How did this happen? How did schools become so vital to our national interests? How did cultures like Brazil, China, and India develop thriving economies in the last decade? How interdependent have these and other national economies become? How has the U.S. economy declined so drastically within the same time period? Will the middle class continue to shrink in the United States? How come children in the United States seem to show declines in math and literacy on international assessments of education? Why do secondary students in Finland outperform U.S. students handily in every measure of math and science? Is it fair to contrast small countries with small numbers of ethnic populations with a multicultural population like that of the United States? Is this question an excuse for poor performance? What is the appropriate question? Is it possible that we don't understand the underlying causes and relationships of failing economies and poor student performance?

In his March 2011 article for the *Educational Researcher,* Condron contrasted 27 highly industrialized countries, and he concluded that "income and wealth are more unevenly distributed in the United States than in any other affluent society (data cited from Smeeding, 2005; Wolf, 2002)" (p. 47). Among these affluent countries, the United States has the second highest percentage of students scoring in the lowest math proficiency level. Condron did not blame public schools in the United States. He noted that as U.S. wealth concentrations increased among a smaller and more affluent population, student achievement declined. Countries with less concentrations of wealth in small portions of their populations had better student achievement (Condron, 2011).

Imagine if Condron is right and much of the U.S.'s failure to compete in the 21st century is the result of public policies designed to favor the rich and ignore the poor. Policy makers at state and federal levels of government are aware of the growing disparity of skill and wealth in America. The new CCSS represent a policy partnership between state governments and the federal government that is designed to raise educational achievement across schools in all of the states in spite of the growing concentration of wealth in America. Increasing concentrations of student failure in poor and urban areas have to be remedied, or America will not have a competitive workforce. Future work requires independent thinking, reading comprehension, thoughtful calculations, and interpersonal skills that schools can teach if their structures and personnel are trained to develop these abilities.

If federal legislation succeeds in encouraging states to educate more students to higher levels of achievement, state governments can increase the wealth, productivity, and overall well-being of their communities. Federal interventions such as those proposed in the Harkin and Enzi 2011 Elementary and Secondary Act shift the focus in the right direction when federal dollars for education focused on the poorest performing school districts in each state. Senators Harkin and Enzi have been joined by Alexander and Kirk in a federal effort to stop spreading inconsequential mandates and rules to improve all schools by testing students (Dillon, 2011a, b). Schools that have more than 90 percent of their students achieving proficient to mastery-level performance may need to focus on more mastery-level performance. Certainly, they do not need more mandates from the federal or state government. The nation should celebrate success-ful schools. All adults have to stand against declaring schools with small numbers of failing students from subgroups within a single grade as the determinant factors for the schools being designated as failures. Nonsense has to be recognized as nonsense.

Only a small percentage of schools with large numbers of students in urban, poor areas are producing most of the failing students. The federal and state governments need to focus on those schools. Certainly, some rural and suburban schools fall into these highly challenged schools, where less than 80 percent and in some cases less than half of the children meet state or CCSS in math, English, social studies, and science performance. All of these challenged schools need national incentives assigned to their states that produce changes and supportive structures so that teaching, assessing, and learning make a difference in the lives of these children.

Under current federal and state regulations, in 2012, "ninety per-cent of New Hampshire's schools are expected to be labeled as fail-ing" (Winerip, 2011, p. A11). Winerip observes that, in the Oyster River middle school with 100 special education students, about a dozen students who did not score at the proficiency level or better represented the key factor that caused the school to be designated as failing. To avoid foolish results like those about to be broadcast in

New Hampshire, criteria for success must change. In the future, it seems that failing schools will be those that have less than 85 percent of their students meeting the criteria set to measure proficiency and mastery in the CCSS.

In the fall of 2011, the federal government invited states to apply for waivers from the 100 percent proficiency standards of No Child Left Behind legislation and to focus their efforts on the lowest 15 percent of schools (Winerip, 2011). Waivers will not make better schools. Rewards for excellent academic performance in schools and a focus on mastery of the CCSS in all schools will change the academic and problem-solving skills of America's public school graduates.

By 2012, 45 states had adopted the CCSS. Many of these states had their own state standards. The greatest difference that the CCSS presented from the majority of state standards was greater emphasis on analytical thinking, connecting themes and patterns, and making use of creative and inventive thinking by students.

The CCSS are designed to reduce the disparities in access to quality instruction and learning that the United States has fostered during the last 30 years as greater portions of wealth continued their progression toward smaller portions of the population. Between 1980 and 2010, 80 percent of the wealth in America moved from 23 percent of the population to 5 percent of the individuals who earned more than $250,000 annually. As wealth became more concentrated in the United States, student academic achievement declined in large measures across America's cities and rural areas.

The standards are part of the solution insofar as they offer school leaders and teachers a common vision of what students must be able to do at every grade level to compete on the world stage. The standards do not offer a way to merge local curricula, teacher training, and new technology into a new educational system that would benefit many more students. The more difficult work ahead is to change the mental models that educators hold about how students should learn and who can learn.

The CCSS offer students in every state a high-quality curriculum. Teachers and school leaders have to determine the strategies and interventions they will employ to help all children achieve these important and necessary expectations, especially those related to applications of knowledge in the core subjects.

THE PROBLEM AND THE SOLUTION: EDUCATION

While politicians and pundits in the United States are quick to blame education and educators for all of society's ills, it is clear that there is plenty of blame to go around. Our present educational, social, economic, and technological state of affairs has been partially caused by educators. Surprisingly, those educators do not live in the United States.

We are suffering the international effects of gifted educators armed with rigorous curricula and training, supportive governments with coherent educational and social policies, and citizens who live in cultures where teachers are revered. The people in those countries are eager to have what we too frequently take for granted. They are our global competitors. They adopted the United States' work ethic and core beliefs: You can be free to believe in whatever you like and to become whoever or whatever you wish as long as you work hard and serve the common good while you serve your own benefit (Huntington, 2004).

In a flattened world fueled by technology, our American dream has spread like a virus. The more people there are who know what we have, the more people who want it for themselves, their families, and their countries. And, while this is a dream worth sharing, we need to find a way to rekindle our quintessential American spirit.

Clearly, American educators need to lead the development of a new, shared vision for our public schools. If they do not create an inclusive vision for our schools and learn how to raise many more students to mastery levels of learning, the American dream and the quality of life we have cherished will be unsustainable in a global economy.

At the beginning of the second decade of the 21st century in the United States, the fastest-growing segment of the population is Latino, and the highest proportional dropout rate from high school occurs among Latinos, especially Latino males (Fry, 2010). Reformers want to dismantle the public school system and create charter schools and voucher systems. In many cases, U.S. reforms are reactionary and thoughtless efforts to stem the tide of multiculturalism in the United States. Elected leaders tend to reflect local prejudices more than collective wisdom. They contribute to the myth that Americans barely understand who they are and how dependent they are upon the Protestant ethic (Huntington, 2004).

There are many myths about diverse groups in the United States that mask the powerful dream of freedom and equal treatment before the law that these immigrants seek. America promised to those who would come to serve her purpose and common goals of life, liberty, and the pursuit of happiness a refuge from religious and political persecution. Nevertheless, large numbers of Americans seem to know little about anyone who differs from their own ethnic or racial group. Much mythology has been written about Latinos in the United States that reflect prejudices about this recent wave of immigrants.

According to Fuentes (in Ramos, 2006), there were more than 45 million Hispanics in the United States in 2000. They would represent approximately one sixth of the entire population and "by 2050 they will grow to 103 million according to the calculations of the Census Bureau" (p. 194, Manley, Trans.). Fuentes takes issue with Huntington's thesis presented in an essay, "The Hispanic Challenge (March/April 2004)," published in *Foreign Policy* in which Huntington observed: "The persistent inflow of Hispanic immigrants threatens to divide the United States into two peoples, two cultures, and two languages" (in Ramos, 2006, p. 195). Fuentes believes that many members of white culture in America cannot "see themselves in the mirror and recognize that they are a mixture of many colors and not white or black" (p. 196). He offers multiple examples of the rapid adaptation of the Hispanic and Mexican immigrants to the society of North America.

- Second-generation Hispanics are more comfortable speaking English than Spanish.
- Third-generation Latinos tend to marry outside the Hispanic community.
- Nearly 90 percent of all Latinos in the United States are bilingual.
- About 56 percent of Latinos in the United States were born there.
- Latin-American immigrants learn English and better their salaries the more time they have in the United States.
- Poverty levels for Hispanics decline, mastery of English increases, home ownership increases, and naturalized citizenship increases as Hispanics spend more time in the United States.

- In 2004, 4 million Hispanics were in the process of becoming citizens of the United States.
- More than 500,000 Hispanics in the United States are doctors or lawyers or have earned a master's or doctoral degree.
- There are 1.2 million businesses in the United States owned by Latinos.
- More than 30,000 Hispanic soldiers fought for the U.S. military in the Iraq War (in Ramos, 2006, p. 196)

Ramos (2006) observes:

What unites the United States is not English. No. What unifies the United States are the concepts that comprise the North-American creed—equality, liberty, social justice—and the basic principles that hold together the American society: tolerance of diversity, acceptance of immigrants and the constant search for the new and the innovative. These elements made the United States a prosperous and powerful nation. (p. 197)

In spite of the good news about the Latino communities in the United States that Ramos presents in his book, *La Otra Cara de America,* the facts remain that Latino immigrants present twice the high school dropout rate of all other minorities (Fry, 2010). How can CCSS bring us together and enable students of color, students raised in poverty, and middle-class students to prosper? Educators must come together with parents and community leaders to adopt a new vision for our children and their schools, and this vision must be informed by the CCSS.

CAN GOVERNMENT RESCUE OUR SCHOOLS?

Standards in and of themselves do nothing. The more precise question is how the United States of America, with 50 diverse states and narrowing concentrations of wealth, can achieve a national consciousness about public schools. Can a new national vision translate into local action where school leaders and teachers assume responsibility for the continuous growth of every student within their schools? Can small communities across America and individual public schools buck the national trend to pander to the wealthy and ignore the poor? Can educators reignite among their students a desire to learn and to master new skills? Can school leaders get policy makers to listen and to follow their wisdom? Is there a way for American educators to reverse the trend in American schools that diminishes the value of trade schools and forces higher numbers of Americans to drop out of school and join unemployment lines as 17-year-olds?

Media pundits are having field days demonizing teachers for their pensions, benefits, and failures to raise all students above the benchmark of state exams. Tenure is blamed for all of society's ills, and educators are depicted as the major reason that property taxes are too high. State pensions require more of the taxpayer dollar because politicians have mismanaged state pensions. In some cases, such as New York, legislators reduced the level and length of time that civil service workers must contribute to their pensions to the first 10 years of their employment (Chapter 126, 2000).

In New York, legislators inaccurately estimated future revenues from state-invested pension funds and failed to increase reserves and lower return estimates on investments when the U.S. economy was growing. Many other states suffer public pension challenges from politicians who are unwilling to affix any pain to their wealthy supporters and who are searching for revenue and cost reductions. Certainly, pension reform is required in most states, not defined pension replacements with 401k programs that could destroy the base for all pensions. State legislators need to enact programs that will permit the gradual replenishment of the pension losses that occurred during the Great Recession and give local communities 10 years to invest additional dollars rather than the thin envelope of 5 years that they require for localities to be fully funded in their pension obligations. As former President Clinton stated in his speech nominating President Barack Obama for a second term, balancing a budget is simple arithmetic.

Federal and state programs designed to use student test scores to evaluate teachers seem like simple ways to identify less-able teachers and to remove the costly, ineffective teachers from the ranks. This is ludicrous criteria to evaluate teachers. It assumes that teachers have equal distributions of skilled students in each of their classes. More importantly, it denies the primary leadership role that school leaders must play to make schools work for the benefit of students. Yes, teachers should be evaluated for how well their students learn on multiple measures such as formative tests, standardized tests, and criterion-referenced exams as well as performance goals adjudicated by independent judges.

The goals to help all students achieve mastery of valuable curriculum understandings, dispositions, and skills and to apply competitive knowledge in a variety of situations have been fractured by political ideologies. The CCSS offer educators a pathway out of the maze of conflicting ideologies that have confused and distracted them from their main mission. School leaders and teachers must evaluate the common core standards at the local school level, determine how to employ and merge their goals with local school goals, and convince the local public community that these goals are valuable and worthy of their support.

Teachers have to work diligently and collaboratively to identify gaps in student learning, to initiate interventions, to redesign instructional strategies and rewards for learning, and to hold each other accountable for the students that they share. School leaders have to evaluate teachers fairly and honestly regarding the growth that students are making in learning. They must use appropriate, explicit evidence, such as locally produced formative assessments, criteria-referenced assessments, and standardized state examinations, alongside independent judges who evaluate performance exhibits such as a speech, a rendition of a musical piece, a science or math or technological experiment, or a research paper.

Certainly, incompetent teachers and those whose performance is weak are well known in a school, especially to competent school leaders who visit classrooms regularly and who can document the strengths and weaknesses that they observe. School leaders must ensure that incompetent teachers exit, help improving teachers, celebrate competent teachers whose students meet CCSS, and reward master teachers.

Politicians who scapegoat the public schools use wedge issues like charter schools and annual standardized tests results to drive educational policies that adversely affect the types of change that could restore our nation to global competiveness. Charter schools siphon funds from public schools. Testing outcomes do not improve production or learning (Deming, 1986, p. 15). Testing verifies one's status in the same manner that a blood pressure gauge identifies that one's blood pressure is within or beyond normal ranges. No matter how many times the blood pressure gauge is applied to one's body, it will not improve one's blood pressure.

Magazine and newspaper editors, state and federal legislators, governors, and the powerful and wealthy have co-opted the public forum to denigrate teachers, public schools, and the mission of public service. Stephen Moore (2011), senior economics writer for the *Wall Street Journal*, belittled the work of teachers from 1970 to 2005 with specious analysis. He claimed that, after being adjusted for inflation, school spending doubled, and standardized achievement scores were flat. What he failed to note was that most of those new dollars for education were assigned to special education students because of the inflexible, mandated services attributable to federal and state legislative acts and to equally restrictive, mandated services for growing numbers of immigrant and English Second Language (ESL) children in the schools. Funds for general education students actually declined.

The nation and its elected officials should be celebrating the great accomplishment that public school teachers have achieved as they held constant the level of achievement among these diverse general education, immigrant, and special needs students. Our nation needs a new vision of education.

Should the new vision promote separate, unequal schools, driven by individual choice, or offer children of a democratic society the opportunity to learn among diverse students in their communities with equal opportunities, resources, and demands for quality education?

Moore (2011) and his editorial cohorts are part of the problem. They lack a true respect for teachers and education. They make their money bashing other professions with claims like "We've Become a Nation of Takers, Not Makers." What has an editorial writer ever made? At least, the National Governor's Conference made an attempt to level the playing field for all children when they sponsored the CCSS.

Blaming teachers will not improve education. Improving how teachers work together, providing them with continuous professional development to advance mastery learning among their students, and supervising the changes school leaders initiate are the only ways to transform our current system of education. Given the political rhetoric about the importance of education in a flat world, coupled with the irony of diminished educational funding and the opportunities funding secures, the question one must ask is this: Who serves the legitimate interests of our nation's children?

It is time for educators to go on the offense and design the high-quality educational environment that our children require to sustain our nation's ability to compete academically, socially, economically, and politically on the global stage. The CCSS can fuel this noble effort. School leaders, teachers, and school boards should not wait for others to lead. They should not limit themselves to political regulations of poorly informed politicians. They should take charge of their own schools and work above and beyond the dictates of state education regulations so that every child seeking to master the knowledge required in the CCSS at every grade actually can do it.

We must reframe our thinking about government interventions. Let us be frank; regulations will not go away, and while most are not helpful, it is up to the educational community to make them work and to engage students at their current levels and bring them far above where government intervenes. In fact, the greatest peril to the children that we educate is politicians who dictate educational policy, standards, and curriculum development without listening to highly experienced and capable school leaders and teachers. The true skills politicians possess are to make laws and to award incentives. Politicians should enact policies that reward efforts and results that build our nation's capacity to learn. They should abandon their foolish endeavors to design schools and teaching according to some mythological story about what works in a few schools. They have no real knowledge or insight into how schools work. They do know what they want to see as far as outcomes from investments in schools. Let them reward those schools that achieve desired outcomes. Let them set the criteria and not the methodology.

Educators must use their educational associations to stage a national dialogue about what a 21st-century education should entail and what children and youth should be able to do in truly responsive and futuristic public schools. What are the civic virtues and the reading, math, writing, technologically innovative, and creative skills that we need students to master?

The CCSS state some of the knowledge and skills that are required to be competitive on the global stage. This conversation about the future of U.S. education opened with the publication of the National Common Core State Standards, I (2010a) in Reading, Writing, Historical and Scientific Writing, and Mathematics.

As of February 2012, 45 states had adopted the National Common Core State Standards as the framework for education in their states. Many educators and researchers view the CCSS with their emphasis on critical thinking, analysis, synthesis, evaluation of information, the application of knowledge, and the inventive and creative use of knowledge as very high standards for schools to achieve. In truth, the common core standards are the basic standards for the 21st century.

Educators, at every school, need to learn how to redesign their curricula and their instructional strategies so that the CCSS are absorbed. School leaders have to engage faculty teams in the visionary and practical work of making new schools for children of poverty as well as children of wealth.

All children should experience learning as a process that begins with what they already know and moves to what they do not know. Learning should be the only goal of effective schools, and all school assessments should be designed to measure learning and to inform teachers about the success of their instructional practices.

Teachers need extensive training in the design of local curricula aligned to the CCSS. They need to collaborate in the development of their own formative and summative tests. Teachers have to administer commonly designed formative assessments to students so that they can evaluate and critique their students' and their own work. Teachers have to become self-reflective learners if students are to learn how to modify strategies that enhance their own learning.

We recognize that our rationale for the CCSS is deeply ingrained with economic and political beliefs. We believe that these economic and political beliefs are practical judgments and not partisan assumptions about the status of American education and the role teachers, school leaders, and school board members must play in the 21st century. If America is to remain the land of the free and the home of the brave, we must seek mastery of the CCSS for all students.

Our book is designed in four parts or dimensions. In each part, we explore key considerations or domains by which the CCSS must be viewed to ensure the transformation of American education and the continued prosperity of our country and its people.

In the first part of this book, we address the rationale underlying the common core standards and role of the school leader and teachers in the creation of new visions for their schools. In the second section, we examine practical efforts of school leaders and teachers to merge the CCSS and local curricula in English language arts and mathematics. The implementation of a new common core local curricula and state standards in English language arts and mathematics is presented in ways that encourage teachers to work together in the assessment and verification that all children in their classes can demonstrate progress in their learning. In order to ensure that the CCSS are not interpreted or assessed through a 20th-century lens, we provide educators with various pathways, viewpoints, and practices to guide their dialogues and design their work.

In 2011, there are CCSS available for social studies and science that teachers and school leaders can examine and merge with improved local curricula designed to meet the needs of local students who will have to work in a global economy. The beauty of the CCSS is their high level of expectations for students and their flexibility and ease of adaptation to teacher-driven curricula and teaching strategies that address specific students at the point of development. The difficulty arises in the exchange of ideas, practices, and perceptions of meaning that the common core standards elicit. For this reason, teachers and school leaders need time for extensive professional training and dialogue that will allow them to design and redesign their efforts to meet the needs of the actual students at their school and not some mythical representation of students.

In the third section of the book, we discuss the challenges that educators face at local schools and in their communities as they move up to and beyond the basic expectations for academic knowledge contained in the CCSS. We provide educators with insightful examples of how they should guide their students, parents, and teachers to adopt new mental models that reflect expectations that all students will master what must be learned at each grade level. We describe how educators can use formative assessments to engender capacities for all members of the school community to conduct informed inquiries and engage in passionate and respectful dialogues that help to construct relevant knowledge. Also, we present a methodology for school districts and school leaders to take advantage of the diversity among faculty, parents, and students to differentiate instruction and achieve higher levels of mastery for all students through the artful use of inquiry, guiding principles, and double-loop feedback (Senge, 1990).

In the fourth part of this book, we examine multicultural issues, school improvement systems, and public policy changes that must be addressed for greater school competitiveness. We explore how to help students discover and acquire knowledge beyond the CCSS. Finally, we discuss the role of teachers, school leaders, school board members, and business leaders in the national dialogue that must inform politics and policy designs and implementations associated with effective schools where almost all children master the common core standards.

All in all, we have attempted to provide practical advice, examples, and design considerations that are modifiable for any culture, school, or district that is serious about being part of the new age of American achievement and prosperity. While this is not an easy task, it is doable. Translating CCSS into world-class curricula and using transformative instructional strategies have the potential to return American education to the world-class status that made our country prosper and flourish. Being competitive in a global community is not only a very worthy goal; it is a lifeline to a sustainable future.

SECTION I

Designing Competitive Curriculum for a Global Economy

CHAPTER 1

Common Core State Standards

What Are They?

U nlike most imposed programs and policies, the committee for the Common Core State Standards (CCSS), sponsored by the National Governors Association (NGA) and the Council of Chief State School Officers (CCSSO), worked diligently to gather grassroots support for a common core curriculum. "The standards were developed in collaboration with teachers, school administrators, and experts to provide a clear and consistent framework to prepare our children for college and the workforce" (Common Core State Standards, I, 2010a).

In addition to working with a wide variety of diverse stakeholder groups, the designers of the common core "have also received initial feedback on the draft standards from national organizations representing, but not limited to, teachers, postsecondary educators (including community colleges), civil rights groups, English language learners, and students with disabilities" (CCSS, I, 2010). The committee for common standards explained how members sought effective models for high standards: "The standards are informed by the highest, most effective models from states across the country and countries around the world, and provide teachers and parents with a common understanding of what students are expected to learn. Consistent standards will provide appropriate benchmarks for all students, regardless of where they live" (CCSS, I, 2010a).

In order to ensure that the common core standards would hold practical benefits for students, the committee examined what knowledge and skills were necessary for career and college-level opportunities. "These standards define the knowledge and skills students should have within their K–12 education careers so that they will graduate high school able to succeed in entry-level, credit-bearing academic college courses and in workforce training programs" (CCSS, I, 2010a).

The committee for the common core standards identified the six characteristics of the CCSS that were most valuable. They stated that the standards:

- Are aligned with college and work expectations;
- Are clear, understandable, and consistent;
- Include rigorous content and application of knowledge through high-order skills;
- Build upon strengths and lessons of current state standards;
- Are informed by other top-performing countries so that all students are prepared to succeed in our global economy and society; and
- Are evidence based. (CCSS, I, 2010a)

COMMON CORE STATE STANDARDS: MORE THAN STANDARDS WITH AN INTERNATIONAL FLAVOR

The CCSS have been created with the world stage in mind. They borrow heavily from standards across many states and nations. They are designed to mirror the rigor and relevance of standards used in those countries with whom we are competing globally. There is a stepwise design relating to content, skills, and process that builds sequentially on the content, skills, and dispositions that must be acquired in prior grade levels. Starting with kindergarten and ending with high school graduation, the CCSS provide a pathway for students to follow that enables high school graduates to have the requisite capacity to enter college or progress directly to the world of work. Practical, technical, and vocational education programs require these same skills in graduates who wish to enter the trades or be self-employed entrepreneurs.

The CCSS have also been designed with curriculum and assessment as integral partners to the standards themselves. As we have seen with many state standards, the quality of implementation often varies from school to school and district to district. In some locations, the standards themselves are perceived as curriculum rather than a roadmap to guide curriculum development, instruction, and student assessments.

If not ultimately accompanied by a local core curriculum, poor and inconsistent implementation of the common core and weak assessments will lead to irregular responses to student evidence and failure to achieve mastery. The result would be the same negative consequences of previous reform efforts that left large numbers of students without the requisite skills to compete on the world stage.

In the local core curriculum, teachers and school leaders must plan for specific evidence that constitutes *success* in meeting the standards. Without agreed-upon rubrics and evidence for students' successful acquisition of the standards' criteria, teachers will continue to teach children blindfolded. They will cover the curriculum, check off the standards that were taught, and forget to ensure that each child has mastered the behavior, thinking, and dispositions required by the standard criteria.

The CCSS should form the requisite baseline for content, skills, and processes that new and experienced teachers alike must learn and master to fully practice their profession. Teacher preparation programs as well as locally generated professional development must avoid an emphasis on developing surface knowledge and rote skills. Teachers need to learn how to merge the CCSS and local curriculum. They need training in the design and use of formative assessments to more precisely identify which students need help in specific areas of the curriculum.

Teachers need ongoing professional development in the use of varied strategies to help their students explore the applications of knowledge. Teacher preparation programs and in-service courses should focus on developing deep capacity among new and experienced teachers to move students from a current state of learning to mastery level applications of the CCSS.

Schmidt, Houang, and Cogan (2011) examined data from the 2010 Teacher Education and Development Study in Mathematics, a 16-country survey of math teachers in training near the end of their final semester. They concluded that "U.S. middle school math teacher preparation does not produce teachers with an internationally competitive level of mathematics knowledge" (p. 1266). At least 60 percent of U.S. math teachers' preparation was dedicated to pedagogical knowledge related to teaching math and general pedagogical knowledge related to instructional practices. Only 40 percent of their preparation was dedicated to "generally agreed upon cognitive competencies necessary for teaching mathematics" (p. 1266). The Russian Federation and Taiwan, with highly competitive math students, dedicated 50 percent of their math teacher preparation to math knowledge, 30 percent to math pedagogy, and only 20 percent to general pedagogy (p. 1266).

Therefore, using the common core standards to design curricula and assessments for college teacher preparation programs, although a good approach in itself, will not be sufficient unless the CCSS frameworks are treated as the minimum standard that all children must learn at mastery level. By mastery level, we mean that all children must be able to consistently solve problems and use mathematics and language in ways that the CCSS require.

No excuses should be tolerated for teachers who fail to grow their students' skills equal to and beyond the CCSS at their grade levels. Naturally, some students will require more time and more intensive interventions than others to achieve mastery knowledge. Schools must be structured so that teachers can provide appropriate differentiations in time and instructional options for every student. To show progress toward grade-level common core standards in mathematics and language arts, students must be assessed weekly and monthly with locally developed formative assessments. Teachers have to be trained to be competent designers of formative assessments and to work collaboratively in the interpretation of their results.

Currently, the United States has adequate protections and guarantees for children with special needs and English language learners to receive special support and interventions to ensure they learn in the least restrictive environment and gain sufficient knowledge to be productive students. Every school community and each state has to conduct constant vigils to ensure that those with the greatest needs receive effective instructional programs that benefit their social, emotional, and cognitive needs. We also advocate that the theories, methods, and tools to enact the CCSS must be constantly honed and refined in a collaborative, research-informed, national consortium of practitioners.

The implementation of these standards will require nothing less than a sincere, well-articulated national commitment to education and supportive social policies accompanied by significant national resources.

In the United States, K–8 school leaders encounter many newly graduated teachers with minimal training in language arts who require many hours of additional instruction and training to develop their skills as teachers of literacy and writing. The training and backgrounds of these same common core teachers in mathematics are woefully inadequate. The common core standards need to be the foundation of teacher preparation programs as well as the basis for professional development programs for in-service teachers.

When all is said and done, the CCSS should create a framework to guide the development of 21st-century educational curricula, programs, and assessments. Many decisions required to give life to the common core framework should be made locally. Teachers must be given important roles in the design of local curriculum and formative assessments. In the 21st century, teachers have to transform curriculum, instruction and learning, and student formative assessments into a systemic process that leads to all children mastering the CCSS in the public schools.

The CCSS present challenges to redesign and reframe curriculum. These new requirements demand changes in mental models among school leaders, teachers, parents, and students regarding how children learn and who can learn. The structure of relationships, school schedules, differentiation of instruction, time specialists spend with children, and co-teaching must fit the needs of the students. The design and intent of our book are to provide educators, school leaders, and parents with practical assistance and guidance in the restructuring of their schools for the 21st century.

A QUICK TRIP AROUND THE WORLD

When reviewing the educational structures, policies, and cultures of those countries with whom we seem to be competing, one notices several patterns that emerge. With some notable exceptions, social, educational, and economic policies seem to dovetail nicely. Teachers are afforded status in those competitive economies and societies appropriate to the importance of the profession and its contributions to the future of the nation. Culturally, in the nations with the highest student achievement, the value of an education is unquestioned, and teachers enter the profession from the top third of the college graduating classes (Domenech, 2011).

In the most competitive nations, there are national standards and curricula that appear to be far more rigorous than those that appear in most American schools. World languages and cultural awareness are not considered optional or elective learning events. Social emotional literacy is embedded within all curricula. Every child is expected to master curricula expectations at high levels of mastery and apply new knowledge in fresh circumstances (Schmidt, Houang, & Cogan, 2011). The CCSS in language and mathematics present school leaders and teachers (K–12) with precise and powerfully linked expectations for what students should be able to do after instruction.

Porter, McMaken, Hwang, and Yang (2011b) suggest that the CCSS offer all states four benefits: (1) shared high expectations; (2) greater focus on quality curriculum; (3) greater efficiencies in the development of curriculum materials, assessments, and teacher training; and (4) better delivery of quality and electronic common core assessments. They analyzed alignment of CCSS with 16 state standards in math and English language arts (ELA) using data of state standards stored at the Wisconsin Center for Educational Research. They found only moderate alignment between the common core and the majority of local state standards.

In mathematics, the CCSS "represent a modest shift toward higher levels of cognitive demand" (Porter et al., 2011b, p. 106) with greater emphasis on demonstrating understanding and less emphasis than state standards on memorization and performing procedures. In ELA, the common core standards put much greater emphasis on analysis, evaluation, and language study, while states tend to stress that students "perform procedures" and "generate ideas" (Porter et al., 2011b, pp. 105–108). In many cases, local State standards do not align well with CSS (Porter et al., 2011a).

In most high-performing countries, the U.S. federal and state government-sanctioned, grade-by-grade obsession with testing is virtually nonexistent. Other competitive countries seem to believe in and design for Deming's (1986) notion of building quality into the initial process and continuously developing stakeholder capacity so that they assess quality throughout each stage of development rather than test the end result and find how many errors have been produced.

Exit exams are prevalent in most of these countries at Grades 8 and 12. Many of these countries employ educational inspectors who visit schools and classrooms to verify that school leaders manage appropriate instructional designs and supervise teachers effectively.

They verify that instructional and managerial processes at the school produce desired results, and they seek innovative adaptations if results are less than desired.

In highly competitive countries, teacher training programs are very competitive, rigorous, and highly aligned to the skills that teachers must acquire to make independent decisions about their students' learning processes. In those countries, there are no jokes made that those who cannot make it in the "real world" become teachers. Teachers are among the most respected professionals within their society.

In fact, as opposed to teacher salaries in the United States, where frequently teachers earn much less after seven years than other professionals, the gap between teacher salaries and those paid to other professionals is markedly less in the most competitive countries in Asia and Europe (Paine, 2010). In many countries competing with the United States, teachers are expected to be professional and are therefore treated professionally. In South Korea, teachers are referred to as *nation builders*.

Condron (2011) examined inequalities of wealth among 27 affluent countries and demonstrated that the United States, which ranked among the top five countries for income concentration in the hands of the smallest portion of citizens, also ranked among the top four countries with the greatest portion of students who did not achieve math proficiency. He concluded that school-based reforms "place the burden of boosting achievement and reducing economically based disparities on the education system rather than the broader economic system" (p. 54). He noted that affluent countries with less income inequalities contend with less economic disparities among their students and achieve higher performance in science and math along with higher-order cognitive processes.

Teachers and school leaders cannot wait for politicians to get the economic balance right in their communities. In high-wealth communities, more than 95 percent of the students graduate and attend college. In high-poverty communities, more than 30 percent of the students fail to graduate. Poverty cannot be an excuse for student failure. It is a condition within a community that schools must overcome with inventive and collaborative work designed to engage all students in learning activities. Teachers and school leaders must partner with each other and find new ways to organize students within the classroom so that peer tutors and co-teachers can help differentiate instruction and the students' school-day experiences.

Principals and teachers must win the support of parents for changes that their children must make in how they approach learning. For some children, learning must be extended every day, and in some cases, their learning must be guided by precise formative assessments and one-to-one instruction.

Individual patterns of student performance, when examined as the products of the whole economic and social system in the United States, present a more accurate picture of the clusters of school failure that school leaders, teachers, and parents face. Failing schools are associated with high-poverty communities because they are structured to serve a middle-class population with all of the enriched opportunities, language assumptions, and family support that middle-class families enjoy. Certainly, it is obvious that it is much more difficult to teach and to identify ways to help poor children acquire prior knowledge and learn new material at mastery level than students who come to class with the prior knowledge already mastered. America has great teachers and school leaders, caring professionals seeking to make a difference in the lives of every child in their schools. No matter how hard they try to make the middle-class model of learning work in non-middle-class schools, they will be ineffective. School leaders and teachers have to redesign the school day to fit the needs of their students if they are going to help more students achieve mastery of the common core standards. It is also interesting to note that, despite their higher test scores, these high-performing countries look to the American education system with envy because it seems that we produce a greater portion of students who are creative and innovative. The creative and innovative elements of our schools often are associated with the fine and technical arts, clubs, activities, sports, and projects that teachers use to engage students.

Translated into a cognitive comparison of students competing with American high school graduates, the United States tends to have proportionately more children who are capable of performing at the upper levels of Bloom's taxonomy, where students must analyze, evaluate, and create solutions. We could have many more students operating at these highly creative levels if we had systemic rewards for them and did not rely mostly on our individualistic culture to produce our entrepreneurs and risk takers.

All students must be expected to master the building blocks to independent and creative problem solving. The common core standards represent a national effort to raise expectations, to improve instructional practice, and to expand teacher training for greater content mastery across the core curriculum. Clearly, the benefits that the CCSS promise are something we do not want to lose.

Yet, truth be told, many of our students are not even close to performing at high levels of mastery in even the basic skills. There is much work still to be done within the context of 21st-century schools. Friedman and Mandlebaum (2011) in their new book, *That Used to Be Us,* cite an Education Trust report that 23 percent of the U.S. high school graduates who take the military enlistment test do not achieve the minimum score for any branch of the military (p. 220). Teachers and school leaders should reflect on this statistic because only 75 percent of our cohort age group graduates high school. Almost half of our current high school age-appropriate graduates are not prepared to achieve proficient scores on the military enlistment test.

MOVING FORWARD

The CCSS are the closest we will come to national standards in the United States. Given the process used to seriously engage stakeholders as well as the intent and design of the standards and their indicators, they can and should serve as a springboard to transport American students onto the global stage in a position to perform competitively. School leaders and teachers must insist on mastery of the common core.

Every child, no matter where one is born or resides, is inextricably linked to a world where traditional boundaries are disappearing. Every country, no matter its geography or culture, is finding its people have more in common with people from other countries than ever thought possible a decade ago. Our students no longer are in competition with the community next door. Their ability to maintain the standard of living Americans have enjoyed for many decades depends on their capacity to grow, to change, and to reinvent themselves. What our public schools engender today is what we will reap tomorrow. The world is indeed becoming flatter and flatter, and our students must be global citizens in a world economy.

It is up to our educational leaders working in collaboration with their faculties, staff, and other internal and external stakeholders to write the story about America's continued prosperity throughout the 21st century. It is a challenge we can meet if we stop the blame game and seek to reframe the work of teachers and students in terms of lifelong learning, the process of discovery, and the application of knowledge and critical reasoning skills. School leaders and teachers must cease their emphasis on covering curriculum and focus their efforts on helping students master the essential curriculum at each grade level.

In 2011, the United States faces an uncertain future and multiple opportunities to create a new world where educators lead in the development of science, technology, engineering, mathematics, and creative arts instruction. We are at a critical juncture in our country's history. Perhaps American educators and citizens need to adopt a vision of educators as nation builders. As citizens of a global community in need of greater equality and opportunities to learn, all students should receive the appropriate guidance that leads to mastery of the skills and dispositions they need to be a free people.

As we design high-quality schools that enable children to compete on the world stage and demonstrate their mastery of the CCSS, we will need to reject old mental models of teaching with chalkboards, rows of desks, and teachers talking. We must create a new vision of how teachers, students, technology, and the community interact.

We have an espoused national vision that places before us a clear goal that all children be prepared to enter the world of college or work ready to meet the contextual challenges of the 21st century. We expect that our children will graduate high school and be prepared for full citizenship. We want them to have the skills and flexibility to ensure that they may work and live happy lives.

Frankly, we believe that to merely prepare students for work or college is too limiting, and we encourage local schools and districts to think bigger. Each community school needs to create a vision for itself that paints a picture of what children who complete its educational experience can do. Schools must raise their own expectations. As Jim Collins (2001) advocates, create Big Hairy Audacious Goals (BHAGs) that motivate and inspire all stakeholders. School leaders, teachers, and parents should aspire to accomplish that which others say is impossible. Developing creativity, imagination, talents in the arts and sciences, and team leadership must be part of any curriculum that children are asked to pursue.

At your school, merge the CCSS with your curriculum in ways that lead students to take joy in learning new things. Create engaging discovery opportunities with nature. Use imagery, sound, touch, and movement that help students experience what they do not know. Let them experiment with technology to create messages of what they do know and to explore what they do not know.

We hope to inspire you to think bigger than you ever imagined possible. It is our goal to explore the CCSS in four ways. First, we will examine them through the lens of how the standards look and feel when fully implemented and connected to your local curriculum. Second, we will view the CCSS through the lens of professional development and explore how to best teach the standards to all stakeholders. Third, and perhaps most importantly, we will discuss how to supervise all aspects of the CCSS initiative.

Finally, in the fourth section, we will explore ways to pursue the CCSS as pathways to new worlds for children of many cultures and languages in the United States. In fact, in that section, we will offer a school evaluation model where members of an intervention team use the collective wisdom of the personnel, parents, and students at a school to help the school design more effective teaching and learning processes.

Our system will serve to deepen the understanding of all stakeholders about the CCSS. We will help to ensure the fidelity of the common core standards implementation by leading you through a process in which a shared vision of the value of the CCSS is created. We will share ways that the common core should impact many educational domains including, but not limited to, curriculum, assessments, instruction, pedagogy, supervision, technology, and community involvement.

We seek to make the application and merger of common core standards with local school curriculum as practical as possible for anyone involved in any stage of the CCSS process whether you are a teacher, administrator, member of the board of education, or an interested student or parent. Please enjoy the journey we have planned for you.

CHAPTER 2

The School Leader's Role in Making the Common Core State Standards Work

In this chapter, we will outline a process, or model, for using the CCSS to transform our schools into 21st-century learning institutions. Like many models, we express our model in a linear, stepwise fashion that makes it easier to transmit our thoughts. In reality, the process will be organic and quite dynamic in nature. Our model uses inquiry to promote dialogue. We advocate spending a great deal of time discussing why change is necessary and what needs to be done as opposed to how it should be done. With the exception of setting context, our model can be modified, and the time lines should be adjusted based upon organizational needs and the readiness of the personnel to implement the CCSS.

One thing we are sure of is that each step in the model is necessary to create the context and necessary circumstances to transform a school. Begin the dialogue and inquiry at the point where your organization is ready to start. Make sure every step is completed. There are no shortcuts.

We know that *how* is a function of collaborative design and continuous feedback from the users. In our case, the main users would be principals, teachers, and students. How a new system grows can best be described as an organically developed garden of ideas sprinkled throughout by well-informed stakeholders.

Friedman and Mandelbaum (2011) cite Hewlett Packard's CEO, Leo Apotheker, who observed that "a lot of innovation now happens on the shop floor" and, assuming a well-conceived and executed design, the factory "will be more productive a year later because the workers themselves on the factory floor are critical thinkers and can improve the process along the way" (p. 95).

The key role of educational leaders is to engage teachers so that they become critical thinkers and problem solvers. All personnel must function in the 21st century as flexible, adaptable problem solvers. Innovation in education will largely emanate from dedicated, well-trained teachers guided by well-trained, collaborative leaders.

Our model is largely a synthesis of the body of work available on creating learning organizations, professional learning communities, systems thinking, and change theory. It is dependent upon our notion of *leading with inquiry*. Leading with inquiry speaks to the notion that leaders are more effective when they balance advocacy with inquiry. There is clearly a role for advocacy in our organizations. We should advocate for treating everyone with dignity and respect and not advocate for one answer to a problem.

Educational leaders should advocate for and value fairness, transparency, collaboration, communication, and the arts and sciences and create opportunities for all children to be taught by well-educated, dedicated, and self-reflective teachers. What educators should not advocate for is "do it my way or else." This method stifles creativity, ensures compliance-only behavior, and kills trust. Inquiry, on the other hand, creates trust, common understanding, and a shared vision and unleashes loyalty and creativity within an organization. Lead with inquiry.

Our model outlines a collaborative process that implements the CCSS by focusing on the creation of a respectful, data-informed, professional learning environment. We seek distributive leadership where everyone leads and follows, depending upon the circumstances and the mastery required completing a task.

The environment we seek to create devalues blame and values continuous inquiry, communication, professional development, and learning. In our view, teachers and school leaders should align professional training within a shared vision they hold for students and the needs of the educators who must implement the vision. All stakeholders should be engaged at every stage in the process.

We also advocate the creation of specific outcomes and behaviors that one associates with achieving the vision and goals.

The leader's role is to assist the teachers and remove all barriers to their success. Leaders monitor explicit benchmarks and coach to the desired outcomes—the outcomes that are indicative of student success academically, socially, and emotionally. The assistance that the school leader offers is authentic, necessary, and at times, brutally honest about the gap between where student performance is and where it must go.

Bob, a principal, had a conference with a teacher who had 50 percent of his students score about the same on a formative assessment as they had on their quarterly grade. Bob thought, "Those results are horrible." He observed, "Wow, what a challenge; half the class learns, and half do not." He then asked, "What can you do to change those results?" The teacher gave Bob a quizzical look and replied, "That's the way those kids are." Bob asked, "If you had a child in this school, would you place him in your class when you know that only one out of two students will demonstrate proficiency on any topic you teach? Parents expect you to be more creative. How could you reteach what most students failed to learn?" The teacher replied, "I don't know what you mean." Bob knew he must be pleasant and persistent in his inquiries. He suggested, "Let's share some ideas and strategies to regroup students in the class and have peers help each other. What are some of the ways you might do that?"

Later, in the team discussions, Bob brought up the difficulties some students were having with certain questions that required justifications and the use of evidence from the text. Several teachers offered suggestions about strategies they used to get more students to master the building blocks required to answer the question. The teacher with the low passing rate observed his peers' enthusiasm about strategies they were using to raise mastery rates in their classes. In the ensuing weeks, he began to adopt some of their strategies. Months later, he told Bob, "You know I'm not a bad guy. No one ever asked me to try to improve. I thought my failure rate was authentic."

Our inquiry-based model creates the learning environment necessary for what Collins (2001) describes as "tight vs. loose" leadership. This is where the real transformation of American education into world-class schools takes place. The negative connotation of tight leadership references the top-down archetype where leaders are micromanagers and solely responsible for decision making (at least until something goes wrong and they seek a scapegoat).

Loose leadership connotes a more collaborative and distributive style. In reality, however, this is not an either-or proposition. All competitive and sustainable organizations in the 21st century require both tight and loose leaders who know how and when to be either.

The tightness we are after is the persistent commitment to create and lead toward an organization's desired future as expressed in the organizational vision, mission, and goals. This requires a laser-like focus on achieving organizational goals using methods aligned with organizational values. Tight leaders align all resources—knowledge, human, financial, material, and spiritual—to the organization's core business and principles.

Loose leadership is more a means of interacting with internal and external stakeholders. It spurs loyalty and commitment and unleashes creativity among stakeholders. Through the creation of common understanding and a shared vision and guiding ideas (GIs) and explicit goals, loose leaders monitor and foster success and sustainability.

We need leaders who are simultaneously comfortable and skilled in when to be tight and when to be loose. This is precisely the kind of leadership that is essential if faculty and staff are to become innovators. It is also essential for the transformation of schools into world-class learning centers.

CREATING GUIDING IDEAS TO IMPLEMENT THE COMMON CORE STATE STANDARDS

The CCSS create a vision of what 21st-century teaching and learning must look like. Yet, they are only the beginning. The CCSS, like GIs, start with the big picture, and they are refined as one travels deeper through organizational architecture to the place where the work is actually performed—in the classrooms and other arenas of art, physical activity, and leadership. The process of creating GIs starts at the macro level and is then followed down to the micro levels of schools, departments, grade levels, and even individuals. By design, GIs are not highly prescriptive, yet they provide explicit pictures of success that are communicated to and expected of all stakeholders. Once the description of success is clear, evidence of success and failure can be found in a manner consistent with organizational values. When success has been achieved or remains a distant or near reach, teachers and principals can redesign their current practices to address the gaps in learning within a class, often using current resources that have been restructured.

Guiding Ideas and Evidence

A *guiding idea* is much like it sounds. GIs literally and figuratively guide the change you espouse. They are often based on data, research, and best practices. GIs are hard to disagree with if they are crafted well. This is particularly important at the macro level of change, where a school leader tries to build support and common understanding. For instance, one GI that everyone knows well and on which there is little disagreement is that we want no child left behind. Few, if any, want to leave a child behind his or her peers. No one opposed this GI. The No Child Left Behind initiative failed because few knew how to make this happen, and those who were in charge adopted an impossible strategy to achieve the GI: Test excellence into the teaching system, and punish or embarrass those who teach students with low scores.

If leadership creates context well, GIs can be more specific and focused, and the likelihood of people supporting them increases. The key to successful change initiatives is how well a leader facilitates the work of stakeholders who must discover the gaps between the current reality and the desired future reality; then they will feel capable of designing an intervention.

GIs are expressed as beliefs such as these: "We believe all children can achieve academic mastery" or "We believe all children are capable of mastery performance in every core subject." They create the parameters that enable those doing the work to innovate (or be "loose") within acceptable limits that are known to all stakeholders. We feel that the key to unlocking the capacity and creativity among teachers that can transform our schools depends on trust in their desire to be successful in helping children learn.

An underlying premise to earn their trust is admirable institutional values and commitment to continuously develop their skills. Teachers must feel that they partner in the process of change and transformation of themselves and the school leaders. Both members of the partnership must participate fully in the transformation and the professional development of their knowledge, dispositions, vision, and practices. They must renew themselves if they are to bring forth new behavior, dispositions, and performances from their students.

The "tight" aspect of change comes through the explicit and detailed evidence associated with every GI. So, whether the GI is intuitively designed or extracted from CCSS, specific evidence that is formal or informal, quantitative or qualitative, document based or archival, must define successful measurements of progress toward the GI. In the GI, "We believe all children are capable of mastery performance in every core subject," evidence of having met this GI is "mastery or an average summative grade of 85 percent in every core subject."

The evidence that the school leader and teachers accept should be determined at the school: It should reflect rigorous expectations and be demonstrated in a relevant and authentic way. Evidence could, and many times will, represent benchmarks over time. It is also best that evidence not be solely relegated to test scores or only one measure of success. Within the context of the CCSS, remember that evidence that reveals both content and process is required. Explicit evidence enables supervisors and colleagues to self-regulate their performance or *supervise to the evidence*. Central organizational leaders retain the duty to evaluate and endorse the rationale for evidence and the criterion measures.

Consider the task of revamping your reading curriculum to reflect the CCSS. First, it helps to have clear understandings about the design parameters. What are the big ideas around which the CCSS are centered? Knowing the big ideas enables us to know how they might influence our curriculum design. If we examine a section from the Common Core State Standards Initiative website (National Governors Association & Council of Chief State School Officers, 2010), such as the section titled *Key Points In English Language Arts,* pertaining to reading, it states:

> The standards establish a "staircase" of increasing complexity in what students must be able to read so that all students are ready for the demands of college and career-level reading no later than the end of high school. The standards also require the progressive development of reading comprehension so that students advancing through the grades are able to gain more from whatever they read.

Assuming you have done the preparation within the workforce necessary for teachers and principals to answer the question "Why are we doing this," you are ready to turn the CCSS into grade-level reading curricula. The curricula design teams typically include diverse stakeholder representation. If your intention is to create vertical and horizontal alignment or cross-content alignment, there could be several working groups or one large group—the choice is yours and depends upon the participants and their capacities.

You can elect a completely different structure that reflects your needs. Whatever the structure, all curriculum writers need guidance about the products they will create. The CCSS present explicit guidance for teacher curriculum teams to use as a framework.

On the macro level, it would be wise to turn elements of the text above into guidance for everyone associated with turning the CCSS into a core ELA curriculum. Several GIs might be formed. These GIs will ultimately provide design guidance for the writers. For example:

We believe that the standards establish a "staircase" of increasing complexity in what students must be able to read so that all students are ready for the demands of college and career no later than the end of high school.

We believe that the standards also require the progressive development of reading comprehension so that students advancing through the grades are able to gain more from whatever they read.

These statements of belief provide big-picture guidance. Next, it is the time to decide the evidence associated with each of them. Remember, we are setting guidance for the curriculum committee(s), so the evidence must align with the GIs expressed above. For example:

We believe that the standards establish a "staircase" of increasing complexity in what students must be able to read so that all students are ready for the demands of college and career no later than the end of high school.

In this case, the evidence could be the following:

- First draft of the ELA curriculum and curriculum map for every grade level is due on February 1, 2012 (6 months); benchmark meetings will occur monthly at times to be mutually agreed upon.

- Second draft of the ELA curriculum and curriculum map for every grade level is due on May 1, 2012 (3 months); benchmark meetings will occur monthly at times to be mutually agreed upon.
- Final revision of the ELA curriculum and curriculum map for every grade level is due on July 1, 2012 (2 months); benchmark meetings will occur monthly at times to be mutually agreed upon.
- Board of Education adoption of final ELA curriculum for every grade level is due September 1, 2012.

What you define as evidence of meeting GIs is totally up to you. For the practitioner charged with accomplishing the task, the evidence provides a window into what the students will be able to produce as a result of instruction. Teachers know what the evidence should look like from the start. The illustration above is *process* evidence.

Academic evidence should be more reflective of multiple measures and indicative of appropriate academic rigor, relevance (developmentally and culturally), and authenticity when possible and also include process expectations. Examples of academic evidence could be the following:

- All students will achieve mastery (85 percent or higher) on all summative assessments.
- All students will be reading on or above grade level by the end of second grade.
- All formative assessments will demonstrate student growth and mastery of all instructional goals.
- All formative assessments will be used to measure effect size changes greater than .4 for each class.

Wiggins and McTighe (2005) note that assessment evidence must be drafted in terms of the goals of the curriculum and the standards: "We are obligated to consider the assessment evidence implied by the outcomes sought, rather than thinking about assessment primarily as a means for generating grades" (p. 148).

Getting to How: Operationalize Your Guiding Ideas

Up until this point, our efforts have been focused on the why and what aspects of the change process. As we move from dialogue to action, every step is designed to produce greater clarity in the descriptions of the desired change. Now, we begin to address the how part of change. This aspect of the model, as with all others, is intended to be collaborative and to include all relevant stakeholders.

From GIs and evidence, our journey brings all of the new found data and information illuminated through inquiry into focus by establishing operating principles (OPs). *Operating principles* take the aspirations obtained from the GIs to create a picture of the new behaviors necessary for the desired change. The OPs are created within all of the relevant instructional and noninstructional domains that play roles in the achievement of the GIs. The OPs help to inform, at a deeper level, all stakeholders about the innovations they need to seek if school transformation is to take place.

For instance, if our GI is "We believe all children are capable of mastery performance in every core subject," and we define evidence of having met this GI as "mastery (an average summative grade of 85 percent) in every core subject," the school leader and teachers need to make this operational throughout every domain. Here is where the discussion and creativity are paramount. If a school leader has created (and frequently revisited) the context for the change, people may surprise him or her with their levels of engagement and talent. They will make unique and valuable contributions to the developing thinking process.

The OP could look like this: "If we believe all children are capable of mastery performance in every core subject, then . . ." The then part of the equation starts bringing us into the how part of change. By identifying the then, we begin to see the new behaviors or content associated with the evidence we want to produce. These behaviors guide the innovation necessary for transformation. In this exchange, strong leadership, advocacy, data-driven analysis, and careful listening skills must be paramount within all partners. Current reality may restrict the partners to an analysis of current practices and resources, jettisoning some so that a few may be redesigned and reallocated to high-impact behaviors and use of time and money. Rather than bring in more staff or create another service industry, such as a remediation crew, teachers may have to reallocate class time to differentiated groups working to achieve mastery at multiple levels, such as peer tutoring and modeling, exploratory team projects, and co-teaching moments. No one knows the limits of teacher creativity once it is unleashed.

If we were members of the reading department, and the district's GI was "We believe that all children should achieve high levels of literacy to succeed in the 21st century," we would need to deeply examine our role in achieving this goal within the context of the effects of globalization and instructional technology on our nation's educational programs. We would discuss how to shift our expectations and professional practice, professional development, curriculum, materials, budget, schedules, and general interactions and exchanges regarding student performance to achieve our GI. Based upon what research indicates about success in school, one discussion might look something like this:

GI: We believe all children must be reading at a mastery level by the end of second grade.

Evidence:

- Kindergarten
  - All children will exit K at or above Level D.
  - All children will score at mastery levels in phonemic awareness, and rate and fluency subtests.
  - All children will demonstrate mastery on CCSS #s . . .

- Grade 1
  - All children will exit Grade 1 at or above Level x.
  - All children will score at mastery levels in phonemic awareness, decoding, and rate and fluency subtests.
  - All children will demonstrate mastery on CCSS #s . . .

- Grade 2
  - All children will exit Grade 2 at or above Level x.
  - All children will score at mastery levels in phonemic awareness, comprehension, and rate and fluency subtests.
  - All children will demonstrate mastery on CCSS #s . . .

- Grade 3
  - All children will exit Grade 3 at or above Level x.
  - All children will perform at or above mastery on state ELA assessments.
  - All children will demonstrate mastery on CCSS #s . . .

Of course, there would need to be other GIs in later grades that amplify this first GI.

OP: If we believe all children are capable of all fundamentals of literacy at a mastery level by the end of second grade, then . . .

Teachers

- All elementary classroom teachers must realize that literacy is at the core of our instructional program.
- All elementary classroom teachers must have deep knowledge of the reading process.
- All elementary classroom teachers must have deep knowledge about the learners they teach (learning styles, strengths, deltas).
- All elementary classroom teachers must have access to a rigorous, relevant, and user-friendly curriculum.
- All elementary classroom teachers must have deep knowledge of the CCSS and be able to use them to promote rigor and relevance in both professional activities of planning and delivery of lessons in whole and small group processes.
- All elementary classroom teachers must have the ability to diagnose, prescribe, and remediate the reading needs of typical primary readers.
- All elementary classroom teachers must have deep knowledge of available data and their use in guiding instruction.
- All elementary classroom students must have adequate theories, methods, and tools to differentiate instruction.
- All elementary classroom teachers must design their class schedules to maximize time on task for reading instruction (whole and small group).
- All elementary classroom teachers must have time to plan collaboratively and to create grade-level baseline and benchmark formative assessments that emphasize student understanding and critical thinking.
- All elementary classroom teachers must have access to and availability to work with reading teachers, facilitators of learning, and reading directors.

Leaders

- All leaders must have deep knowledge and understanding of the reading process and ability to coach teachers when required.

- All leaders must foster collaborative learning environments.
- All leaders must provide every teacher with uninterrupted instructional time for literacy.
- All leaders must monitor and collect data points on all baseline and benchmark assessments.
- All leaders must provide teachers time to access adequate training and to consult with peers and resource personnel.
- All leaders must provide adequate financial and human resources to achieve set goals.
- All leaders must supervise to the evidence.

And so it continues with other affected domains. The goal is to create a clear picture of each partner's role in achieving the GI:

Support Services

Special Education

Students

Parents

Budget

Curriculum

Technology

It is always better to have no more than three to five GIs with associated operating principles that are deeply developed and implemented across the grades than have numerous deployments of many objectives done poorly. In some school districts with whom we share consulting services, administrators and boards were proud of the 25 goals that they had adopted for the school year. The chance of anyone remembering 25 GIs, whether well done or not, is zero. Go for quality, not quantity.

Given the process described thus far, and within the context of the need for 21st-century schools to compete on an international playing field, what GIs, evidence, and OPs would you create to:

- Introduce the CCSS to your faculty?
- Design a process of cross-walking the CCSS into curriculum?
- Design a process that ensures that the curriculum, instruction, and assessment processes are rigorous, relevant, culturally sensitive, and authentic?

In every organization's culture, personnel possess different levels of understanding, expectations for results, capacities for change and stability, leadership, and sustained attitudes, beliefs, biases, and assumptions that support the status quo. Whatever the beginning circumstances may be, creating a new context is step one in the change process. The crafting of the GIs and OPs will vary depending on where leadership can apply the greatest leverage for the changes required. There is no right or wrong unless you borrow a change model from a neighboring district without discussion and try to customize it to your culture and its needs. That is flat out wrong and truly a fix that will fail.

Operating Rules

Operating rules further tighten supervision by explicitly expressing the behaviors that the organization reserves as nonnegotiable. These are sacrosanct and should be limited in number but potentially wide in scope. We view operating rules as setting cultural norms that are transparent and to which every member of the organization must commit. The sampling of operational rules below is extracted from Rich's former district, where he served as superintendent for 11 years.

- We will not blame children, parents, and teachers for any deficits we may perceive.
- All students will be engaged in standards-rich instructional lessons and activities.
- All student assignments will reflect the format and rigor of the state assessments.
- All teachers should know the performance levels of their students at all times and be able to present evidence of same upon request.
- We must remove all professional educators or staff from our district who feel that our mission is futile and our students are incapable.

As you might expect, the last operating principle received the most attention by a certain group of teachers who ran to the union leaders asking what they thought of Rule 5. Because the union leaders were well aware of this document from its inception and participated in several revisions, they simply said that they saw little to argue with and asked why anyone would want to work beside someone who thought that the mission was futile.

IDENTIFYING THE INNOVATION

When all of the data are available in transparent form and easily reviewable by stakeholders, almost everyone understands the need for change. The process of identifying gaps between current reality and a desired future for the school is simplified. Stakeholders develop GIs and evidence statements that they will use to evaluate progress toward the attainment the GIs. OPs and operating rules shape the trajectory for making the necessary changes that will create a world-class school district. When a clear vision of what stakeholders at the school want is developed, the innovations to create the desired reality emerge.

Innovations are not necessarily new inventions, although they can be. What is important to know is that they are new to your school. Here is where Einstein's well-known definition of insanity requires consideration. If you were filling the gaps between current and desired curriculum, teaching, learning, and assessment, then you would already be producing the results you desire. You simply cannot do the same thing you have always done and expect a different result. It's time to search for the means to make your aspirations come true. If significant numbers of students fail to master the curriculum, it is time to change what you think and do.

It is also critical to note that the innovations you decide upon must be systemic. Everyone has a role in making your system world class. Here again, if you have been faithful to the process of creating deep understanding among all stakeholders, they have a road map with the new landmarks that they can identify to transform the school.

Given the context of schools internationally that are outperforming America's schools and our understanding of globalization and the information technology revolution, there are many innovations that we must research more deeply to change our organizational cultures. There are schools in America where many poor children are meeting high standards, and there are many more schools where poor children barely approach proficiency standards. While we would contend that any standard of proficient is too low, many schools need to pass through proficient on their way to mastery.

All of the successful schools share a vision of high expectations for students, high commitment from teachers to meet the needs of students, high professional efficacy and self-regulating instructional behavior among teachers, and high levels of professional development offered by school leaders to the staff as needed (Dalley, 2012; Passi, 2010).

Doug Reeves (2011) presents research on 90/90/90 schools that is quite inspiring and informative. Reeves worked with numerous schools that have 90 percent of the school population living in poverty, 90 percent of whom are minorities, and 90 percent of whom have reached proficiency. Reeves is now moving toward 100/100/100 schools. His work can inform faculty dialogue, planning, and execution about change endeavors, especially if they focus on his guidelines for data teams. Reeves is the first to give credit to collaborative teams of teachers that engage one another in authentic inquiry, data analysis, experimental treatments, feedback loops, and commitment to continuous improvement of instruction and learning.

Robert Marzano's (2003) ideas in *What Works in Schools* are worth investigating, especially how to establish challenging goals and receive effective feedback. Once you now know what you want, you can easily search out the how to fit your needs. It will never be as hard as you think. Getting started on a new endeavor and operating in a new way introduce heightened but constructive anxiety into work and make for a dynamic and exciting workplace. The most difficult disposition to change is fear of the unknown and of failure. The only way to overcome fear is to be excited and thrilled about a new adventure and exploration and to embrace the autonomy to select alternate choices about ways to work together.

For instance, if we want to be deeply focused on literacy and ensure that all children are reading above grade level (mastery) by the end of second grade, the answer may not be in a new reading program. Reeves (2011) and his colleagues have done studies on effect sizes of various typical "innovations" and found that the one that had the most effect was learning how to implement what you are currently implementing more deeply.

This is not to say that you should stick with what you have, especially if it is not reflective of best practices and the latest research on teaching and learning. However, the implication for continuous, highly aligned professional development seems self-evident. Essentially, when you have a poorly executed innovation or strategy, redesigning the process of implementation with GIs and OPs may actually create a truly new innovation and higher mastery learning among students.

Technology allows us to assist teachers in assessing, diagnosing, and differentiating instruction for students with different needs. It can provide the latest training for teachers targeting the things they want to know. It can offer the latest visual support for critical understandings that students must master, such as 1,000 video clips that the Kahn Academy offers free on the Internet.

Castle Learning Systems (2001) and others have embedded in their software simple commands that allow teachers to post inventive creative-thinking questions directly related to curriculum. The software analyzes student responses collectively and individually and publishes distribution histograms for each test item and test. Within an instant, the tedious task of analyzing 30 to 300 test responses can be accomplished. There are two critical practices that must be adhered to:

1. Teachers must design and select questions that scaffold up the criteria of performance so that more than recall cognition is being measured, and

2. The teachers must use the differentiated performance data to stop the race through the curriculum and to attend to the mastery needs among students within each class.

Tony Wagner, quoted in Friedman and Mandelbaum (2011), defined a "better" education as one that focused on "the three C's" . . . critical thinking, effective oral and written communication, and collaboration" (p. 139). Others think critical-thinking skills are now a baseline skill for any sustainable employment, whether on an assembly line or in the office. We know that the huge shift our educational system needs is one that changes focus from what the teacher does to what students master.

The former emphasis on isolated learning and rote, memory-centric instruction became obsolete with the digital expansion of knowledge. Google and a variety of other search engines render recall capacity less valuable. We need students who can access information, assess its value, and see patterns and connections to use what they have learned in new and different ways.

In short, curriculum, teaching, learning, and assessment must be designed for students to play at the higher levels of Bloom's taxonomy. Creativity and interpersonal skills are the talents that keep one employed in the 21st century.

It is therefore ironic that we see arts programs being cut across the country at record rates since the Great Recession. These programs tend to operate at the very top of Bloom's taxonomy because they are performance based, and the music, art, and technology associated with the web and computer-generated designs encompass multiple high-level cognitive skills and personal disciplines. Here again, don't lose focus or take wrong turns because you have accepted a fad or fallen prey to fearmongering about budgets and abandoned very strong GIs and OPs that your community values. Parents and grandparents know what they value. They can see high performance in their children in these creative programs. They cherish the hard work and the rewards of solid performances that their children enjoy. They will invest in these opportunities given that the school leaders and teachers can communicate the vision and power of these programs. We know because we faced steep cuts in the state aid allotted to our districts and grew all of these programs anyway because parents and residents valued them. They knew the dollars spent on these children produced visible effects and did not pay for bridges to nowhere.

The education program that fits best is the one your community values based on the research and wisdom you share with stakeholders. Leaders who share valid research and insightful wisdom win support from constituents.

TEACHING THE CHANGE

As mentioned in the previous chapter, context is necessary for any design to be approached in the proper frame of mind. The 21st century demands a workforce wherein critical-thinking skills are the baseline and where workers must frequently address new and unfamiliar situations requiring adaptation of existing knowledge for a new purpose or outright innovation (Friedman and Mandelbaum, 2011). This context must be maintained when teaching your stakeholders how to achieve success with the new design.

Thus far, we have moved from awareness of the CCSS and why they exist to common understanding to creating guidance for the changes we envision. Lastly, we start taking action. Because the core business of schools is teaching and learning, curriculum forms our culture, and curriculum forms our structural underpinnings.

Actualizing the CCSS into curriculum that is developmental and culturally sensitive and that promotes application, analysis, synthesis, and evaluation—the sum of which enables creativity (Bloom & Krathwohl, 1956)—is largely an academic exercise. Many schools do this aspect of change reasonably well.

What they do not do well is teaching the changes required by new curricula or programs to those who enact and supervise them. Our notion of Senge's (Senge, Ross, Smith, Roberts, & Kleiner, 1994) deep learning cycles is depicted below. We will focus on the theories, methods, and tools our faculty and staff require to effectively implement the innovation (in our case, curriculum) that contains the evidence that signals fulfillment of our GI (see Figure 2.1 below).

If you're developing a 21st-century curriculum (in whatever subject you choose), you should have already created several GIs around the development process itself and the need for developmentally appropriate, 21st-century knowledge, skills, and dispositions (the CCSS). You should also have defined the 21st-century evidence (rigorous, relevant, and authentic) that each innovation must yield. The GI and the evidence you wish to produce inform your choice of innovation.

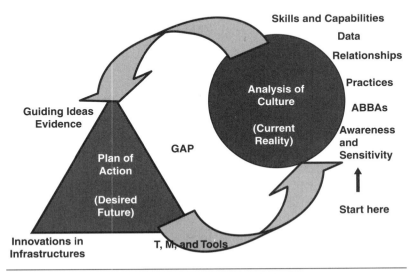

Figure 2.1   Moving From Current Reality to Desired Future

Source: Adapted from Senge et al. (1994).

The theories, methods, and tools necessary to actualize an innovation effectively must be taught. Every stakeholder who holds responsibility for implementation must learn what is expected. Expectations must be taught. In our fictional case, the major leverage for implementing a new curriculum comes from teachers, coaches, and leaders.

For instance, if you have identified a new innovation that requires different knowledge, skills, and dispositions than your workforce presently possesses, initial professional development should concentrate on providing your personnel with the information they require in advance of implementing the change. The basic GI here is that workers and supervisors must be prepared for success.

If economic or political pressure demands change, modify and adjust time lines, expectations, and perhaps the magnitude of the change you have selected. Pilot projects or beta testing is always a good idea. A pilot project, staffed with personnel who seem to possess the talents required for a successful implementation, allows your organization to work out the kinks and create more specificity about training needs or adaptations not previously considered. This is akin to the bottom-up innovation concept illuminated by Friedman and Mandelbaum (2011).

Pilot projects also provide insight to those in supervision about what they need to know and how to supervise the change effectively. They too must be trained, preferably alongside those implementing the initiative. Teachers and supervisors should train together and separately, never only separately. This is recommended for a number of reasons, not the least of which is that the training provides a vehicle to build trust with the workforce and provides valuable insights into the work that is required and the potential barriers to success.

The other major factor to consider is that professional development must be continuous and data informed. As Michael Fullan (2001) has pointed out, *implementation dips* are common to all change initiatives, and all too frequently the dip is recognized too late, and recovery becomes difficult.

Inexperienced leaders at the helm of a change initiative typically panic when they encounter resistance and discouragement among employees, and frequently, they call for a new program. They are convinced that the problem is the program; it rarely is. Generally, the needs and capacity of personnel, the school culture, and the support required of supervisors to implement the change have been misjudged. Personnel need a great deal of help to adapt to the desired change. Fear, a lack of knowledge and training, little confidence, little time to experiment and practice innovations inhibit success. School leaders must frame the initiative as experimental learning for everyone. They must be partners in the learning process and be seen as adapting and changing their own practices.

These patterns of decline in desired performance occur as personnel encounter difficulties implementing new behaviors, and some teachers and school leaders may experience *initiative fatigue*. Far worse, skepticism and cynicism may spread, and as cynicism increases, performance decreases. As a result, in a pattern of poorly conceived and designed innovations, feelings of hopelessness and blame permeate the workforce. Figure 2.2 depicts the problem of resistance and ineffective leadership. Figure 2.3 shows how leaders should remain focused on data-informed decisions and continuous professional development.

When data suggest a dip in achievement or in support for a change, this is a signal to ramp up dialogue and professional development. This assumes you have data (evidence) that signal a true dip in the first place—a big if in many instances. More importantly, if the data collection process is designed well and appropriate benchmarks are in place, the dip can be quickly recognized and diagnosed. Most importantly, partners in the initiative must face the brutal

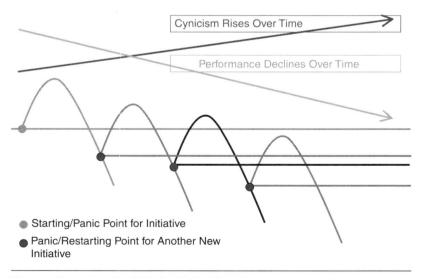

Figure 2.2   Dealing With the Dip Ineffectively

Source: Adapted from Senge et al. (1994).

fact that a dip in performance is occurring and facilitate dialogue, inquiry, and renewed efforts to forge ahead with the innovation. Soon after the dip in performance occurs, if it is properly addressed, personnel rally around new and better-designed initiatives, and they redirect the results toward the desired reality. At this point, all personnel learn that they have the capacity to change and to improve their results. From here on, a spirit of continuous improvement will drive multiple innovations and greater success.

It is simply not enough to train anyone once (and usually poorly) on any new innovation and hope for the best. As Rich is fond of saying, "Hope cannot be your primary strategy!" We especially love the horror stories about textbook salespeople training teachers for an hour the day before school begins in September about how to implement their new "curriculum." This is hopeless from the start, not to mention grossly irresponsible.

THE SOCIAL AND EMOTIONAL LITERACY COMPONENTS OF THE COMMON CORE STATE STANDARDS

We know that one of the most essential skills required to live in a global world and compete in a global economy is emotional

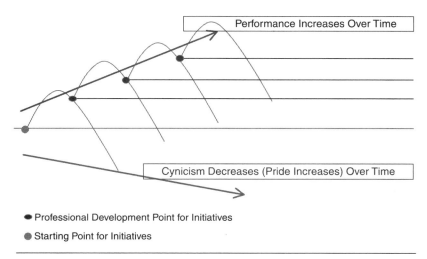

Figure 2.3   Dealing With the Dip Effectively

Source: Adapted from Senge et al. (1994).

intelligence (Goleman, 1998). It will be easy for teachers and leaders to focus on the content aspect of the CCSS while ignoring the social and emotional strands embedded in them. It is our task as leaders to maximize the learning associated with content and process in both the academic and social domains represented by the CCSS. A cognitive emphasis without a focus on the social and emotional development of children will diminish our capacity to compete in the global environment.

This is one of the reasons we believe that the process we have outlined here is so necessary for implementing the CCSS in the way they are intended. We have provided a means of establishing the why, what, and how to implement the CCSS. The process itself models the behaviors one associates with the ability to function effectively on a team. Other than in schools, teams are the way the world gets things done. Working in isolation guarantees obsolescence, and educators here in America have a massive amount of evidence to support how teacher isolation has fostered the current state of most of our schools.

Social and emotional literacy must be taught and modeled in everything we do and as a part of everything we teach and learn. Robinson (2010) noted that the world of commerce values one's capacity to collaborate, yet in school we call this cheating. Putting aside his tongue-in-cheek comment, there is so much truth in his observation. The specific implications for teaching, learning, and assessment, and more generally the design of American schools, are pretty clear—teachers are isolated, long-distance runners driving students across flat curricula. Teachers and leaders must model the change in behavior that we seek from our students. They must collaborate, plan, and assess student performance and seek peer review to achieve new outcomes. Our schools must become true learning communities (Hord, 1997).

SCHOOLS LEADERS AND TEACHERS
PARTNER TO HELP STUDENTS

The CCSS require a major shift in our American view of education and in the biases that impact our current design. The fact is that few teachers know how to diagnose and prescribe learning challenges. It's not their fault. Largely, they haven't been trained to behave this way. Few college programs emphasize a rigorous clinical approach toward teacher education.

In NYS and many other states, to be licensed as an elementary teacher requires one course about reading. It usually exposes the prospective teacher to the various methods available for teaching reading. A special educator might need two classes in reading instruction, popularly described as *literacy*. Neither one requires a clinical setting. Should we be shocked that the numbers of children classified under the Individuals With Disabilities Education Act (IDEA) have grown exponentially, especially those classified as *learning disabled* (LD)?

We remind you that, by definition, a child classified as LD has average or above-average intelligence (this capacity is still measured mostly through IQ scores), and the discrepancy between his or her actual performance in school and expected performance differs by two or more grade levels. Casting aside the fact that most of the students classified as LD are male and predominantly students of color or students whose primary language is other than English, the vast majority of these students were labeled as persons with learning disabilities because they could not comprehend what they read and did not respond to traditional instruction.

So, we have teachers who have limited knowledge about how to teach a child to read and teaching children who are quite different from them, and they have little or no capacity to diagnose, prescribe, and remediate the child's challenges with reading. Should we be shocked that children whose language is other than English falter in our schools? Teachers simply do not have the skills to help these children, and therefore, the system, as most schools work, allows teachers to refer the students to special education committees so that the children can be passed off to another set of teachers who may or may not be able to help them overcome the gaps that they have in basic knowledge. Once again, the special education label isolates many children into groups where their teachers have been acculturated to believe that they cannot meet the CCSS.

Unfortunately, the CCSS cannot remediate the reality we just described. It takes leaders who possess 21st-century skills, the least of which are courage and passion. We must develop the skills of inquiry and dialogue and the ability to listen and hear deeply. Leaders should understand the complexity within systems and model critical thinking salted with humility. The fact is schools need effective teachers to partner with effective school leaders. When students present patterns of success, all partners in their success should celebrate. When segments of the students demonstrate a lack of mastery, teachers and school leaders must ask what we should do differently, select a course of action, and commit to execute new behaviors to get new results.

To lead a school is to promote learning. For teachers to use thought-provoking, engaging, and interactive instructional strategies and assessments that bring the best out in their students, principals must model that behavior (Parkay, Hass, & Anctil, p. 373). Figure 2.1 presents an outline of the model that we believe depicts one of the best ways to take the benefits and the content of the CCSS and merge them with local curriculum at the school and school district level.

INSPIRING TRUST, CREATIVITY, TRANSPARENCY, AND SUCCESS: A FRAMEWORK FOR LOOSE VERSUS TIGHT LEADERSHIP

Part I: Building Understanding About the Issue and Its Impact on Your Organization

This section focuses on defining and understanding the issue your organization faces through the lens of every affected stakeholder group. The goal is to understand the issue deeply and to prepare the organization for the need for change and the anticipated solutions. The overarching focus is on the what, not the how.

Step 1: Analyze the Issue Confronting the Organization

- Determine the level of importance
- List who is affected
  - What is the level of their awareness
  - What is their current capacity to successfully challenge this issue
  - Identify points of leverage

Step 2: Design a Dialogue Among Stakeholders

- Make it specific to the audience and level of awareness
- Create context for the change considered
  - Focus on the big picture
  - Tell a story using real events, data, and facts
    - Patterns will emerge
      - Areas of common understanding
      - Areas requiring further discussion and investigation

Step 3: Creating Guiding Ideas

- Begin by focusing on areas of common understanding
  - Merge the patterns of agreement into belief statements (GIs)
    - Macro
      - Start with the big picture impacting all stakeholders
      - Begin each domain with, "We believe . . ."
    - Micro
      - End with the smaller picture impacting individuals and groups
      - Begin each domain with, "We believe . . ."
- Refine understanding in areas of disagreement requiring further discussion and investigation
  - Merge the patterns of agreement into belief statements (GIs)
    - Macro
      - Start with the big picture impacting all stakeholders
      - Begin each domain with, "We believe . . ."
    - Micro
      - End with the smaller picture impacting individuals and groups
      - Begin each domain with, "We believe . . ."

Part II: Moving From Understanding to Action

This section focuses on developing and converting your beliefs or GIs into OPs and operating rules. The goal is to transform your beliefs into actions that address the issue your organization faces and to guide innovation among all stakeholders. The overarching focus is on the how from a behavioral sense. Note: You do not want to get too prescriptive. You want to inspire change and innovation from the bottom up.

Step 1: Shaping Your New Culture by Developing Operating Principles

- Convert your GIs to OPs
  - Transform your GIs into OPs that begin to define the behaviors your organization must adopt to enable your beliefs to be realized
    - Move from "We believe . . ." to "If we believe . . ., then . . ."

- The then aspect of the equation begins to define the actions and behaviors necessary to adopt to overcome the challenges that face your organization.
- Involve multiple stakeholders and the various domains within your organization in developing OPs.

Step 2: Guiding Your New Culture Through Operating Rules

- Identify your culture's nonnegotiables
  - Define aspects of behaviors which are expected or for which there is no latitude or tolerance
    - Positive
      - "Everyone will . . ."
    - Negative
      - "No one will . . ."
  - Operating rules should be as limited as possible (no more than ten and preferable five or less)

Step 3: Identify the Gaps Between Your Desired Future and Your Current Reality

- Continue adding new data and conducting dialogues
- Compare and contrast your desired OPs with your current behaviors and practices
  - Identify positive behaviors
  - Identify barriers and negative behaviors

Step 4: Design for Your Desired Future

- Using gap analysis, identify changes and innovations that might address your needs and propel your organization forward using the lens of stakeholders in every domain (diversity breeds productivity)
  - Evaluate options
    - Choose those that best align with your new shared beliefs and goals
    - Modify selected options where necessary for your culture
  - Identify specific evidence of success
    - Target specific goals and time frames
    - Be explicit
      - Adopt or develop metrics to monitor goals
        - Establish baselines and benchmarks

Step 5: Teach All Stakeholders How to Achieve the Success They Envision

- Identify capacity and knowledge gaps between the current reality and desired future
  - Identify specific theories, methods, and tools every employee in every department must possess to enable the innovation under consideration to succeed
    - Address the gap through highly aligned continuous professional development
      - Adopt an artist-in-residence model
      - Avoid assembly programs

Step 6: Supervise to the Evidence

- Develop and use a system of metrics that provides sufficient baseline and benchmark data that are transparent and accessible to all
  - Everyone must own and use the data

Step 7: Congratulate Your Organization

- You have started your journey toward transformation

Step 8: Repeat Steps 1 Through 8

In the next three chapters, we address explicit examples of how schools merge the CCSS with local ELA and mathematics curricula. We examine specifically the challenges that are associated with implementing the CCSS, especially the mental models, beliefs, mores, and values that represent internal and external obstacles to children's success in schools. In the last section of this book, we address the ever-expanding multicultural issues in our schools, a proven method to improve schools with long-term joint intervention teamwork, and finally, we offer recommendations for public policy issues that school leaders, teachers, parents, and citizens must address.

SECTION II

Helping Communities Create a New Future

CHAPTER 3

Designing Local Curriculum to Absorb the Common Core State Standards in English

If we want to have all children reading grade-level materials with comprehension by third grade, curriculum must be designed to achieve this goal. Obviously, the curriculum must be guaranteed and viable; developmentally appropriate; rigorous; and attendant to pacing, process, and content (Marzano, Waters, & McNulty, 2005). Teachers should control the viability, rigor, pacing, process, and content of curriculum. They must be deeply involved in its design if they are to acquire profound understanding and commitment to the curriculum. They must articulate explicitly what their students will be able to do as they guide students through the curriculum much in the manner that Sacagawea guided Lewis and Clark as they explored North America. To serve as curriculum guides, teachers must be involved intimately in mapping the curriculum and designing local assessments that verify where students comprehend and fail to comprehend.

School leaders and teachers must learn how to apply the wisdom inherent in Bloom's taxonomy (Bloom & Krathwohl, 1956; Bloom, 1981) and Wiggins and McTighe's (2005) *Understanding by Design* to improve the capacity of all children to learn (Manley & Hawkins, 2010).

In 1981, Benjamin Bloom published his book, *All Our Children Learning*, in which he offered a system to ensure that all children would learn. He presented five theoretical components that a unified curriculum system should incorporate:

1. Stimulate children to perceive aspects of the world about them and fix the aspects in the child's memory by the use of language.

2. Develop more extended and accurate language. The child's comments must be extended by the teacher's responses. The interaction between the teacher and the child and among children should lead to more precision, complexity, and variety in the use of language.

3. Develop a sense of mastery over aspects of the immediate environment and an enthusiasm to learn for its own sake. The primary goal is to learn how to learn, to explore, and to interpret increasingly complex environments.

4. Develop thinking and reasoning and the ability to make new discoveries for oneself. Some problems should be presented in the forms of games and play that encourage children to discover their own ways to solve.

5. Develop purposive learning activity and the ability to attend to issues for longer periods of time. Encourage the child with feedback and reinforcement as she or he engages in various cooperative activities and solves problems successfully (adapted from Bloom, 1981, pp. 82–83).

Bloom offered these systemic guidelines to help culturally disadvantaged nursery school children gain the knowledge and dispositions they would need for a lifetime of learning. His system works at every level of learning because teachers who adopt the system promote self-regulated learning in students of all ages. Teachers who use Bloom's approach ask constantly, "What must I change in my instructional process to get more students to master the curriculum?"

Wang and Holcombe (2010) examined data from 1,000 eighth grade students in Maryland to investigate if any school-related practices were associated with their academic achievement. They reported, "Greater school participation, school identification and use of self-regulation strategies were positively associated with GPA" (p. 650). School participation was measured using statements about students being attentive in class. School identification employed statements that asked students to express how comfortable they felt at school. Self-regulation strategies employed statements about students' use of prior knowledge, anticipation strategies, and self-correction by checking their work or seeking help. When these practices were pervasive across a middle school in classroom after classroom, students achieved higher grade point averages, especially if their efforts were attached to mastery-level goals for each grade-level curriculum (Wang & Holcombe, 2010). Dalley (2012), in his study of 300 teachers, found that those in high-poverty and high-achieving schools distinguished themselves as self-reflective and efficacious people who changed what they were doing to get more students to master what they taught.

In schools with weak curriculum designs, the teacher is the focus, and the curriculum is a large lesson plan. Such curriculum statements guide the teacher's behaviors and fail to identify how the student will demonstrate learning. Excellent curriculum designs include statements that describe the cognitive applications and the operational dispositions and actions that students will be able to achieve with instruction.

Grant Wiggins and Jay McTighe (2005) in their book *Understanding by Design* propose six facets of student expressions of understanding: explanation, interpretation, application, perspective, empathy, and self-knowledge (pp. 76–77). They contend that curriculum design must attend to how instruction enables students to explain what they've learned. Students should be encouraged to offer an inventive or fully justified account of a historical event, a literary work, or a scientific or mathematical process.

Wiggins and McTighe (2005) want students to interpret events or phenomena, to analyze meaningful connections, and to identify significance within events. The school experiences of every child who is learning to read, write, and speak should be enriched with these expectations in a planned and collaborative instructional process that teachers and school leaders adopt.

Wiggins and McTighe (2005) note that the application of knowledge is evident when students adjust understandings to diverse, complex, and difficult contexts. Students achieve personal perspective by effectively criticizing other viewpoints and offering penetrating or novel assessments of events. Instruction should lead students to achieve empathy so that they are disposed and able to see and feel as others do, and so that they are open to diverse and even unusual people and events.

Finally, Wiggins and McTighe (2005) pose the challenge that instruction should lead students to become deeply aware of the boundaries of their own and others' understanding, their own integrity and courage, and their prejudices and projections. Without using the term *self-regulation strategies,* they offer the most profound descriptions of self-regulated learning and curriculum strategies that promote students to make judgments about their own learning. They remind us that teacher sensitivity to student learning has to be embedded within the curriculum and should be the focus of supervision.

Curriculum design matters to students. The aim of the curriculum must be clear and must focus on what students will be able to do if it is to have lasting meaning for them. How we encourage students to learn matters also. Students are willing to pursue learning when it has some social aspect such as the interpersonal relationships that collaborative work offers. Curriculum that promotes independent and self-directed dialogue and collaborative exchanges among students and faculty fosters a learning community among teachers and students. Teachers need school structures and support to build learning communities (Passi, 2010).

Curriculum is effective when teachers engage in creative brainstorming at their grade levels. DuFour (2011) identifies one of the key ingredients of successful learning communities when he observes that a collaborative school culture raises student achievement, while there is no evidence to support that teachers who work in isolation raise student achievement in schools.

Teachers can produce a hierarchical engagement of students in learning activities that involve multiple cognitive and dispositional levels. By working together to design curriculum and collaborative assessments, teachers can expand their own creative and innovative practices.

Peter Senge (1990) proposed in his book *The Fifth Discipline* that a learning organization employed systems thinking, personal mastery, mental models, shared vision, and team learning. Senge (1990) stated that the "essence of mastering systems thinking as a management discipline lies in seeing patterns where others see only events and forces to react to" (p. 126). Passi (2010) examined high- and low-performing high schools and compared patterns of structure, collaboration, and assessment. He found that teachers who worked in schools with supportive structures that required them to collaborate about curriculum, instruction, and formative assessments actually produced higher-achieving students (Passi, 2010).

Personal mastery is a developing skill that all teachers need to address continuously as they attend to the needs of students that they teach at common grade and subject levels. Senge (1990) defined personal mastery as a discipline that allows us to continually clarify and deepen personal vision, focus energies, develop patience, and see reality objectively (p. 7). Mental models, he stated, are "deeply engrained assumptions, generalizations, or even pictures or images that influence how we understand the world and how we take action" (p. 8).

Senge (1990) tries to guide us in our work of building a shared vision when he writes that a shared vision begins with multiple personal visions that, during many inquiries and dialogues, come to be shared and grow "as a by-product of interactions of individual visions" (p. 217). He offered that leaders should allow multiple visions to coexist and listen for the right course of action that transcends and unifies all of our individual visions. He suggested that leaders should be enrolled in the mission, be honest, and offer others the option to choose, or if choice is not an option, be open about the need for compliance.

Vision in Senge's (1990) lexicon is the future we seek, purpose is what we value that drives our actions, and core values are the beliefs that prescribe how we will act. Virtues represent personal mastery efforts that comprise the disciplines that enable us to act. He explains that team learning "starts with dialogue, the capacity of members of a team to suspend assumptions and enter into genuine thinking together" (p. 10). Dialogue is not discussion. Dialogue is a discipline that "involves learning how to recognize the patterns of interaction in teams that undermine learning" (p. 10) and letting these defensive patterns emerge, surface, and be addressed creatively so that new learning can occur. Truly collaborative enterprises master these five disciplines and build a system in which students can collaborate among themselves, with their teachers, and with the larger community in which they dwell.

In their book, *Quality in Education: The Quality Circle Way*, Sharma and Kamath (2006) observed, "Teaching and learning quality processes require a significant degree of interaction among academic staff. Good teaching does not stem only from individual performance. Quality systems require leadership, well-designed processes, diligent follow-up, and continuous improvement" (p. 87).

Collaboration is not an easy practice to foster. Briggs (2007) found that some colleges in the United States made the mistake of initiating a campus-wide effort at collaboration that created tension, anger, and animosity among faculty members. She examined four highly collaborative campuses in the United States and found that "individual, disciplinary and other differences need to be taken into account when instructing others about collaborative work" (p. 17). Her finding should apply to any faculty in a K–12 environment.

Briggs (2007) identified successful efforts as those that struck a balance between top-down and bottom-up efforts and where an integrated infrastructure that supported collaboration helped to redesign the college and not reform the whole campus. Even in these settings, college leaders had to support continuously the sense of priority that they assigned to collaboration and repeatedly state the role of collaboration in the mission of the college. All school leaders could learn how to lead collaborative efforts at their schools from her research. Her most critical recommendation is that school leaders respect the collective wisdom of the faculty.

Charlotte Briggs (2007) studied examples of curriculum collaboration in 44 continuous-planning college academic departments in the United States, and she noted how department chairs and senior faculty "encouraged voluntary initiative and curriculum collaboration by fostering an ethos of curricular exploration and experimentation" (p. 13). Briggs noted that members of continuous-planning departments did not expect everyone to be involved at all times. She wrote, "Contrary to such a formula for faculty burn-out, continuous planning in a department appears to be sustainable precisely because it is characterized by faculty engagement in curricular collaborations that, at the individual level, fluctuates over time" (p. 14).

Briggs (2007) summarized her analysis in these words: "In addition to enjoying strong community, faculty who engage in extensive curriculum collaboration have a firm sense that they share responsibility for a particular curricular domain and that they are educational practitioners as well as disciplinary experts" (p. 21). Briggs cautioned administrators to recognize that climates conducive to curricular collaboration were created by "enculturation, freedom and support to experiment and informal opportunities and individual actions that provide examples and inspiration to others to strive for excellence in curriculum practice" (p. 25). She concluded that, in all successful cases, the faculty shared a commitment to improve learning for their students.

Passi (2010), in his study of high school learning communities, reported that, when collaboration among and between faculty was authentic and focused on instruction and learning, teachers changed their patterns of instruction, students engaged in more learning activities, and they evidenced more mastery learning.

To implement the Common Core State Standards (CCSS) effectively, each school leader and all faculty members must share a profound understanding that their work goes far beyond the adoption of the CCSS. Adoption is a first step, similar to buying a map to plan a trip. The real task is to make the trip with precise stops for nutrition, rest, recreation, fun, and learning. In this vein, teachers and school leaders must decide how to connect the common core standards to locally developed curriculum.

Teachers must know the needs of the actual students at each grade level, and teachers must align instruction to student needs and to a merger of common core standards and local curriculum. Teachers have to adapt instructional strategies to student patterns of response in their formative assessments. Precise and engaging local curriculum, collaborative and adaptive teaching, and formative assessments are some of the strategies that school personnel must master to bring the CCSS to life in their schools.

Shirley Hord (1997) identified several important attributes among academically successful public schools. Hord noted that principals who shared leadership and invited teacher input into the decision-making processes that affected learning had students that were more successful. She noted that, when teachers had a shared vision of learning, they continuously referenced their work in terms of how well children were learning; they engaged in collective learning and found solutions to individual students' needs.

Finally, Hord (1997) observed that, in effective schools, principals distributed facilities and resources so that teachers had specific times to meet and to collaborate. She offered a professional element that contributed to high performance among teachers and students: "the visitation and review of each teacher's classroom behavior by peers as a feedback and assistance activity to support individual and community improvement" (p. 18). The transition from adoption of the CCSS to the merger of the standards within local curriculum and new implementation strategies requires formative assessments, targeted collaboration about learning and teaching, and continuous feedback.

The CCSS represent a national effort in the United States to alter curriculum expectations so that all children will have equal opportunities to pursue a rich and rigorous curriculum with teachers dedicated to their success. The common core standards state: "The following standards offer a focus for instruction each year and help ensure that students gain adequate exposure to a range of texts and tasks. Rigor is also infused through the requirement that students read increasingly complex texts through the grades. Students advancing through the grades are expected to meet each year's grade-specific standards and retain or further develop skills and understandings mastered in preceding grades" (Common Core State Standards, I, 2010a).

In order to illustrate how the CCSS may be absorbed into local school curriculum, we have chosen to place examples of common core standards on the left side of our tables (see Tables 3.1 through 3.9) and to show how teachers in local schools have absorbed those standards into particular school curriculum. On the right side of each table in this chapter, we present examples of local school curriculum that teachers and school leaders have aligned with the CCSS. We present these examples from local school curriculum where we worked with teachers, school leaders, and supervisors to illustrate how teachers might approach the merger of common core standards with local curriculum expectations.

Normally, in the middle of the table, the local school places the themes that represent the scope and sequence of the grade-level curriculum. When school leaders and teachers collaborate in the process of adapting local curriculum to the standards, they adopt a greater variety of assessments for student learning and become more critical of the quality of their assessments. In fact, they constantly criticize their own assessments and improve them.

We believe deeply that principals must afford teachers a school structure where collaboration and high expectations converge with extensive local monitoring of student achievement in regular formative assessments. Effective teachers examine and criticize how students perform on formative assessments. They identify individual gaps in mastery, intervene, and alter their previous practice. School leaders must engage in this dialogue and facilitate inquiry and adaptations that teachers desire to make. Teachers decide how to ensure that students will master the vital knowledge necessary to proceed through the curriculum. School leaders partner with teachers to evaluate and endorse the local curriculum. School leaders ensure that all inquiry and collaboration efforts focus on improving how children learn. School boards adopt curriculum and monitor student outcomes.

REAL-WORLD APPLICATIONS

The next section of this chapter presents some of the adaptations that teachers and school leaders made in the schools where we had the privilege to guide and with whom we consulted.

Grades K–2: Phonological Awareness (One Topic)

Table 3.1 depicts examples of how teachers merged local curriculum in phonological awareness with the CCSS in the primary grades.

For the Language Common Core State Standard of Key Ideas and Details, we chose to identify three important curriculum outcomes that every student should master, which would indicate that our students were able to perform the behavior that the CCSS required. We chose to focus on key ideas and details and literary

Table 3.1   Grades K–2: Phonological Awareness (One Topic)

Common Core State Standards	*Key Understanding*
Kindergarten	
2. Demonstrate understanding of spoken words, syllables, and sounds (phonemes).	2. Identify sounds of vowels and consonants.
a. Recognize and produce rhyming words.	a. Identify beginning and end-of-word sounds.
b. Count, pronounce, blend, and segment syllables in spoken words.	b. Identify rhyme patterns.
c. Blend and segment onsets and rhymes of single-syllable spoken words.	c. Use double consonant sounds.
d. Isolate and pronounce the initial, medial vowel, and final sounds (phonemes) in three-phoneme (consonant-vowel-consonant, or CVC) words. (This does not include CVCs ending with /l/, /r/, or /x/.)	d. Discriminate sounds and meanings using words that provide imagery.
e. Add or substitute individual sounds (phonemes) in simple, one-syllable words to make new words.	e. Find words with similar meanings.
Grade 1	
2. Demonstrate understanding of spoken words, syllables, and sounds (phonemes).	2. Use sounds and words that create images.
a. Distinguish long from short vowel sounds in spoken single-syllable words.	a. Play with words that change vowel sounds.
b. Orally produce single-syllable words by blending sounds (phonemes), including consonant blends.	b. Play with single-syllable words that sound similar and have different meanings.
c. Isolate and pronounce initial, medial vowel, and final sounds (phonemes) in spoken single-syllable words.	c. Generate complete sentences orally.

d. Segment spoken single-syllable words into their complete sequence of individual sounds (phonemes).

d. Read a complete sentence, and tell what is not true.

Grade 2

3. Know and apply grade-level phonics and word analysis skills in decoding words.

3. Use phonetic analysis to pronounce unknown words.

   a. Distinguish long and short vowels when reading regularly spelled one-syllable words.

   a. Use context clues to interpret new words.

   b. Know spelling-sound correspondences for additional common vowel teams.

   b. Practice spelling common usage words.

   c. Decode regularly spelled two-syllable words with long vowels.

   c. Read nonfiction to find a variety of words in context and decipher meaning.

   d. Decode words with common prefixes and suffixes.

   d. Know common prefixes and suffixes.

   e. Identify words with inconsistent but common spelling-sound correspondences.

   e. Develop appreciation for unique words in context.

   f. Recognize and read grade-appropriate irregularly spelled words.

   f. Establish personal goals for reading, and keep a log of what you learned.

---

structure and comprehension. In addition, we chose craft and structure from the CCSS to serve as the backdrop for our local curriculum in Grades K–2.

Grades K–2: Key Ideas and Details and Craft and Structure

The right sides of Tables 3.2 and 3.3 represent the local curriculum statements that teachers at the school agreed to teach and practice with their students. The goal was to have all students demonstrate these behaviors. Obviously, teachers had to individuate instruction, vary the time they worked with segments of their classes, and differentiate instruction with peer tutors.

Table 3.2   Grades K–2: Key Ideas and Details

Common Core State Standards for Literature	*Local School Curriculum*
Kindergarten	
1. With prompting and support, ask and answer questions about key details in a text.	1. Watch, listen to, and recall information in a shared text, e.g., *Chicka Chicka Boom Boom* by Bill Martin, Jr.
2. With prompting and support, retell familiar stories, including key details.	2. Tell stories through puppetry, role-playing, and dramatizations.
3. With prompting and support, identify characters, settings, and major events in a story.	3. Listen to literature, and clarify ideas about characters, setting, and events in guided discussions with peers.
Grade 1	
1. Ask and answer questions about key details in a text.	1. Identify lead and ending word sounds. Identify main idea in a text.
2. Retell stories, including key details and a message or lesson.	2. Identify structure, sequence, or patterns in a story and within the language in the story.
3. Describe characters, settings, and major events in a story using key details.	3. Interpret a graphic organizer. Use a thinking map to describe a character.
Grade 2	
1. Ask and answer questions such as *who*, *what, where*, *when*, *why*, and *how* to demonstrate understanding of key details in a text.	1. Sequence the events of a story.
2. Recount stories, including fables and folktales from diverse cultures, and determine their central message, lesson, or moral.	2. Contrast the meaning of two stories.
3. Describe how characters in a story respond to major events and challenges.	3. Connect a personal life story to an event in a story.

Differentiated instruction within a class means that the teacher varies activities, time, visualizations, and supportive opportunities for students to demonstrate new knowledge. Every student in the class receives individual teacher support until all students can express personal mastery in a given task.

Craft and structure represent a common core standard at Grades K–2 we chose to depict in the national core format side by side with a locally derived illustration that teachers in real schools developed. All teachers and school leaders should know the CCSS and should play a role in the integration of the CCSS with local curriculum. In fact, the teaching staff should evaluate local curriculum in terms of how well it aligns with the CCSS. There is no better way for teachers to comprehend the CCSS than to work with school leaders to align local curricula with CCSS.

Table 3.3   Grades K–2: Craft and Structure

Common Core State Standards for Literature	Local School Curriculum
Kindergarten	
4. Ask and answer questions about unknown words in a text.	4. Identify vowel and consonant sounds in a text. Identify unknown words.
5. Recognize common types of texts (e.g., storybooks, poems).	5. Distinguish between fact and fiction. Classify literature into categories.
6. With prompting and support, name the author and illustrator of a story, and define the role of each in telling the story.	6. Identify tone and voice of authors.
Grade 1	
4. Identify words and phrases in stories or poems that suggest feelings or appeal to the senses.	4. Use words that create images.
5. Explain major differences between books that tell stories and books that give information, drawing on a wide reading of a range of text types.	5. Evaluate and state opinions about stories and books that give information.
6. Identify who is telling the story at various points in a text.	6. Formulate and express judgments about the content, organization, and meaning of a text.

(Continued)

Table 3.3   Continued

Common Core State Standards for Literature	Local School Curriculum
Grade 2	
4. Describe how words and phrases (e.g., regular beats, alliteration, rhymes, repeated lines) supply rhythm and meaning in a story, poem, or song.	4. Identify rhyming, figurative, and rhythmic patterns in a text.
5. Describe the overall structure of a story, including describing how the beginning introduces the story and the ending concludes the action.	5. Evaluate ideas presented in a text, and offer supportive justifications for one's opinion.
6. Acknowledge differences in the points of view of characters, including by speaking in a different voice for each character when reading dialogue.	6. Suggest possible feelings of a character while reading a text, and offer potential outcomes that predict plausible events.

Grades 3–5 Fluency (One Topic)

In Grades 3–5, fluency in reading texts within the CCSS emphasizes comprehension of grade-level texts in a variety of genres and subject areas including history and science as well as the arts. The local school curriculum should reflect the culture of the community, opportunities the local community has to enrich and make learning meaningful for students, alignment with research, and even hands-on investigations or interviews students can conduct to further their mastery of a topic. Table 3.4 illustrates how teachers merge inventive curriculum with the CCSS.

Table 3.4   Grades 3–4: Fluency (One Topic)

Common Core State Standards	Local School Curriculum
Grade 3	
4. Read with sufficient accuracy and fluency to support comprehension.	4. Read stories, personal experiences, factual literature, poetry, and drama to express diverse social, historical, cultural understandings of community.
a. Read on-level text with purpose and understanding.	a. State the purpose of a newspaper story.

b. Read on-level prose and poetry orally with accuracy, appropriate rate, and expression on successive readings.

c. Use context to confirm or self-correct word recognition and understanding, rereading as necessary.

b. Create a poem, song, rap, or story that reveals a personal vision of one's own experience.

c. Interpret a scientific or historical essay after identifying and defining unique or difficult terms in the text.

Grade 4

4. Read with sufficient accuracy and fluency to support comprehension.

4. Effectively use active prior knowledge, connections to other texts, visualizations, inference, questions, vocabulary, self-monitoring of comprehension, and synthesizing to interpret texts.

a. Read on-level text with purpose and understanding.

a. Employ context clues to understand new vocabulary.

b. Read on-level prose and poetry orally with accuracy, appropriate rate, and expression on successive readings.

b. Use specific evidence from texts to identify themes, contradictions, main ideas, and meaning.

c. Use context to confirm or self-correct word recognition and understanding, rereading as necessary.

c. In an excerpt from a Harry Potter book, show how meaning changes with tone of a reading.

Grade 5: Reading With Fluency and Accuracy

In language arts, students in fifth grade must master the reading process in at least one of multiple ways so that they understand what they read, recognize if they do not comprehend material, select strategies they can use to access meaning, and self-regulate their learning. Children must be taught how to recognize their own levels of comprehension of a text. They must interpret and explain or even contest the veracity of a text to demonstrate mastery (Mullin, 2011). See Table 3.5.

When teachers are highly invested in the merger of the national common core curriculum with their locally developed school curriculum, they build a foundation for future collaborations that align with meaningful improvements of student learning. DuFour (2011) reminds us that teams of teachers need to "gather ongoing

Table 3.5   Grade 5: Reading With Fluency and Accuracy

Common Core State Standards	Local School Curriculum
Grade 5	
4. Read with sufficient accuracy and fluency to support comprehension.	4. Use evidence from stories to identify themes.
a. Read on-level text with purpose and understanding.	a. Describe characters, interpret motivations for actions, and formulate judgments about how the story derives its meaning.
b. Read on-level prose and poetry orally with accuracy, appropriate rate, and expression on successive readings.	b. Read poetry with appropriate expressive and rhythmic emphasis.
c. Use context to confirm or self-correct word recognition and understanding, rereading as necessary.	c. Analyze ideas and information, and contrast events and protagonists to draw meaning from a text.

information regarding the learning of their students through a comprehensive, balanced assessment process that includes common formative assessments developed by the team" (p. 61). He notes that, if a school has a systemic process that ensures students who are struggling receive appropriate help, "the school will create a multi-tiered, coordinated and collective response to support that student" (p. 61).

DuFour (2011) cautions school leaders not to create artificial teams that make excuses for low achievement. He notes that some teams focus on getting along together and do not have the time and resources to intervene with students who need help. These weak and ineffective teams do not build collective capacity for grade-level teachers to make a difference in the learning curve of each student. Explicit actions and outcomes designed to illustrate learning should change the behavior of both students and teachers. Change, growth, and student response to intervention must be the overarching focus and goals of any learning community.

Grade-level teams that have time to gather and examine student results on formative assessments make a difference in the learning of their students. Well-designed formative assessments

are the ingredients for dialogue and inquiry that lead to transformations in instructional practices at schools.

Poorly designed formative assessments have too many curricular aims or standards that they attempt to measure. If there is
one criticism that we must aim at the CCSS, it is that they comprise
too many statements, too many performance goals, and some trivial
expectations. Teachers who intend to merge the CCSS with their
local curricula and their practice for teaching and learning must
determine in a collaborative process what standards are most important to teach, measure, and reinforce.

We selected a few CCSS in English language arts (ELA) at
Grades K–2, 3–5, 6–9, and 10–12 to illustrate the work that teachers
must do to implement the common core standards within their local
school curriculum. We placed a few of the CCSS for each grade
level on the left side of our tables, and on the right side of our tables,
we provided actual adaptations of local school curricula to illustrate
how a group of teachers might interpret the common core standards
that we selected.

Even this merger of CCSS and local curriculum would be
meaningless without a planned and commonly shared formative
assessment system to measure student responses to instruction and
interventions. Particularly, as children progress through a curriculum,
the various topics and expectations for learning at each grade level
must assure alignment and fidelity to mastery goals for all children.

We believe that the debate, dialogue, formative assessments,
and inquiry that collaborative teams of teachers adopt at their
schools are the most important activities that teachers can do to
improve teaching and learning for their students. The local school
curriculum examples that we chose represent the thinking of several
collaborative teams of teachers in a variety of schools.

The interpretation of the common core standards and their merger
with local-level curriculum should be logical and practical. All expressions of the steps and stairs to successful learning at every grade level
should align with a vision of what graduates must know and be able to
do at the end of the process. Evidence depicting the accomplishment
of each standard and the means by which students could demonstrate
mastery should appear within the local school curriculum plan.

The only way to implement the CCSS within a school is for
teachers to analyze the worthiness of every standard by grade level,
assess how to incorporate them into their local school curriculum,

and commit to annual analysis of the curriculum and of student performance on collaboratively designed formative and summative assessments. Students and parents should be aware of the shared vision that school leaders and teachers hold for the students they wish to graduate.

Most schools would benefit from a concerted effort by school leaders and teachers to take a year to analyze the CCSS across the grades at their schools. Teachers should collaboratively identify the gap between their current reality and their desired reality for their students. Teachers need time, inquiry, and discussion to identify and select the CCSS that they wish to merge with the local school curriculum.

In every grade, teachers must develop collaborative formative assessments as well as personal formative assessments for their individual lessons to identify which students are mastering a skill, technique, procedure, critical-thinking process, or self-reflective management strategy. As teachers and leaders work together, they should discover strengths and weaknesses within their own professional practice, and they should be able to ask for targeted professional development.

School leaders must be open to inquiring and listening to what teachers need. Teachers must feel that they should support their opinions and judgments with evidence that is much more substantial than what they think collectively.

In Chapter 5, we will discuss more fully how to help teachers develop collaborative formative assessments that reveal student progress in the CCSS. In the previous discussions, we focused on literacy developmental practices for elementary schools. Secondary schools present their own set of challenges, and curriculum plans must turn to the social and emotional development of the adolescent and the young adult in these settings as precisely as effective plans do in elementary schools.

Grades 6–8: Key Ideas and Details (One Topic)

Table 3.6 presents examples of mergers between the common core curriculum standards and a local school curriculum for one theme within ELA at Grades 6–8.

Teachers need to have curriculum aims. They need a clear vision of what students should be able to do in order for them to adjust their teaching strategies to how students respond to their instructional efforts. Teachers need a viable curriculum system. In 1994, Edwards W. Deming wrote in his book, *The New Economics for Industry, Government, Education:* "A system must have an aim. Without an aim, there is no system. The aim of the system must be clear to everyone in the system. The aim must include plans for the future. The aim is a value judgment" (p. 50). He went on to note, "The secret is cooperation between components towards the aim of the organization. We cannot afford the destructive effect of competition" (p. 50).

Table 3.6   Grades 6–8: Key Ideas and Details (One Topic)

Common Core State Standards	*Local School Curriculum*
Grade 6	
1. Cite textual evidence to support analysis of what the text says explicitly as well as inferences drawn from the text.	1. Analyze, interpret, and evaluate information from academic and nonacademic sources.
2. Determine a theme or central idea of a text and how it is conveyed through particular details; provide a summary of the text distinct from personal opinions or judgments.	2. Demonstrate how a change in point of view affects the narrative. Write a letter to your younger self offering advice for the future.
3. Describe how a particular story's or drama's plot unfolds in a series of episodes as well as how the characters respond or change as the plot moves toward a resolution.	3. Support interpretations and personal opinions about a text with references to outside authorities.
Grade 7	
1. Cite several pieces of textual evidence to support analysis of what the text says explicitly as well as inferences drawn from the text.	1. Identify literary elements in a text such as symbolism, foreshadowing, irony, metaphor, and simile to interpret a work.
2. Determine a theme or central idea of a text and analyze its development over the course of the text; provide an objective summary of the text.	2. Produce a summary about a famous person found in a biography. Show how internal tensions explain the development of this individual.
3. Analyze how particular elements of a story or drama interact (e.g., how setting shapes the characters or plot).	3. Use text features such as format, sequence, details, setting, and internal tension to explain the plot, the characters, and emotional development.

(Continued)

Table 3.6   Continued

Common Core State Standards	Local School Curriculum
Grade 8	
1. Cite the textual evidence that most strongly supports an analysis of what the text says explicitly as well as inferences drawn from the text.	1. Distinguish between fact and fiction, opinion and prejudice, allusions and reality, and relevance and irrelevance from the text.
2. Determine a theme or central idea of a text, and analyze its development over the course of the text, including its relationship to the characters, setting, and plot; provide an objective summary of the text.	2. Identify the distinguishing features of a text and major forms of texts, and use those elements to interpret a text from H. L. Mencken. Write a critique of a book.
3. Analyze how particular lines of dialogue or drama interact (e.g., how setting shapes the aspects of a character or provokes a decision).	3. Evaluate an author's use of language and literary devices to propel the plot and excite the imagination. Critique the characterization and plot development.

Deming (1994) believed that management had to direct the efforts of all components toward the aim of the system. In his terms, school leaders must ensure that all teachers and other instructional staff understand deeply the aim of the system. How a teacher might direct his or her efforts toward the aim—be it math, language, or another curriculum system—will be influenced by how flexible, creative, innovative, and collaborative the principal tries to be.

All curriculum systems should be visible to students, parents, school staff, and school leaders on the school's website. All curriculum systems should support the development of lifelong learners. All children should graduate with the capacity to pursue new and necessary knowledge and to contribute to one's community and nation.

In his book *The Quality School*, William Glasser (1990) noted that quality schools eliminate coercion and promote student self-evaluation. Glasser writes that students must learn this important lesson: "The success or the failure of our lives is greatly dependent on our willingness to judge the quality of what we do and then to improve it if we find it wanting" (p. 159).

Diana R. Cundell (2006), a tenured faculty member at Philadelphia University, in her article titled "Science as a Borderless Discipline," wrote that she incorporated into her microbiology course a comprehensive look at the field and its global, historical, and social impacts. Her idea of a comprehensive look at the field included student collaboration. She expected high school graduates to come to her college classes ready to do independent research; to analyze data; and to draw connections, patterns, and insights from the data. She described her course preparation like this: "In tackling this problem of content versus scope in my own upper-level science courses in microbiology, immunology, and histology, I have used a variety of strategies to make the course borderless, most of which involve considerable extracurricular research by the students" (p. 45).

Professor Cundell (2006) noted that she used various writing assignments and videos like *The Coming Plague* to develop new thinking and to help her students experience new environments that were not readily accessible to them. She required her students to prepare newspaper articles, personal journals, documentations, and formal research presentations as expressions of active writing across the curriculum. Often, she gave them cultural myths and historical diaries to investigate as tools to advance student knowledge of microbiology.

Of course, her students learned many research and reporting skills as well as critical-thinking and decision-making skills at the same time. Reading and writing in intermediate and middle school as well as high school should be more similar to the work that Cundell (2006) describes: less a practice and imitation of someone else's literary style and much more a development of one's own thinking and decision-making skills.

The CCSS try to move high school students toward critical-thinking and analytical processes that would give them the capacity to make informed judgments. The challenge that school systems face is to merge the CCSS and local school curriculum into a balanced and rich curriculum that all students will have the opportunity to pursue.

One question remains: At what point should high school students have the opportunity for greater autonomy to pursue career and creative goals? We favor fewer directives from the state, a more flexible set of curriculum options after Grade 10, and more autonomy for students in Grades 11 and 12.

Grades 9–10: English Language Arts Curriculum

Table 3.7 presents two examples of CCSS for reading and writing at Grades 9–10 and 11–12. We offer local school curriculum statements that mirror the intent of the common core standards.

These local curriculum statements resulted from inquiry and dialogue among teachers and school leaders about what were the most valuable outcomes of a student's year of study in ELA at high school. Teachers and school leaders analyzed and evaluated research related to the acquisition of reading and writing skills and the CCSS. They created their own design for a local Grade 9–12 high school ELA curriculum that addressed reading and writing skills.

Table 3.7   Grades 9–10: English Language Arts Curriculum

Common Core State Standard	Local School Curriculum
Grades 9–10	
Reading	
1. Determine the meaning of words and phrases as they are used in a text, including figurative, connotative, and technical meanings; analyze the cumulative impact of specific word choices on meaning and tone (e.g., how the language of a court opinion differs from that of a newspaper).	1. Analyze and evaluate ideas from editorials, news articles, and court documents about a public scandal. Criticize public conclusions.
Writing: Text Types and Purpose	
1. Write arguments to support claims in an analysis of substantive topics or texts using valid reasoning and relevant and sufficient evidence.	1. Synthesize information from different sources, make connections, and show relationships and causes.
a. Introduce precise claim(s); distinguish the claim(s) from alternate or opposing claims; and create an organization that establishes clear relationships among claim(s), counterclaims, reasons, and evidence.	a. Develop a thesis, and provide support from social, historical, and psychological perspectives.
b. Develop claim(s) and counterclaims fairly, supplying evidence for each while pointing out the strengths and limitations of both in a manner that anticipates the audience's knowledge level and concerns.	b. Generate a list of significant questions to analyze and evaluate texts.

c. Use words, phrases, and clauses to link the major sections of the text, create cohesion, and clarify the relationships between claim(s) and reasons, between reasons and evidence, and between claim(s) and counterclaims.

c. Analyze and evaluate ideas, data, information, issues, and historical lessons to contrast opposing views.

d. Establish and maintain a formal style and objective tone while attending to the norms and conventions of the discipline in which the students are writing.

d. Recognize and use types of language for the forum and audience in which the essay was constructed.

e. Provide a concluding statement or section that follows from and supports the argument presented.

e. Develop a personal voice that can be employed in writing a conclusion to an essay.

Grades 11–12: Reading and Writing

Table 3.8 presents the Grade 11–12 efforts of teachers and principals to merge the national CCSS with local school curriculum in reading and writing.

Table 3.8   Grades 11–12: Reading and Writing

Common Core State Standard	Local School Curriculum
Grades 11–12	
Reading	
4. Determine the meaning of words and phrases as they are used in a text, including figurative, connotative, and technical meanings; analyze how an author uses and refines the meaning of a key term or terms over the course of a text (e.g., how Madison defines *faction* in *Federalist No. 10*).	4. Analyze a poem by T. S. Elliot to interpret figurative language. Analyze and evaluate a scientific article in a science journal on global climate issues.

(Continued)

Table 3.8   Continued

Common Core State Standard	Local School Curriculum

Writing Example

2. Write informative or explanatory texts to examine and convey complex ideas, concepts, and information clearly and accurately through the effective selection, organization, and analysis of content.	2. Evaluate the consistency of a hypothesis with information, substantive evidence, and logic.
a. Introduce a topic; organize complex ideas, concepts, and information so that each new element builds on that which precedes it to create a unified whole; include formatting (e.g., headings), graphics (e.g., figures, tables), and multimedia when useful to aid comprehension.	a. Analyze and critique the elements of effective writing in a published news article. a.1. Present a more thorough article on the topic using graphics and data to support your thesis.
b. Develop the topic thoroughly by selecting the most significant and relevant facts, extended definitions, concrete details, quotations, or other information and examples appropriate to the audience's knowledge of the topic.	b. Write a personal analysis of a theme that includes an investigation of relevant facts and details.
c. Use appropriate and varied transitions and syntax to link the major sections of the text, create cohesion, and clarify the relationships among complex ideas and concepts.	c. Present a cohesive analysis of a historical and social issue in the United States.
d. Use precise language, domain-specific vocabulary, and techniques such as metaphor, simile, and analogy to manage the complexity of the topic.	d. Analyze and evaluate a poem by Maya Angelou, Margaret Atwood, Elizabeth Bishop, or Gwendolyn Brooks using literary form and critics to substantiate your theme.
e. Establish and maintain a formal style and objective tone while attending to the norms and conventions of the discipline in which the students are writing.	e. Write a literary or film critique.
f. Provide a concluding statement or section that follows from and supports the information or explanation presented.	f. Defend or attack a public policy in a newspaper editorial or column.

As discussed previously, the local-level interpretations of the CCSS require an overarching vision of what the school community stakeholders believe every student must achieve before exiting the school. While a fine start, teachers and curriculum leaders must also have a clear picture of how they will measure the local expression of the standards.

Teachers and school leaders must address other questions as well. Is the local expression of curriculum developmentally appropriate? How do we know? Is there appropriate grade-level rigor and relevance? Is there proper alignment of the standards and evidence retrieval systems of student mastery between grade levels and subject areas? Does the school assessment process produce clarity about student progress and curriculum fidelity? The answers to these questions will largely determine whether our graduates possess actual 21st-century skills or 18th-century skills dressed in 21st-century attire.

Anyone reading this chapter about the implementation of the common core standards in language arts must realize that we do not believe that a common core set of standards can be adopted at a central office or by the board of education or by the state board of regents and actually ensure quality implementation. Those distant agencies can do no more than offer guidance and support to the principals and teachers who have to do the daily adjustments in instruction.

Interactions with students and parents make a difference in how students learn. For the CCSS to have any meaningful impact on the schools, there must be explicit involvement of school leaders and teachers at the local school in curriculum design and formative assessments. Teachers must share their analyses of instruction and student responses to interventions within their professional learning teams if they are to discover new ways to help specific students master the core curriculum. Technology and interactive software open to teacher input should allow teachers to spend less time marking papers and more time interpreting patterns of mastery and gaps in learning. The Castle Learning System (2001) software, among many others, offers this option to teachers. The problem with most vendors of software to support learning is that their representatives try to make their digital learning systems teacher proof so that everyone must follow the same formula. Teachers have to inquire about the options embedded within all software learning systems. When teachers pursue options within digital learning systems, they should find that the engineers have offered them the same intelligent options engineers want for their own software.

In Chapter 4, we take up the question of how one might implement the national common core standards in mathematics. As we progress through the chapters, we will address the challenges of creating coherence and alignment in the curriculum, how to continuously improve teaching and learning with each set of students one encounters in a class, and how assessment of student growth leads to collaborative discoveries of innovations and training that teachers need.

CHAPTER 4

Designing Local Curriculum to Absorb the Common Core State Standards in Mathematics

The Common Core State Standards (CCSS) in mathematics require students to master all of the basic operations of algebra by Grade 9.

> One hallmark of mathematical understanding is the ability to justify, in a way appropriate to the student's mathematical maturity, *why* a particular mathematical statement is true or where a mathematical rule comes from. There is a world of difference between a student who can summon a mnemonic device to expand a product such as $(a + b)(x + y)$ and a student who can explain where the mnemonic comes from. The student who can explain the rule understands the mathematics, and may have a better chance to succeed at a less familiar task such as expanding $(a + b + c)(x + y)$. Mathematical understanding and procedural skill are equally important, and both are assessable using mathematical tasks of sufficient richness. (Common Core State Standards, I, 2010b, p. 4)

In this chapter, we present the challenges that America's teachers and school leaders face in their efforts to improve math curriculum, instruction, and mastery of the underlying principles of mathematics.

COMPARISON OF STATE AND COMMON CORE STATE MATH STANDARD EMPHASIS

Porter, McMaken, Hwang, and Yang (2011b) reveal in their article, "Common Core Standards: The New U.S. Intended Curriculum," that existing state standards and the CCSS for math differ in that the Common Core State Math Standards (CCSMS) have less memorization, procedural performance, and conjecture efforts and greater emphasis on student capacity to demonstrate knowledge and solve nonroutine problems. Porter and colleagues (2011b) present a contrast between state and common core standards in Table 4.1.

What does this difference mean for teachers in the primary and intermediate grades? They will not be able to follow the rubrics in the textbooks any longer. They will have to know the underlying math principles attached to every topic that they teach. They will have to require their students to demonstrate higher levels of understanding of these mathematical principles and to apply them in solving nonroutine problems.

Solving nonroutine problems with mathematics might be fun, and students might enjoy using math skills in these adventures as long as their guide is a knowledgeable teacher. An unprepared

Table 4.1   Comparison of State and Common Core State Math Standard Emphasis

Cognitive Demand	State	Common Core
Memorize	12.11%	9.5%
Perform procedures	48.82%	43.74%
Demonstrate understanding	28.66%	35.65%
Conjecture	7.78%	5.96%
Solve nonroutine problems	2.63%	5.16%

Source: Porter et al. (2011b, p. 107).

teacher would be a nightmare for students. Even well-intentioned teachers who do not grasp mathematical principles deeply engender fear of math and frustrate their students' explorations of math adventures.

Are U.S. teachers in the elementary schools trained sufficiently in mathematics to lead lessons beyond memorization of multiplication tables? Can elementary teachers lead their students beyond the practice of routine math procedures in subtraction, division, fractions, and decimals? The accurate answer to both questions is no. Brent Davis (2011) in his article, "Mathematics Teachers' Subtle, Complex Disciplinary Knowledge," provides a sharp critique of American math teachers:

> Teachers' tacit knowledge includes many instantiations invoked to introduce and elaborate concepts, e.g. analogies, metaphors, and applications. Such instantiations are important in early mathematics learning. Teachers in high performing jurisdictions, such as Hong Kong and Japan, were roughly twice as likely as U.S. teachers to invoke varied interpretations of concepts. (p. 1506)

To illustrate, Davis (2011) shows four different interpretations of multiplication: clustering, array making, compressing, and sloping. His point is that "the mathematician's task is to pack insights into tight formulations (theorems, formulae, and so on), it is the teacher's task to unpack" (p. 1507) these insights with their students. Davis suggests that teachers' mathematical skills should be viewed as learnable and continuously evolving dispositions and that their profound understandings of emergent mathematics have to be developed.

He criticizes America's current approach to early mathematical learning as a linear process with curriculum design and testing that contributes to narrow and rigid conceptions of mathematical instruction. He suggests that teachers should be deeply involved in the identification of useful instantiations of mathematical concepts, combining them into more powerful interpretations and using new insights to inform practice. He envisions early mathematical instruction as an adventure that teachers share with each other and with their students.

Davis favors a shift in math curriculum from a fundamental and linear progression to an involving network of associations and elaborations. The CCSS require an integration of linear and exploratory analysis. Davis (2011) emphasizes the capacity of teachers to learn from one another and to use digital media to network and to develop new ways to think about mathematics with their students. He believes that "in a knowledge-based economy, the development of conceptual fluency is of increased importance" (p. 1507).

School principals are the central source of power from which the energy and tension for change flows. Principals must ask teachers, "How are we thinking about math in each of our grades and in our school as a whole system?" What evidence do we have that students enjoy math? What evidence do we have that teachers have the school support and structure to improve continuously their math knowledge and their initiations regarding math and math instruction and assessment?

The CCSS call for all teachers to work more closely in a collaborative model of grade-level and school-wide instruction in which teachers continuously evaluate how students respond to instruction and demonstrate their understanding of math applications.

Most elementary school teachers received extensive instruction and practice in pedagogical practices for the classroom and child psychological and social development. They received little or no course work in mathematics and science and, for the most part, were required to take one course in math and science pedagogy (education) for the elementary child in their preparation as school teachers.

In a review of elementary school teacher preparation in mathematics in several suburban school districts in New York, we found that many teachers took their last mathematics course in high school, and for some, their last course was Algebra I. In the June 2011 issue of *Science,* Schmidt, Houang, and Cogan compared the preparation of middle school math teachers in the United States to those in Taiwan and the Russian Federation. They reported that U.S. middle school math teachers have 10 percent less course preparation in mathematical knowledge and 10 percent more course preparation in general pedagogical knowledge regarding instructional practices and schooling. Their Taiwanese and Russian Federation counterparts were better prepared in mathematical knowledge. Why is this important?

They examined data from the 2010 Teacher Education and Development Study in Mathematics (TEDS-M) and contrasted math teacher preparation in the two highest-performing countries, Taiwan and the Russian Federation, with the United States. Table 4.2 presents the difference in math preparation for U.S. and Taiwan and Russian Federation teachers.

Table 4.2   Percent of Course Work Related to Mathematical Knowledge

Middle School Teacher Preparation	Taiwan/ Russian Courses	U.S. Courses
Mathematics knowledge	50%	40%
Pedagogy in mathematics	30%	30%
General pedagogy	20%	30%

Source: Schmidt, Houang, & Cogan (2011, p. 1266).

Schmidt and colleagues (2011) concluded: "U.S. middle school mathematics teacher preparation does not produce teachers with an internationally competitive level of mathematics knowledge" (p. 1266). In addition, they noted that some U.S. institutions preparing middle school math teachers were requiring as little as 34 percent of their student teacher course work to be in mathematics.

"The solution for the United States lies in a combination of recruiting those who have strong quantitative backgrounds together with a greater emphasis on rigorous mathematics in teacher preparation" (Schmidt et al., 2011, p. 1267). U.S. school leaders and teachers cannot wait for an evolutionary change to take place in teacher preparation for math instruction. School leaders at the K–6 grade levels need to identify the actual preparation that their teachers have in the three critical areas for math instruction: math content knowledge, math pedagogical knowledge, and general pedagogical knowledge.

Once school leaders identify the baseline preparation that their classroom teachers have in mathematics, they need to establish a professional development program to improve teacher knowledge of mathematics. Secondly, school leaders should strategically place elementary school teachers with more advanced mathematical knowledge across the grades so that they can serve as lead teachers for their colleagues.

In some instances, a grade-level teacher with advanced mathematical knowledge would better serve the needs of the students by teaching the math curriculum to all students at a grade. Many schools have two to four classrooms at a grade level, and within three hours, a teacher could complete four sections of 40 minutes of math instruction Monday through Thursday. Such specialized instructional models require one or more of the other teachers to specialize in literacy and perhaps science or social studies.

Each school is different. The student population, preparation of the teachers, strengths and weaknesses, and even dispositions of the teachers require individualized choices and strategic plans. School leaders are responsible for the quality of the strategic plan and must provide the structure that supports the learning needs of the students while attending to the instructional skills of the teachers.

Almost all teachers want to do well. The few who lack the desire to excel at helping students learn should be removed. School leaders are responsible for the evaluation of teachers, their professional development, and their continuance as teachers. In every school, school leaders should be evaluated and held accountable for the quality of instruction, growth in mastery learning among students, professional development of teachers, and teacher retention.

Most teachers do not lack the desire to help students learn; they lack the knowledge and the training to deal with the student diversity in front of them. The growing complexity of the curriculum and the diversity of the students that they have been assigned to teach require constant professional development. The school leader must take care of the teachers so that the teachers can take care of every child assigned to them.

Elementary school leaders must reorganize their teaching staff and utilize the few grade-level teachers with strong quantitative backgrounds as grade-level math instructors, lead teachers, and math specialists who can demonstrate lessons for colleagues. Elementary school leaders must take charge of the distribution of human resources at the school. School leaders must engage in more precise levels of inquiry, provide more valuable insight into the school assessments of learning, and be responsible for a more effective distribution of teacher potency.

If diverse children from multiple cultures and levels of wealth and poverty are to master the curriculum, school leaders cannot accept children and teacher behavior that results in 35 percent of minority students passing third to eighth grade math tests, as occurred in New York in the spring of 2011 (Otterman, 2011).

Middle school leaders should know precisely the quality of the mathematical knowledge and background training of each math teacher in the school. Middle school principals should encourage teachers to share lesson skills, assessments, and particular interventions for students who exhibit difficulty mastering math concepts. Math teachers in middle school must require their students to demonstrate and explain applications in math problem solving.

In a middle school, math teachers must view themselves as a team of scholars trying to impart math knowledge to groups of students. They should work together to assess how well children are learning at each grade level using formative assessments. They should prescribe interventions for those who are struggling. In every middle school, teachers should develop common formative assessments that are administered by teachers in a preplanned and monthly schedule so that teachers can assess how well children are learning. Such assessment results should be entered into a digital learning program, and frequency of success should be calculated for each class. They must become the basis for renewed teaching and targeted interventions that teachers create within their own classrooms.

School leaders should not permit themselves and teachers to view their success in terms of how a majority of their students pass their courses or how accurate their excuses for student failure reflect the poor behavior of their students. Student failure must be the responsibility of the school leader and the teachers. The only reason to have highly paid and highly qualified teachers and school leaders is for them to make a difference in the learning cycle of every child. When groups of children come to school with a distinctive behavior pattern that serves as a barrier to successful learning, and several years later, the students leave the school with the same failure rates at which they entered, the school failed to make a difference.

New York City is representative of many large cities in the United States that face more rigorous state testing standards as state education agencies try to make student performance on state exams more predictive of success in community colleges and on national or international assessments. New York City reported 57 percent of Grade 3–8 students achieved proficiency on the state math exams in 2011, and only 44 percent achieved proficiency in English language arts (ELA). In mathematics, 63 percent of the Grade 3–8 students in the entire state achieved proficiency, and 53 percent in ELA (Otterman, 2011, p. A16).

More dreadful statistics were revealed when the percent of New York State (NYS) Grade 3–8 black students from mostly poverty-inflicted neighborhoods who were proficient in ELA represented 34.8 percent of the population, and only 44 percent were proficient in mathematics. NYS is not much different from other states with large urban areas and extensive pockets of poor people gathered in small and large cities (Otterman, 2011, p. A16).

Diverse students living in poverty need different school structures than those in middle-class or wealthy neighborhoods. Poor students need teachers who are organized and trained to work in these diverse environments. Extensive testing cannot change results that the old structure and training preserve. Most teachers come from middle-class backgrounds and attend training programs where they learn common practices, theories, and dispositions. Teaching in schools with students of high poverty requires teachers to discover new ways of teaching and learning with their peers and their students.

From 2009 through 2011, in one New York high school in which 61 percent of the students came from English second language (ESL) homes, and more than 50 percent of the students were eligible for free lunch services, we witnessed lead teachers in mathematics initiate a revision of the ninth grade math curriculum. Their efforts merged the common core math state standards, local curriculum, and common formative assessments that teams of teachers aligned with each chapter in the math textbook. The teachers adopted the CCSS for math and integrated them into their local curriculum and assessment plans.

New support structures created by the high school principal enabled teachers to work together to identify student strengths and weaknesses, to regroup students for academic intervention services weekly, to share lessons and specific applications of interactive digital instructional materials, and to reorganize their own teaching practices. School leaders changed the focus of their conversations with teachers from what they planned to do and how well children behaved to how teachers intended to have every child master each lesson and how they would intervene with those who failed to show mastery. Because the new school leader and math coach changed to an inquiry-based professional development process, conversations among teachers changed to how many students achieved mastery and to what teachers needed to do differently. Many more students were successful in the new inquiry model.

In fact, the algebra passing rate for the school's ninth grade cohort rose from 61 percent to 77 percent. In the process, the high school principal and the guidance administrator restructured student data categories to reflect a new emphasis on cohort passing rates among diverse groups within each entering class rather than an analysis of failing rates. Monitoring of student success led to more success.

In this school and others with similar student populations, teachers struggle monthly to adjust what they do and ensure their students master what they teach. They have to have the courage to slow down, to pause, and to regroup students and reteach. They have to have the courage to be masters of their own curriculum pace. Lead teachers, assistant principals, classroom teachers, and guidance counselors should meet and work together to review quarterly performance and to plan interventions that increase the success of students.

At the end of one year in dialogue and inquiry, one year of training in formative assessments, and two years of collaborative work, teachers began to self-regulate their lessons according to the performance of their students. Because of their collaborative efforts, passing rates in core subjects for the ninth grade increased. Nevertheless, there remained many barriers to students' success, such as how homework was valued and used as a sanction or penalty within the grading system. Table 4.3 presents the change in passing rates for the fall quarter in the school year 2011–2012.

Now, teachers are changing their homework systems. Many are moving to a bonus system. There is renewed optimism at the high school that almost all students will be competitive, and teachers can make that happen. One math teacher said, "I changed homework to fewer items; made it a bonus system. I used the items from formative assessments with different numbers in my tests and now I have more students completing homework, less frustration and greater mastery among my students."

Even if state education departments require CCSS in mathematics, the difficulty in the implementation phase becomes more evident as school leaders and teachers misinterpret what the CCSS intend to initiate. They are "explicit in their focus on what students are to

Table 4.3   Change in Ninth Grade Student Passing Rates

Subject	Fall 2009	Fall 2011
Math	Less than 55%	67%
English	Less than 70%	86%
Global studies	Less than 55%	68%
Earth science and living environment	Less than 55%	66%

learn, what we call here 'the content of the intended curriculum,' and not on how that content is to be taught, what often is referred to as 'pedagogy and curriculum'" (Porter et al., 2011b, p. 103). Are the common core standards a national curriculum? Yes, they are, insofar as they set a scope and sequence for student learning, and no, as there are not instructions on how to teach or the building blocks of curriculum that students must master.

The CCSS offer shared expectations, a focus on standards that compete with those of the highest-performing nations and provide for efficiency insofar as they reduce the need for 50 states to determine international competitive standards. They help teachers and school leaders prepare students to excel in international assessments. They represent a national effort to raise curriculum expectations across the United States and, at the same time, allow schools to embrace flexible and innovative instructional strategies for their students (Porter, McMaken, Hwang, & Yang, 2011a).

School leaders and teachers frequently ignore many adopted curricula, especially those in which they had little or no opportunity to share in the design. Nel Noddings (2008) described pedagogical practices in algebra and geometry classes where teachers had little preparation in the design of the curriculum and its application:

> When I first met Margie, she was taking algebra. Looking through her textbook, I thought the course would be wonderful. The textbook was loaded with real-world applications and exercises that invited genuine thinking. But the teacher did not assign even one of these exercises. Not one! The following year, in geometry, Margie was never asked to do a proof. These algebra and geometry classes were composed of kids who, had they had a choice in the matter, would not have chosen courses in academic mathematics. (p. 11)

What happened in Margie's math class too often represents the experience that many students encounter in our public schools. How is such disregard for the learner tolerated? High-stakes testing controls too much of the hard-driving activity of teachers in schools. In two high schools, three middle schools, and two elementary schools where we spent time visiting classes during the last two years, teacher after teacher reported that "I have to cover the curriculum."

In such instances, we ask the teachers how they would like to be a heart attack victim on a flight to Los Angeles and have the pilot state, "Sorry, I know you're sick, but I have to dock my plane in LA by 10:12 p.m. to meet our company's on time regulations?" Every teacher recognizes that the pilot would cover the territory as required, and the sick passenger would never get the proper care.

School leaders must give teachers permission to pause, reflect, and decide how to react to particular students. Teachers and school leaders must agree on only two concepts: Every child must master what I teach, and I will teach to the highest standards in our curriculum. Teachers must adjust the pace of teaching to the evidence of student mastery. Teachers have to employ technology to differentiate instruction and conduct multiple formative assessments.

COMMON CORE STATE MATH STANDARDS

In the next sections, we will present examples of how some schools have coupled the CCSMS with local math curriculum expectations and assessments. We will focus on examples from kindergarten to Grade 2 and Grade 5. For Grades 7–11, we will present a comprehensive overview of the analytical and problem-solving techniques that secondary students are expected to demonstrate. We hope secondary teachers will view these expectations as previews of the content that they must master with their students. These previews should motivate secondary math teachers to undertake deep inquiry into the alignment of CCSMS with the quality of their own local math curriculum and their formative or summative assessments. Academic interventions for students who struggle to master the curriculum should reflect precise formative evidence of a gap in student learning.

In the 21st century, teachers can no longer declare, "These students do not have what it takes to do math." All students need math skills to interpret charts, graphs, statistical data, and information. The global economy and the digital age demand math skills for decision making and for the world of work.

Kindergarten Common Core State Standard and Local Curriculum Math Standards

Table 4.4 presents a comparison of the CCSMS and local school curriculum for kindergarten. The local math curriculum expectations were designed by local school teachers to identify how students at their school could demonstrate the application of a CCSS.

Table 4.4   Kindergarten Common Core State Standard and Local Curriculum
Math Standards

Common Core State Standard	Local Curriculum
Kindergarten	
Know the Number Names and Count Sequence	**Number Sense**
1. Count to 100 by ones and by 10s.	1. Count the items in a collection.
2. Count forward beginning from a given number within the known sequence (instead of having to begin at 1).	2. Explain how one knows the last counting word tells how many items are in the collection.
3. Write numbers from 0 to 20. Represent a number of objects with a written numeral 0 to 20 (with 0 representing a count of no objects).	3. Label a data set 1 to 5.
Operations and Algebraic Thinking	**Algebra Strand**
Understand addition as putting together and adding to, and understand subtraction as taking apart and taking from.	**Understand addition and subtraction**
1. Represent addition and subtraction with objects, fingers, mental images, drawings, sounds (e.g., claps), acting out situations, verbal explanations, expressions, or equations.	1. Use manipulatives to create patterns. Subtract a group of like items. Count remainders. Add back the group missing. Count total items.
2. Solve addition and subtraction word problems, and add and subtract within 10, for example, by using objects or drawings to represent the problem.	2. Use pictures of things (trucks, dolls, and dogs or cats) to add and subtract.
3. Decompose numbers less than or equal to 10 into pairs in more than one way, for example, by using objects or drawings, and record each decomposition by a drawing or equation (e.g., $5 = 2 + 3$ and $5 = 4 + 1$).	3. Use pictures to show which group has equal numbers. Mix dog and cat pictures in sets and select two sets with equal total number of dogs and cats.
4. For any number from 1 to 9, find the number that makes 10 when added to the given number, for example, by using objects or drawings, and record the answer with a drawing or equation.	4. Use checkers to make combinations of numbers that make 10 checkers.

| 5. Fluently add and subtract within 5. | 5. Use checkers to show how 5 checkers can be shared with 2 or 3 friends. Answer the question: can 5 checkers be shared equally with 2 friends? |

Grade 1 Common Core State Standard and Local Curriculum Math Standards

In Grade 1, the CCSS calls for number operations and algebraic thinking. Teachers should lead their students through multiple thinking processes that employ numbers, drawings, and objects that can be organized into patterns and equations. In addition, basic geometric understandings are demonstrated for the first time to these students, and they are expected to explain and contrast shapes and forms in Grade 1 (Table 4.5).

Table 4.5   Grade 1 Common Core State Standard and Local Curriculum Math Standards

Common Core State Standard	Local Curriculum
Grade 1	
Operations and Algebraic Thinking	
Represent and solve problems involving addition and subtraction	**Use addition and subtraction to solve problems**
1. Use addition and subtraction within 20 to solve word problems involving situations of addition and subtraction problems without adding to, taking from, putting together, taking apart, and comparing with unknowns in all positions, for example, by using objects, drawings, and equations with a symbol for the unknown.	1. Solve 1- and 2-digit addition and subtraction problems without regrouping.
2. Solve word problems that call for addition of 3 whole numbers whose sum is less than or equal to 20, for example, by using objects, drawings, and equations with a symbol for the unknown number to represent the problem.	2. Create problem situations that require peers to subtract or add 2-digit numbers to solve the word problem.

(Continued)

Table 4.5   Continued

Common Core State Standard	Local Curriculum
Understand and apply properties of operations and the relationship between addition and subtraction	
3. Apply properties of operations as strategies to add and subtract. *Examples:*	
a. If $8 + 3 = 11$ is known, then $3 + 8 = 11$ is also known (commutative property of addition).	a. Display data in a bar graph and a pie graph. Explain relationships.
b. To add $2 + 6 + 4$, the second 2 numbers can be added to make a 10, so $2 + 6 + 4 = 2 + 10 = 12$ (associative property of addition).	b. Show how data can be combined in a bar graph of student height measured in this one class.
4. Understand subtraction as an unknown-addend problem. For example, subtract $10 - 8$ by finding the number that makes 10 when added to 8.	4. Use combinations of 3, 4, and 5 columns of checkers to show what happens to the total number of checkers when a constant number is added or subtracted from the columns.
Geometry 1	
Reason with shapes and their attributes	**Reason with shapes**
1. Distinguish between defining attributes (e.g., triangles are closed and 3-sided) versus non-defining attributes (e.g., color, orientation, overall size); build and draw shapes to possess defining attributes.	1. Match shapes and parts of shapes to show congruency.
2. Compose 2-dimensional shapes (rectangles, squares, trapezoids, triangles, half circles, and quarter circles) or 3-dimensional shapes (cubes, right rectangular prisms, right circular cones, and right circular cylinders) to create a composite shape, and compose new shapes from the composite shape.	2. Name, describe, create, sort, and compare 2-dimensional and 3-dimensional shapes.

Grade 2 Common Core State Standard and Local Curriculum Math Standards

By Grade 2, students are expected to solve problems and to explain their answers. Teachers must be sufficiently comfortable with mathematical principles to model their own thinking for their students. Table 4.6 presents the higher-ordered thinking process students must exhibit in their use of mathematical principles for the CCSS and examples of how a local school integrated the local curriculum with the common core standards.

Notice that the CCSMS do not direct teachers how to teach a math concept or mathematical application. They provide teachers with a set of sequenced and logical steps to develop mathematically competent children who can use math skills to solve problems.

In many U.S. schools, Grade 5 is the end of elementary school or the beginning of middle school. Grades 6–8 in other school districts comprise the middle school. For the purpose of this review of CSS and examples of how local schools adapted their math curricula to integrate the local curriculum expectations with common core standards, we selected Grade 5 as the last one for which we would provide local curriculum examples. For Grades 7, 9, and 11, we provide the CCSMS models of what teachers and school leaders must address to improve math curriculum understandings in secondary schools.

We want to stress that, if teachers are left out of the equation, their teaching will become mechanistic and lack inspiration. Their students will suffer in their math classes, and only those students with the greatest facility in mathematics will overcome the inadequate instruction, lack of insight, and inflexibility of their teachers.

Grade 5 Common Core State Standard and Local Curriculum Math Standards

As far as the CCSMS are concerned, the designers did not worry about grade configurations of students. They focused on creating highly competitive standards that would ensure that American students would be able to compete with the best international students. Table 4.7 offers an illustration of how local teachers adapted their fifth grade curriculum to meet common core standards.

Table 4.6   Grade 2 Common Core State Standard and Local Curriculum Math
Standards

Common Core State Standard	Local Curriculum
Grade 2	
Operations and Algebraic Thinking	
Represent and solve problems involving addition and subtraction	**Solve problems in equations**
1. Use addition and subtraction within 100 to solve 1- and 2-step word problems involving situations of adding to, taking from, putting together, taking apart, and comparing, with unknowns in all positions, for example, by using drawings and equations with a symbol for the unknown number to represent the problem.	1. Use a variety of strategies to solve addition and subtraction problems using 1- and 2-digit numbers with and without regrouping. Show how to determine if 10 dollars are in a piggy bank and 12 quarters are removed, how many dollar bills must remain in the bank.
Add and subtract within 20	
2. Fluently add and subtract within 20 using mental strategies. By end of Grade 2, know from memory all sums of two 1-digit numbers.	2. Use doubling to add 2-digit numbers. Demonstrate fluency, and apply addition and subtraction facts up to and including 18.
Number and Operations in Base Ten	
Understand place value	
1. Understand that the 3 digits of a 3-digit number represent amounts of 100s, 10s, and 1s; for example, 706 equals 7 hundreds, 0 tens, and 6 ones.	1. Know and recognize coins and values sums of dollars.
Understand the following as special cases:	Estimate and find exact measures in ounces and pounds, grams and kilograms, and inches and centimeters.
a. 100 can be thought of as a bundle of ten 10s called a "hundred."	a. Count by 10s to 100. Subtract 20 four times from 100. Determine remainder of 100.

b. The numbers 100, 200, 300, 400, 500, 600, 700, 800, and 900 refer to one, two, three, four, five, six, seven, eight, or nine 100s (and zero 10s and zero 1s).

b. Visit a large, virtual zoo and separate animals into appropriate classes. Count the number in each category. Determine largest and smallest number in a group and the largest smallest animal by size.

2. Count within 1,000; skip-count by 5s, 10s, and 100s.

Geometry

Reason with shapes and their attributes

1. Recognize and draw shapes having specified attributes, such as a given number of angles or a given number of equal faces. Identify triangles, quadrilaterals, pentagons, hexagons, and cubes.

1. Recognize 2-dimensional shapes of circle, square, rectangle, and triangle (both regular and irregular). Explain and contrast properties of 3-dimensional objects such as cubes, hexagons, pentagons, squares, and rectangular shapes.

Notice that, in fifth grade and forward from there, the focus has changed considerably from the teacher explaining and demonstrating while students repeat operations, describe, re-explain, and apply math principles in new situations to intermediate and secondary students facing expectations that they will use math to solve problems. In the intermediate and secondary grades, teachers must require students to explain data patterns and interpret algebraic formulas and geometric theorems within applicable problems. Students use math skills to solve unique and real-world problems.

Math teachers in secondary schools need to see the breadth of the CCSS for math and decide how they will address the total program given the vision they have developed for their students as math problem solvers. Table 4.7 presents the Grade 5 CCSMS and several examples of how teachers merged local curriculum with the common core.

Table 4.7   Grade 5 Common Core State Standard and Local Curriculum Math
Standards

Common Core State Standard	*Local Curriculum*
Grade 5	
Operations and Algebraic Thinking	
Write and interpret numerical expressions	
1. Use parentheses, brackets, or braces in numerical expressions, and evaluate expressions with these symbols.	1. Translate simple verbal expressions into algebraic expressions.
2. Write simple expressions that record calculations with numbers, and interpret numerical expressions without evaluating them. For example, express the calculation "add 8 and 7, then multiply by 2" as $2 \times (8 + 7)$. Recognize that $3 \times (18,932 + 921)$ is 3 times as large as $18,932 + 921$ without having to calculate the indicated sum or product.	2. Substitute assigned values into variable expressions, and evaluate using order of operations.
Analyze patterns and relationships	
3. Generate 2 numerical patterns using 2 given rules. Identify apparent relationships between corresponding terms. Form ordered pairs consisting of corresponding terms from the 2 patterns, and graph the ordered pairs on a coordinate plane.	3. Plot points to form basic geometric shapes. Collect and record data from a variety of sources. Display data in a line graph to show increase or decrease in a time line.
For example, given the rule "add 3" and the starting number 0, and given the rule "add 6" and the starting number 0, generate terms in the resulting sequences, and observe that the terms in one sequence are twice the corresponding terms in the other sequence. Explain informally why this is so.	Create and explain patterns and algebraic relationships (e.g., 2, 4, 6, 8 . . .)

Number and Operations in Base Ten

Understand the place value system

1. Recognize that, in a multi-digit number, a digit in one place represents 10 times as much as it represents in the place to its right and 1/10 of what it represents in the place to its left.

1. Multiply and divide 3-digit numbers using data from sports and questions about the environment.

2. Explain patterns in the number of 0s of the product when multiplying a number by powers of 10, and explain patterns in the placement of the decimal point when a decimal is multiplied or divided by a power of 10.

2. Show how decimals are used in measurements to construct homes and cook meals.

Use whole-number exponents to denote powers of 10.

Modify fractions to their lowest terms.

Interpret multiplication as scaling (resizing), by comparing the size of a product to the size of one factor on the basis of the size of the other factor without performing the indicated multiplication.

Solve distributions of resources in the classroom with fractions.

Explain why multiplying a given number by a fraction greater than 1 results in a product greater than the given number (recognizing multiplication by whole numbers greater than 1 as a familiar case).

Multiply given numbers by a fraction of 1 and by a fraction greater than 1.

Explaining why multiplying a given number by a fraction less than 1 results in a product smaller than the given number; relate the principle of fraction equivalence $a/b = (n \times a)/(n \times b)$ to the effect of multiplying a/b by 1.

Calculate how to distribute football game tickets to returning alumni classes with different numbers of members in the total class and different numbers of registrants for the alumni dinner.

Geometric measurement: understand concepts of volume, and relate volume to multiplication and to addition

Geometry measurement

3. Recognize volume as an attribute of solid figures, and understand concepts of volume measurement.

3. Calculate the perimeter of regular and irregular polygons.

(Continued)

Table 4.7   Continued

Common Core State Standard	*Local Curriculum*
a. A cube with side length 1 unit, called a *unit cube,* is said to have 1 cubic unit of volume and can be used to measure volume. b. A solid figure, which can be packed without gaps or overlaps using *n* unit cubes, is said to have a volume of *n* cubic units.	Calculate the volume of a cylinder, a rectangular box, and a square box with the same base length.
4. Measure volumes by counting unit cubes, using cubic cm, cubic in., cubic ft., and improvised units.	Identify the ratio of corresponding sides of similar triangles in metrics and feet.
5. Relate volume to the operations of multiplication and addition, and solve real-world and mathematical problems involving volume.	Find a missing angle when given two angles of a triangle.
a. Find the volume of a right rectangular prism with whole-number side lengths by packing it with unit cubes, and show that the volume is the same as would be found by multiplying the edge lengths equivalently by multiplying the height by the area of the base.	Find the centroid within an isosceles triangle and within a right-angle triangle.
Represent threefold whole-number products as volumes, for example, to represent the associative property of multiplication.	Represent the associative property of multiplication.
b. Apply the formulas $V = l \times w \times h$ and $V = b \times h$ for rectangular prisms to find volumes of right rectangular prisms with whole-number edge lengths in the context of solving real-world and mathematical problems.	Apply the formula to find the volume of a soda can and a cereal box. Solve real-world problems to assess weight distributions in a fishing boat.

SIX DOMAINS OF INSTRUCTIONAL STRATEGIES FOR ALL STUDENTS

By Grade 7, we find that many schools have a mathematical curriculum that does not reflect the complexity and higher cognitive operations that the CCSS expect. For instance, in one middle school that we visited, seventh grade math teachers reported that they intended to teach seven basic themes to their students: real numbers; number sense, integers and order of operations; exponents; one- and two-step equations; volume and perimeter; statistics; and angles and polygons.

There was little agreement among the teachers as to what problems students would have to solve or how to assess their understanding and capacity to apply what they had been taught.

Grant Wiggins and Jay McTighe (2005) suggest that each member of the faculty must have a clear and shared understanding of six domains in which students must perform. Table 4.8 presents adaptations of Wiggins and McTighe (2005) domains and key understandings. The constructs are processes that we adapted from actual efforts by teachers in a variety of schools.

Table 4.8   Six Domains of Instructional Strategies for All Students

Domain	Key Understanding	Construct
Explain	Accurate and Coherent Justified and Systematic Predictive	• Tell the big idea, make connections, explain reasoning, create a theory, and make a judgment and justify it. • Use 2 data charts to draw a conclusion.
Interpret	Meaning and Insight Significance and Illustration	• Make sense of stories, artworks, photos, graphs, charts, and data, and translate information in one medium to another. • Collect data from the class, and create a picture of the data.
Apply	Connect and Fluency Adapt, Make, and Design	• Use knowledge and skill in a new situation. • Design or draw models. • Use rules to solve problems. • Select a community problem like public transportation, and analyze bus routes and population density, age, and income to create pictures and histograms of high need and low service.

(Continued)

Table 4.8   Continued

Domain	Key Understanding	Construct
Express View	Reveal and Insight Belief, Reasons, and Feelings	• See things from different points of view. • Solve problems in different ways. • Organize assumptions. • Create an alternative approach. • Estimate outcomes. • Select a community issue such as uncared-for property, and determine how to motivate owners to care for property.
Empathies	Open and Receptive Tactful and Sensitive	• Appreciate differences in patterns, categories, human groups, animals, and nature. • Explore new ideas, and solve real-world problems. • View real people solving problems. • Explain how polio is controlled in the world. • Look at world patterns, and identify dangers.
Reflect	Assess and Adjust	• Know strengths and weaknesses of past performance. • Measure muscle strength in the class compared to daily exercise minutes. • Identify challenges to finding the truth and strategies to measure this relationship.

Grant Wiggins (2011) wrote a sharp critique of the common core math standards in *Education Week:*

In my view, unlike the English/language arts standards, the mathematics components of the Common Core State Standards Initiative are a bitter disappointment. In terms of their limited vision of math education, the pedestrian framework chosen to organize the standards, and the incoherent nature of the standards for mathematical practice in particular, I don't see how these take us forward in any way. They unwittingly reinforce the very errors in math curriculum, instruction, and assessment that produced the current crisis. (p. 22)

Wiggins (2011) noted that the CCSS in math do not show how curriculum should build backward from rich, nonroutine, interesting, and authentic problems. He reminds teachers that results on National Assessment of Education Progress (NAEP) and Trends in International Mathematics and Science Study (TIMSS) exams as well as state math exams show that "our students are woefully deficient in solving any problems that require a transfer of learning, as opposed to the plug and chug of simple rules and algorithms" (p. 22).

He criticizes the lack of challenge in the common core with real problems that require thought and clever approaches. Wiggins (2011) writes that a discussion of "how to pose problems and, more generally, how to ask powerful questions" (p. 23) is missing from the standards.

In our opinion, the power of the CCSS lies in their capacity to provide a road map to competent math knowledge. No one who follows a map of the United States and drives across the country in a single week would dare to claim that she or he knows the country. To comprehend the United States, one must stop and visit the small towns and medium and large cities, spend time there, and get to know the people who live, work, and own businesses in those communities. For this reason, we have presented a variety of examples from actual local curriculum and current teacher efforts in schools with economically, ethnically, and racially diverse students. We focused our attention on teachers who were making a difference in the learning curves of their students.

To use the CCSMS as a road map to raise local curriculum to world-class standards requires teachers to stop and reflect about where their students are and where they want to take them. Teachers need to know their students individually to assess their strengths and weaknesses regularly and to help them master what they have not understood.

PURPOSE OF THE MATH COMMON CORE

The CCSMS are designed to raise the topographical map of math curriculum in the United States. Local school communities must address how their curricula must improve so that student capacity to solve problems and transfer math knowledge to real and interesting problems expands. The merger of local math curriculum and the CCSMS is a local school problem that must include a careful analysis of the math knowledge that teachers in the school hold. Even more importantly, a clear and precise professional development plan must be in place to expand the math capacity of teachers to teach what children need to know in ways that enable students to apply math knowledge and to solve real problems.

Hung-His Wu (2011), professor emeritus of mathematics at UCLA, Berkeley, writes in the *American Educator* a well-reasoned defense of the CCSMS: "The main difference between these standards and most of the others is that the CCSMS are mathematically very sound overall. They could serve—at long last—as the foundation for creating proper school mathematics textbooks and dramatically better teacher preparation" (p. 3).

Wu notes that two of the most widely used math textbook series in schools within the United States have math errors in 50 percent to 40 percent of their pages, and they are considered rigorous if they accelerate math topics to lower grades. He observes that the CCSMS "do not engage in the senseless game of acceleration—to teach every topic as early as possible" (Wu, 2011, p. 4). The CCSS in math spread such topics such as adding fractions across Grades 3–5 so that the developmental process of thinking with numbers occurs in a developmental process for each child.

Wu (2011) criticizes how teachers are prepared to instruct mathematics in our colleges, stating that U.S. colleges provide future teachers with rigorous math courses that deal with topics that are not taught in the K–12 curriculum or with pedagogy-laden courses that avoid the math knowledge that teachers need to know. The poor preparation of math teachers in the United States, he claims, prolongs the poor level of math instruction in our schools. He writes:

The pressing need now is to provide all future mathematics teachers with content knowledge that satisfies both of the following requirements:

A. It is relevant to teaching—i.e., does not stray far from the material they teach in school.

B. It is consistent with the following five principles of mathematics: precise definitions are the basis for logical deductions; precise statements clarify what is known and what is not known; every assertion can be backed by logical reasoning; all the concepts and skills are woven together like a tapestry; and each concept and skill has a purpose. (p. 11)

According to Wu (2011), the CCSMS are a clear conception of what K–12 mathematics should be: "mathematical engineering that enables students to use abstract scientific principles to realize an objective or a function" (p. 11). Wu concludes: "Because failure in math education has far-reaching consequences, the worthiness of successfully implementing the CCSMS is clear" (p. 13).

The common core standards in mathematics in Grades 7–12 offer many powerful expressions of mathematical knowledge of which math teachers in middle schools and high schools should have a complete and thorough knowledge. Each secondary math team needs to examine the CCSS in mathematics and determine what applications and understandings they will prepare their students to demonstrate. Teachers must discuss how they will help their students exceed these standards. Every teacher must remember that the CCSS are an expression of the minimum standards that students must achieve to compete with their peers in a global educational environment.

In order to facilitate dialogue, consensus, and profound understanding of the challenges that secondary teachers face as they attempt to implement the common core standards, we have presented in the next section a brief outline of the math frameworks for Grades 7, 9, 10, and 11. Math teachers at the secondary grades should examine these examples and make a commitment to collectively review the CCSS and to rewrite local curriculum expectations that express how students will be expected to demonstrate mastery of these standards.

Teachers should design creative applications and challenges for their students to demonstrate the math knowledge that these CCSS embody. School leaders should initiate a dialogue with teachers and supervisors in secondary departments to ensure that a local curriculum exceeds the expectations of the CCSS.

Grade 7 Common Core State Math Standards: Ratios and Proportional Relationships

Table 4.9 presents the CCSMS for seventh grade. Teachers should meet to discuss how their local math curriculum will exceed the CCSM standards and how they will provide common formative and summative assessments of student mastery of their math curriculum. Teachers should determine together at the outset of each year what real-world problems they will assign to students that will motivate them to transfer knowledge of math taught in class to situations that interest them.

For the remaining examples of odd-numbered grade-level 7–11 CCSS in mathematics, we are not presenting local curricula that schools are using. We are challenging math teachers to work together to develop common problems for students to solve and common formative assessments to capture evidence of student mastery of the curriculum.

Table 4.9   Grade 7 Common Core State Math Standards: Ratios and Proportional Relationships

Analyze proportional relationships, and use them to solve real-world and mathematical problems.

1. Compute unit rates associated with ratios of fractions, including ratios of lengths, areas, and other quantities measured in like or different units.

For example, if a retail store can purchase 100 school team shirts for $7.50, and the retail store must charge an additional $2.50 to cover overhead and provide $.50 in profit, how many shirts must be sold at what dollar amount for the retailer to earn a profit of 4.5 percent?

2. Recognize and represent proportional relationships between quantities.

    a. Decide whether two quantities are in a proportional relationship, for example, by testing for equivalent ratios in a table or graphing on a coordinate plane and observing whether the graph is a straight line through the origin.

    b. Identify the constant of proportionality (unit rate) in tables, graphs, equations, diagrams, and verbal descriptions of proportional relationships.

    c. Represent proportional relationships by equations.

For example, if total cost t is proportional to the number n of items purchased at a constant price p, the relationship between the total cost and the number of items can be expressed as $t = pn$.

    d. Explain what a point (x, y) on the graph of a proportional relationship means in terms of the situation with special attention to the points $(0, 0)$ and $(1, r)$ where r is the unit rate.

Use variables to represent quantities in a real-world or mathematical problem, and construct simple equations and inequalities to solve problems by reasoning about the quantities.

   a. Solve word problems leading to equations of the form $px + q = r$ and $p(x + q) = r$, where p, q, and r are specific rational numbers. Solve equations of these forms fluently. Compare an algebraic solution to an arithmetic solution, identifying the sequence of the operations used in each approach.

For example, the perimeter of a rectangle is 54 cm. Its length is 6 cm. What is its width?

   b. Solve word problems leading to inequalities of the form $px + q > r$ or $px + q < r$, where p, q, and r are specific rational numbers. Graph the solution set of the inequality and interpret it in the context of the problem.

For example, as a salesperson, you are paid $50 per week plus $3 per sale. This week you want your pay to be at least $100. Write an inequality for the number of sales you need to make, and describe the solutions.

Solve real-life and mathematical problems involving angle measure, area, surface area, and volume.

3. Know the formulas for the area and circumference of a circle, and use them to solve problems; give an informal derivation of the relationship between the circumference and area of a circle.

4. Use facts about supplementary, complementary, vertical, and adjacent angles in a multistep problem to write and solve simple equations for an unknown angle in a figure.

5. Solve real-world and mathematical problems involving area, volume, and surface area of 2- and 3-dimensional objects composed of triangles, quadrilaterals, polygons, cubes, and right prisms.

Grades 9–10 Common Core State Math Standards: The Real Number System

In Grades 9–10, the CCSMS provide expectations for the use of rational and irrational numbers, the structure of expressions, and the use of equations to solve problems. Ninth and tenth grade math teachers must agree about the content of their local curriculum, its inclusion of the CCSS, and its reach beyond the common core standards. These teachers must develop common methodologies to assess student mastery of these standards, such as collaboratively developed formative assessments. Table 4.10 presents the CCSMS's expectations of what all students will be able to do as a result of math instruction in all high schools.

Table 4.10   Grades 9–10 Common Core State Math Standards: The Real
                     Number System

Extend the properties of exponents to rational exponents

1. Explain how the definition of the meaning of rational exponents follows from extending the properties of integer exponents to those values, allowing for a notation for radicals in terms of rational exponents.

For example, we define 51/3 to be the cube root of 5 because we want (51/3)3 = 5(1/3)3 to hold, so (51/3)3 must equal 5.

2. Rewrite expressions involving radicals and rational exponents using the properties of exponents.

Use properties of rational and irrational numbers

1. Explain why the sum or product of two rational numbers is rational, that the sum of a rational number and an irrational number is irrational,; and that the product of a nonzero rational number and an irrational number is irrational.

Perform arithmetic operations with complex numbers

1. Know there is a complex number i such that $i2 = -1$, and every complex number has the form $a + bi$ with a and b real.
2. Use the relation $i2 = -1$ and the commutative, associative, and distributive properties to add, subtract, and multiply complex numbers.
3. Find the conjugate of a complex number; use conjugates to find moduli and quotients of complex numbers.

Represent complex numbers and their operations on the complex plane

4. Represent complex numbers on the complex plane in rectangular and polar forms (including real and imaginary numbers), and explain why the rectangular and polar forms of a given complex number represent the same number.
5. Represent addition, subtraction, multiplication, and conjugation of complex numbers geometrically on the complex plane; use properties of this representation for computation.

For example, (–1 + √3 i)3 = 8 because (–1 + √3 i) has modulus 2 and argument 120°.

Algebra

Interpret the structure of expressions

1. Interpret expressions that represent a quantity in terms of its context.

   a. Interpret parts of an expression, such as terms, factors, and coefficients.
   b. Interpret complicated expressions by viewing one or more of their parts as a single entity.

For example, interpret P(1 + r)n as the product of P and a factor not depending on P.

2. Use the structure of an expression to identify ways to rewrite it.

For example, see x4 – y4 as (x2)2 – (y2)2, thus recognizing it as a difference of squares that can be factored as (x2 – y2)(x2 + y2).

Write expressions in equivalent forms to solve problems

1. Choose and produce an equivalent form of an expression to reveal and explain properties of the quantity represented by the expression.

   a. Factor a quadratic expression to reveal the 0s of the function it defines.
   b. Complete the square in a quadratic expression to reveal the maximum or minimum value of the function it defines.
   c. Use the properties of exponents to transform expressions for exponential functions.

For example, the expression 1.15t can be rewritten as (1.151/12)12t ≈ 1.01212t to reveal the approximate equivalent monthly interest rate if the annual rate is 15%.

2. Derive the formula for the sum of a finite geometric series (when the common ratio is not 1), and use the formula to solve problems.

For example, calculate mortgage payments.

Represent and solve equations and inequalities graphically

1. Understand that the graph of an equation in 2 variables is the set of all its solutions plotted in the coordinate plane, often forming a curve (which could be a line).

11. Explain why the x-coordinates of the points where the graphs of the equations $y = f(x)$ and $y = g(x)$ intersect are the solutions of the equation $f(x) = g(x)$; find the solutions approximately, for example, using technology to graph the functions, make tables of values, or find successive approximations. Include cases where $f(x)$ and/or $g(x)$ are linear, polynomial, rational, absolute value, exponential, and logarithmic functions.

2. Graph the solutions to a linear inequality in 2 variables as a half plane (excluding the boundary in the case of a strict inequality), and graph the solution set to a system of linear inequalities in 2 variables as the intersection of the corresponding half planes.

Interpreting Functions

Understand the concept of a function, and use function notation

1. Understand that a function from one set (called the domain) to another set (called the range) assigns to each element of the domain exactly 1 element of the range. If f is a function and x is an element of its domain, then $f(x)$ denotes the output of f corresponding to the input x. The graph of f is the graph of the equation $y = f(x)$.

2. Use function notation, evaluate functions for inputs in their domains, and interpret statements that use function notation in terms of a context.

(Continued)

Table 4.10   Continued

3. Recognize that sequences are functions, sometimes defined recursively, whose domain is a subset of the integers.

For example, the Fibonacci sequence is defined recursively by f(0) = f(1) = 1, f(n+1) = f(n) + f(n-1) for n ≥ 1.

Construct and compare linear, quadratic, and exponential models, and solve problems

1. Distinguish between situations that can be modeled with linear functions and with exponential functions.

    a. Prove that linear functions grow by equal differences over equal intervals and that exponential functions grow by equal factors over equal intervals.
    b. Recognize situations in which one quantity changes at a constant rate per unit interval relative to another.
    c. Recognize situations in which a quantity grows or decays by a constant percent rate per unit interval relative to another.

2. Construct linear and exponential functions, including arithmetic and geometric sequences, given a graph, a description of a relationship, or 2 input-output pairs (include reading these from a table).
3. Observe using graphs and tables that a quantity increasing exponentially eventually exceeds a quantity increasing linearly, quadratically, or (more generally) as a polynomial function.
4. For exponential models, express as a logarithm the solution to $abct = d$ where a, c, and d are numbers and the base b is 2, 10, or e; evaluate the logarithm using technology.

Grade 10 Common Core State Math Standards for Geometry: Congruence

By Grade 10, CCSS for geometry require students to know precise definitions of terms, processes, and procedures to prove geometric theorems and describe the underlying mathematical principles that comprise the basic knowledge of solid geometry. Teachers must examine their local school curriculum and determine how to introduce real problems into the curriculum that will interest and challenge their students. They must identify the building blocks, the goals, and the scope and sequence of important objectives, problems, and issues that they will connect to the CCSS.

Finally, teachers have to agree about common assessments that they will use to provide evidence that their students are mastering appropriate math knowledge. Assessments must require students to present evidence that they can use their math knowledge to solve real problems. Table 4.11 presents the CCSMS for geometry that teachers should examine and contrast with local curriculum.

If American school students are to compete in the global economy, math teachers must lead the way. They must determine the quality of problems that students will be required to solve and the innovative and creative thinking that they will pursue with their students. Math teachers must analyze the scope of the CCSMS in geometry and determine the best ways for them to lead their students beyond mastery of these expectations.

Table 4.11   Grade 10 Common Core State Math Standards for Geometry: Congruence

---

Experiment with transformations in the plane

1. Know precise definitions of angle, circle, perpendicular line, parallel line, and line segment based on the undefined notions of point, line, distance along a line, and distance around a circular arc.
2. Represent transformations in the plane, for example, using transparencies and geometry software; describe transformations as functions that take points in the plane as inputs and give other points as outputs. Compare transformations that preserve distance and angle to those that do not (e.g., translation vs. horizontal stretch).
3. Given a rectangle, parallelogram, trapezoid, or regular polygon, describe the rotations and reflections that carry it onto itself.

    a. Develop definitions of rotations, reflections, and translations in terms of angles, circles, perpendicular lines, parallel lines, and line segments.
    b. Given a geometric figure and a rotation, reflection, or translation, draw the transformed figure, for example, using graph paper, tracing paper, or geometry software. Specify a sequence of transformations that will carry a given figure onto another.

Understand congruence in terms of rigid motions

    c. Use geometric descriptions of rigid motions to transform figures and to predict the effect of a given rigid motion on a given figure; given 2 figures, use the definition of congruence in terms of rigid motions to decide if they are congruent.
    d. Use the definition of congruence in terms of rigid motions to show that 2 triangles are congruent if and only if corresponding pairs of sides and corresponding pairs of angles are congruent.
    e. Explain how the criteria for triangle congruence (ASA, SAS, and SSS) follow from the definition of congruence in terms of rigid motions.

(Continued)

Table 4.11   Continued

Prove geometric theorems

   f. Prove theorems about lines and angles. *Theorems include: vertical angles are congruent; when a transversal crosses parallel lines, alternate interior angles are congruent and corresponding angles are congruent; points on a perpendicular bisector of a line segment are exactly those equidistant from the segment's endpoints.*
   g. Prove theorems about triangles. *Theorems include: measures of interior angles of a triangle sum to 180°; base angles of isosceles triangles are congruent; the segment joining midpoints of 2 sides of a triangle is parallel to the third side and half the length; the medians of a triangle meet at a point.*
   h. Prove theorems about parallelograms. *Theorems include: opposite sides are congruent, opposite angles are congruent, the diagonals of a parallelogram bisect each other, and conversely, rectangles are parallelograms with congruent diagonals.*

Apply geometric concepts in modeling situations

1. Use geometric shapes, their measures, and their properties to describe objects (e.g., modeling a tree trunk or a human torso as a cylinder).
2. Apply concepts of density based on area and volume in modeling situations (e.g., persons per square mile, BTUs per cubic foot).
3. Apply geometric methods to solve design problems (e.g., designing an object or structure to satisfy physical constraints or minimize cost or working with typographic grid systems based on ratios).

Grade 12 Common Core State Math Standards for Statistics: Using Probability to Make Decisions

In many high schools, eleventh and twelfth grade mathematics may address issues concerned with advanced algebra, trigonometry, precalculus, and calculus. Each high school differs in how advanced mathematics is organized and taught. Much of the instructional math curriculum at Grades 11–12 depends upon the sequence of offerings students received in the lower grades, especially middle school. Within the current middle school accelerated curriculum, students who want to achieve success in advanced placement courses in calculus and statistics have to accelerate their mastery of mathematics by Grade 7 and complete their first full year of algebra in Grades 7 or 8. Within the CCSMS, students might take an elective in statistics and another elective in advanced placement calculus in twelfth grade.

The CCSMS expect that students will acquire a mastery level of basic statistical theory and its applications by Grade 12. This assumption is rooted in the belief that, as our society becomes more driven by digital information and data, citizens will need more complex understandings of statistics to guide their own decision making. High school math teachers should evaluate the CCSMS for statistics and merge their local curriculum with these standards.

The merger of local, state, and the CCSS requires teachers at the school level to present a vision of what students should be able to do with their mathematical skills at the end of their statistical studies, including their capacity to provide interesting, unique, and important solutions to problems using statistical processes. Table 4.12 presents the CCSMS for Grade 12 statistics.

Table 4.12   Grade 12 Common Core State Math Standards for Statistics: Using Probability to Make Decisions

---

Calculate expected values, and use them to solve problems

1. Define a random variable for a quantity of interest by assigning a numerical value to each event in a sample space; graph the corresponding probability distribution using the same graphical displays as for data distributions.
2. Calculate the expected value of a random variable; interpret it as the mean of the probability distribution.
3. Develop a probability distribution for a random variable defined for a sample space in which theoretical probabilities can be calculated; find the expected value.

For example, find the theoretical probability distribution for the number of correct answers obtained by guessing on all 5 questions of a multiple-choice test where each question has 4 choices, and find the expected grade under various grading schemes.

4. Develop a probability distribution for a random variable defined for a sample space in which probabilities are assigned empirically; find the expected value.

For example, find a current data distribution on the number of TV sets per household in the United States, and calculate the expected number of sets per household. How many TV sets would you expect to find in 100 randomly selected households?

(Continued)

Table 4.12   Continued

Use probability to evaluate outcomes of decisions

5. Weigh the possible outcomes of a decision by assigning probabilities to payoff values and finding expected values.

    a. Find the expected payoff for a game of chance. *For example, find the expected winnings from a state lottery ticket or a game at a fast-food restaurant.*
    b. Evaluate and compare strategies on the basis of expected values.

For example, compare a high-deductible versus a low-deductible automobile insurance policy using various, but reasonable, chances of having a minor or a major accident.

6. Use probabilities to make fair decisions (e.g., drawing by lots, using a random number generator).
7. Analyze decisions and strategies using probability concepts (e.g., product testing, medical testing, pulling a hockey goalie at the end of a game).

The purpose of this brief review of the CCSMS was to set the stage for the levels of work and training that school leaders must support for their teachers and to offer teachers a quick overview of what they face in the future.

Our national interests require that teachers and their students create a new vision of math education embedded within the CCSMS if we are to compete in the new global economy. The diversity, freedom, and extensive resources that our citizens enjoy in education place the United States in a unique position to lead and to share in the development of new wealth and work within the United States and across the globe.

If school leaders and college preparatory programs prepare our teachers so that they have the skills and collaborative professional dispositions to help their students meet the demands of the global economy, American teachers will prepare their students for productive citizenship. If we continue to fail in the proper preparation of our teachers, we will fail our nation and our children.

Diversity and freedom are the hallmarks of productivity (Page, 2008). American citizens should cherish their education system, their diversity, and their freedom. The CCSS represent the best efforts of the governors of 50 states and their selected commission members to protect the capacity of our citizens to be free and to sustain our democracy by expanding the depth of knowledge that our students master in our schools. The CCSS offer cohesive power for goals and standards while protecting the inherent strength of local and national diversity.

School leaders must require teachers to prove their students master what they are taught. Teachers and school leaders must learn not to settle for proficiency when it often translates to about 65 percent accurate answers. Students and teachers must share a desire to use math in realistic ways that evaluate how things occur and how things are made and to improve how we think with mathematics.

In the next chapters, we will take up the questions of how teachers and school leaders must change their beliefs and mental models about effective teaching. We will discuss how teachers should assess student progress, what school district leaders have to do to create the conditions for fundamental change, the role of learning teams in the engagement of students within their schools, new assessment systems for the CCSS to take hold, and multicultural issues among students in the changing face of America. In addition, we will offer several recommendations for our state and national public policy authors, guidelines for citizens to influence their futures, and actions all of us must undertake to support the CCSS.

CHAPTER 5

Challenges to the Implementation of Rigorous Common Core State Standards

Beliefs, rituals, mores, and values are confusing in many of our schools. School leaders drive teachers to have "growth" test results at all costs. We have no time to look at root causes for student failure. We rush through the curriculum. We work mostly alone with our students. We examine results and blame the students and their parents for failure. In some cases, we reserve for ourselves the credit for whatever successes students achieve, and we accept none of the failure. In many cases, students learn tricks to get certain correct answers on particular formulaic questions. Understanding is not required.

In one case we know, an assistant principal proudly stated: "I never take credit for the success of our students. Their successes and failures are their own." If that is true, we do not need school leaders; we need time clocks to start and end the day.

It is time to stop, pause, and think about what we want to do, why we want to act in a certain way, and how we can know if our actions are valid. Can we change the politicians in our state or our federal government and get them to stop dictating how public schools should operate, spend resources, compete with poorly regulated charter schools, and intervene with challenged learners? Not likely in the short term. Many politicians who never led a school believe they possess the wisdom to dictate behavior that will change failing schools into successful schools. Only sophomores believe in their own wisdom. A few politicians recognize that most school failure occurs in the United States where most poor people live.

Student failure of any kind requires unique interventions for the failing student. In communities with high ratios of student failure, creative, unique, and different interventions should address the needs of failing students and not impede the progress of successful students. Too often, educational leaders and politicians try to find a panacea, a single legislative act or policy that will correct student failure. The world does not respond to one-way-or-the-highway philosophies. Communities, schools, parents, and educators must find their own ways out of the frontiers of failure. The CCSS provide a map to higher educational success. They are tools to more competitive skills and knowledge for U.S. students. The hard, pioneering work that educators and community leaders must do to raise student success in a failing community requires the same pioneering spirit that America's first settlers used to sustain themselves in a wilderness. Cooperation, collaboration, inventiveness, and persistency must imbue continuous trail, error, and success efforts.

TESTING POLICIES DO NOT IMPROVE SCHOOLS

State and federal education departments and state boards of education should stop issuing policy and pause to think deeply about the problems of educating diverse students and the children of the poor who are underemployed and unemployed. They should disaggregate the data about failing schools in each state and see how schools with high failure rates cluster close to poor communities. These policy makers might realize that they do not have a pervasive problem. They have pockets of highly successful, successful, and highly unsuccessful schools.

Highly successful schools, where 90 percent or more of the students achieve proficiency on state exams, need to be commended and rewarded with annual grants for innovative efforts. They will respond to rewards for moving greater segments of their student population to mastery performance on state exams. Unsuccessful schools need to have long-term state interventions, preferably orga-nized as intervention teams of experienced educators who've proved they raised achievement in their own schools.

An educational expert should lead a joint intervention team (JIT) with clear intervention powers and a commitment to serve as a cata-lyst for change during a three- to five-year effort. Every procedure, expectation, and practice in an unsuccessful school must fall under scrutiny. All practices must be justified in terms of how they contrib-ute to learning. State boards of education should take the initiative to identify and provide intervention teams to failing schools.

In 2012, failing schools should be those that have less than 85 percent of their general enrollment students, including racial sub-groups, meeting proficiency and mastery levels of performance in literacy skills, mathematics, science, and history studies. Successful schools must have general education students, including gender, ethnic, and racial subgroups, perform at the 85 percent minimum cri-teria for proficiency or mastery performance. At successful schools, 75 percent of English language learners (ELL) and special education students should show sustained annual growth. The most severely challenged students with Individualized Education Plans (IEPs) should show progress toward their annual goals. Schools should have to prove these growth patterns to state education officers.

ELLs should not be counted in the general subgroup categories as they have special needs and take between five to seven years to complete acculturation processes in which they master the intricacies of the second language. At a successful school, more than 75 percent of ELL and special education students must demonstrate growth in learning from their first year of measurement. Growth in learning means that students tested in Grade 3 show sustained performance in Grade 4 by performing on the ensuing grade-level tests at a similar level, stanine, or percentile when contrasted to their previous year's performance. Progress that is more emphatic can be demonstrated with math, science, reading, writing, and native language projects that ELLs and children with IEPs produce. Exceptional growth would be greater than the previous year's performance criteria mea-surement on a more difficult standard or criterion-based measure-ment. Exceptional growth is the goal for every child, and mastery level performance is the ultimate goal.

The federal role in education should be to promote rewards in states for schools with high student success and to appropriate funds for interventions in unsuccessful schools. In New York State (NYS), there are slightly more than 700 school districts, and approximately 140 of these districts have failing schools where less than 80 percent of the students achieve proficiency. These districts are located in predominantly urban areas with high unemployment and poor health care and dental services (Cantor, 2010).

Do we need testing policies to improve achievement in these schools? What a ridiculous response to an endemic problem. We need new leadership, new curriculum, new instruction, new teacher development strategies at these schools, new supportive structures within the schools, and closer partnerships with parents and social and health agencies. In challenged schools with high percentages of academic failure, school leaders have to redesign the school day for students and teachers. In some extreme cases, schools should close if they have had three years of targeted staff development and they continue to show little or no improvement in student performance. We do not favor charter schools. On the other hand, we recognize some school personnel exhibit recalcitrant attitudes, and they will not change unless they must change. For such staff, we recommend a three-year intervention plan that has a time line for an adjudication that the school may be shut and reopened as two charter schools with one headmaster and two separate staffs if improvements in teaching and learning are not verifiable.

At the outset of the intervention in failing schools, personnel need to know that they must make effective changes within 36 months or the school will close. All employees will have to compete for new jobs with a separate contract established for the charter school, including new hours and compensations and fixed benefit allotments from the community. In failing schools, there should be no doubt that the school personnel must change what they do and get better results from their students. Failing schools cannot sustain themselves as they are.

What is the role of state tests? They are thermometers that measure the academic temperatures of the students at a school. They provide a picture of the academic health of the students. State tests are instruments that measure current reality in terms of Common Core State Standards (CCSS) and norms. They can do nothing to improve student academic health. In fact, standardized tests are poor measures of intellectual proficiency and correlate with a narrow band of learning (Kohn, 2006). Currently, they are the only measures that states have to distinguish failing and successful schools. State tests are like thermometers. They report a current state of health. They cannot improve health nor diagnose its contributing factors.

Teachers and school leaders who believe that they can improve student learning are those who improve their own learning about how students differ in proficiencies. They know how to use formative assessments. When teachers improve their own use of formative tests, they correct the ones they design, and they devise new ways to respond to individual differences among their students. They diagnose and prescribe. They act as professionals.

THE COMMON CORE STATE STANDARDS: OPPORTUNITIES FOR EQUITY AND EXCELLENCE

Are CCSS the problem? We suggest that the CCSS represent an opportunity for every school district in the nation to become part of the solution to America's poor-performing students. First, all school leaders and teachers must commit to having students master the body of knowledge that the CCSS present. Second, school leaders must commit to extensive training of teachers to ensure that they have shared knowledge of the curriculum and common planning time at each grade level to collaboratively develop formative and summative assessments of student learning and fair and regular observations of their work with students.

The CCSS represent the basic knowledge that our students need to master. Proficiency is a low performance standard. Yet, we need to start there and move from proficiency to mastery measurements. Schools that have more than 60 percent of their students achieve mastery should receive federal awards, as they are nation builders within our current patterns of academic success. School boards should award all students who achieve mastery on state exams with academic pins of excellence.

If our federal government, the president, and Congress want to help improve education in America and make our graduates more competitive on the world stage, they should do one and only one policy change: Provide rewards to states and school districts where more than 60 percent of the students achieve mastery-level performance on state or national exams. They should add significant incentives to states and schools for every increment of 10 percent of the student population above 60 percent mastery. Imagine the outcomes if government rewarded mastery-level performance and did not give away sundry dollars to intervene in failure.

Schmidt and colleagues (2011) note that 100,000 new science, technology, engineering, and mathematics teachers will be needed in middle and high school classrooms in the next decade. Add to this number of secondary teachers and elementary teachers at every grade level with extensive training needs in science, technology, engineering, and mathematical concepts, and a picture of the challenge appears. School boards need incentives to promote science, technology and engineering, math skills, and language and literacy skills. Let government provide the incentives and financial rewards for high school graduates to complete math, science, and engineering degrees and to excel on advanced placement tests in these subjects as well as history, language, and literacy.

Beyond the preparation of teachers who raise student performance to mastery levels lays the actual work that they will do and how they will be acculturated into this work. Here is where the CCSS present the glue to bond local curriculum to high-quality national and international competitive standards in mathematics, literacy, science, and social studies. American schools need to improve student mastery of mathematical, science, and engineering concepts and applications. Teachers and school leaders must work together to expand literacy and the historical, creative, and innovative thinking capacity of our students from the earliest grades forward.

The foundation for greater academic achievement starts at preschool to primary grades where teachers and school leaders adopt the CCSS and integrate them with local curriculum. Teachers have to do this integration if they are going to be master artisans. They need extensive training in professional and collaborative teamwork and team learning. They have to make a transition or transformation from long-distance runners in single classrooms to teammates working with unique combinations of human talent and learning needs. They must become learning teams (Senge et al., 2000).

One of the unique strategies that school leaders can employ to help teachers form learning teams is to train them in the design and use of formative assessments to guide and transform their instructional practices for the students that they have in front of them. They need to learn how to conduct regular analyses of student performance on common formative assessments in the same way teams of clinical doctors and nurse practitioners monitor patient results and alter treatments according to timely readings of each patient's health status.

Recently, we witnessed a dialogue between two special education teachers serving on an instructional intervention team. The team was discussing collaborative formative assessments that general education and special education teachers designed in core subjects. One special education teacher offered the following observation: "You know, our students have learning disabilities, and they don't learn as quickly as the general education population. I think we should develop our own tests and make them fit our children better."

A colleague replied: "We can't do that. These students have to pass state exams to graduate. The formative assessments align with the CCSS and our state standards. We need to know how our kids will perform—what they know and don't know on the standards. I prepare my classes with the necessary vocabulary for each of the five items that make up the core collaborative formative assessment. I administer segments of the assessment during several days. The data I get back show me exactly what they can and cannot do. I adjust my teaching accordingly. We all have to do this. We can't go back to the old way of creating easier tests for our kids."

Friedman and Mandelbaum (2011) concluded there were five elements that America had to address to improve its economic strength: education, infrastructure, immigration, research and development, and regulations. Education is the foundation for all of the others (p. 355). The challenges to rigorous implementation of the CCSS are those that lie within our own assumptions, mental models, and beliefs.

To change our own assumptions, teachers and school leaders must diversify the talent and training within teacher teams and encourage debate and constructive conflicts so that the school staff can change. We should not be fearful of parents and community members with unique skills and experiences who can join ad hoc curriculum teams for short periods. Adding diverse people to ad hoc committees will help reframe our curricula and our teaching processes. The more open and transparent educators are with experts within their own community, the more likely they are to create responsive and unique learning communities for their students.

Learning communities for schools may appear to be a natural metaphor. The truth is that few schools have leaders who foster learning communities where teachers and students accelerate learning.

We know of a small city high school where many diverse children select magnet-learning opportunities. The students spend one third of their day in one of four specialized colleges of science and technology, fine arts, performing arts, and liberal and governmental studies within the school.

Unfortunately, each subdivision has a staff focused on its own priorities and not the general development of students. In one case, a student leader told us he was elected president of a club that met one hour after school each week. The band leader told him he had to leave the band if he missed one hour of practice each week. What do you think the student did? He left the band.

In a second case, a Spanish-language, third-year student told us he received a gift from his grandfather of a Spanish novel written by Miguel de Unamuno. He brought it to class to read after he finished his Friday chapter tests, while he waited for other students to finish. His teacher told him not to read that book because she taught it in Level 5 Spanish. Guess what he did? He quit Spanish language studies after Level 3.

How have so many teachers become robot like in their work? Why can't they see each child as unique and respond in kind? Have they been trained and acculturated to treat everyone the same in spite of living in an age of corporate individualization? In order to change fundamental approaches teachers employ with students, we must change how teachers judge each child. School leaders have to encourage teachers to differentiate instruction and to address disparities in their assessment results. Teachers must feel authorized to slow the pace of curriculum to meet the needs of some students while providing creative ways for others to accelerate their own learning.

Teachers must rethink their planned process, such as counting homework for 20 percent of the quarterly grade when their results indicate 40 percent or more of their students fail. Homework should be a formative assessment. The teacher's final grade should comprise summative assessments that assess exactly what students were taught and their levels of mastery.

In the next chapter, we present a process by which all teachers can adopt formative assessments to assess their students' mastery of the CCSS. We explore formative assessments and demonstrate their value. We provide clear and precise examples of the use and power of formative assessments when teachers commit to their design, control their use, and change instructional practices based upon the results their students deliver. The shared wisdom of teachers regarding student mastery begins with collaborative inquiry about current reality as evidenced in formative assessments. When teachers contrast where students are to where teachers want to take them, teachers begin the creative and professional work of designing interventions and removing gaps in learning.

Great teachers do what great surgeons do. Great surgeons remove cancerous cells, bypass blocked arteries, and find ways to return many people to good health. Great teachers encounter obstacles to learning among their students, and they find ways around them.

SECTION III

Helping Teachers Redefine Their Profession

CHAPTER 6

How to Assess Mastery of the Common Core Curriculum State Standards

The common core curriculum state standards have been designed as a pathway toward successful functioning in a complex democracy in which citizens must contribute to the well-being of their communities and families. Four qualities that the Common Core State Standards (CCSS) assume teachers will address are creativity, flexibility, self-control, and discipline. Diamond and Lee (2011) report that children in the 21st century need to be prepared to "think creatively to devise solutions never considered before" (p. 959). They continue:

> They will need working memory to mentally work with masses of data and see new connections among elements, flexibility to appreciate different perspectives and take advantage of serendipity, and self-control to resist temptations and avoid doing something they would regret. Tomorrow's leaders will need the discipline to stay focused, seeing tasks through to completion. (p. 959)

Diamond and Lee (2011) distinguish between core and complex executive functions that the human brain must learn to employ. They describe core executive functions as dependent on neural circuits in which the prefrontal cortex is central. Core executive functions are learned cognitive processes such as flexible thinking, inhibitions such as self-control and self-regulation, and working memory.

More complex, executive functions include cognitive processes such as problem solving, reasoning, and planning. "The most effective way to improve executive functioning and academic achievement is probably not to focus narrowly on those alone but to also address children's emotional and social development . . . and physical development" (Diamond & Lee, 2011, p. 963).

Fu, Raizen, and Shavelson (2009) report that the National Assessment of Education Progress (NAEP) 2009 science framework recommends the employment of four new science assessments:

Concept maps that require students to draw and describe connections among science concepts.

Probes of student mental models, e.g. (What forces can act on an object at rest?).

Predictions students are asked to make about a presented situation and, following an observation or summary of what actually happens, students provide an explanation of the result such as if a given object will float on water.

Interactive computer tasks in which students are asked to resolve a variety of challenging tasks such as organizing a data base into useable information, conducting an empirical investigation, working one's way through a simulation or creating a concept map. (p. 1638)

Each of these processes could be the foundation of within-class and short-term formative assessments. We favor frequent formative assessments in the classroom where teachers have students complete three tasks related to a single theme. Each task should reveal what the student knows or assumes and how the student uses data or facts and descriptions to create information in numerical, written, and visual formats. The quality of information arrangement reflects the student's decision-making process. Teachers working with formative assessments should require students to justify their decisions, verify or support their findings, and explain the implications of their results.

The collaborative nature of effective school environments cannot be underestimated. Wang and Holcombe (2010) conducted a longitudinal study of 1,000 adolescents who were asked to assess their perceptions about their Grade 7 perceived school environment and their Grade 8 grade point averages, school participation, school identification, and use of self-regulation strategies. The students represented 23 public school districts within a large, ethnically diverse county on the East Coast of the United States. Wang and Holcombe found that teachers who promoted positive student identification with their school and who offered positive and improvement-based praise that emphasized effort and mastery of knowledge and skills had more highly motivated students who were higher academic achievers (p. 652).

The more students participated in school, identified themselves as belonging in the school, and regulated their own learning with strategies to assess how they were doing and how to obtain appropriate help when needed, the greater the likelihood that students would be high achievers. Self-regulated learning has to be taught to teachers, and teachers have to teach students how to use these powerful learning tools (Mullin, 2011).

Formative assessments that provide students with three to five opportunities to demonstrate competence or mastery within a subject theme promote continuous learning (Popham, 2008). Students who have acquired self-regulated learning strategies use formative assessment results to guide their own pursuit of knowledge.

> Instead of simply indexing students against external normative standards, mastery approaches foster students' sense of competence by emphasizing and highlighting what students have mastered. A mastery goal structure provides more opportunities for students to work together rather than compete against each other. (Wang & Holcombe, 2010, p. 652)

Hung-His Wu (2009) offers multiple ways to teach and assess student mastery of adding two whole numbers in Grades 2 and 3. "The difficulty here is mostly in motivating and engaging students so that they come to understand the standard additional algorithm and, as a result, develop a deeper appreciation of place value . . ." (p. 4). Wu criticizes much of what takes place in American elementary schools in the area of mathematical teaching as uninvolved learners memorizing what teachers want them to know. He presents a simple problem to students. "Alan has saved 45 pennies and Beth has saved 31. They want to buy a small packet of stickers that costs 75 cents, and they must find out if they have enough money together" (p. 5).

Wu provides several directions for students:

1. Count all of the pennies.

2. Accept Alan's bag of pennies with 45 pennies and count all of Beth's pennies.

3. Show the students a progression. Using Alan's 45 pennies take three pennies from Beth and add them to Alan's count 46-47-48. Do the same with all 31 of Beth's pennies.

4. Show students they are adding $45 + 31$.

5. Have students put Alan's pennies into four bags with ten pennies each and leave 5 pennies in a pile. Then have students put Beth's pennies into three bags with ten pennies each and leave one penny alone. Ask students how many bags of ten they have and how many pennies they have that are stragglers (not in a bag).

6. Show students

   4 bags of 10 pennies + 5

   3 bags of 10 pennies + 1

   Explain that these sets of numbers depict the number of pennies. Ask them to add the number of pennies in the bags and the number outside the bags. They will find 7 bags of 10 pennies = 70 pennies + 5 = 75 + 1 = 76.

7. Show students $45 + 31$ (pennies) =

   Ask students for the total number of pennies.

8. Show students
   $$\begin{array}{r} 45 \\ + 31 \\ \hline \end{array}$$

   Ask for total ____ (Wu, 2009, p. 5)

Wu (2009) notes that many educators

> believe that the real difficulty of this algorithm arises when 'carrying' is necessary, but conceptually, carrying is just a sidelight, a little wrinkle on the fabric. The key idea is contained in the case of adding without carrying. If we succeed in getting students to thoroughly understand addition without carrying, then, they will be in an excellent position to handle carrying too." (p. 5)

Most second and third grade teachers can use Wu's procedural approach to addition or whole number computations. By changing the numerical elements, these same teachers could create five formative assessments to determine which students mastered the concepts, and which ones needed more specialized tutoring or simply an opportunity to explain what they know and do not know.

A child we know, who is finishing her K–5 experience in the public schools of an affluent community, summed up her school experience with these words: "My school is a place where teachers only care about what you know and what you get correct. They don't want to learn what you don't know." If this high-performing school where students achieve the highest proficiency ratings has a student criticize its practices so aptly, what are other schools like?

Sadly, many schools have teachers who are without the support and continuous learning that an ever-changing and challenging curriculum requires. Wu (2009) calls for a radical change in how mathematics is taught in elementary schools: "I hope you will join me in calling for the creation of a cadre of teachers who specialize in the teaching of mathematics in Grades 4–6 (p. 5).

We believe that all elementary schools need to expand the skills of their teachers in the instruction of reading, expository and creative writing, mathematics, and science and technology. Teachers need to work in teams at every grade level. They need to specialize in content areas, to learn from one another, and to experiment with new technologies to help children master the curriculum. Most of all, teachers need to learn how to use formative assessments to guide and transform instruction.

Formative assessments should be ongoing and frequent in every classroom. Teachers also need to assess their own progress in helping their students learn by developing collaborative assessments that measure agreed-upon standards. In several schools in which we see movement toward important teaching and learning changes, we see teachers coming together to identify an espoused scope and sequence for their curriculum and to develop shared formative assessments that give students regular opportunities to demonstrate what they know and do not know.

Mike Rose, writing in the *American Teacher* (2011), noted "standards based reform can only succeed in tandem with other essential components—particularly high quality curriculum, strong professional development, appropriate resources, and assessments tied into curriculum and standards and comprehensive stakeholder buy-in" (p. 12). One critical issue Rose identifies is that teachers have to be involved in the examination of how the CCSS fit with what they are doing already. Teachers have to be part of the dialogue about what necessary support and resources are needed to successfully implement the standards.

In one high school that we visited, ninth grade teachers in math, science, social studies, and English established learning teams to write formative assessments that the entire ninth grade teaching team used throughout the year. Each subject and grade-level team used the shared formative assessments to assess at least monthly the progress and mastery-level performance of their students on the critical curriculum priorities. They identified challenges that their own formative assessments revealed and used them to request additional training in the use of technology at the school as well as content-related instructional strategies.

Later in this chapter, we will present and discuss some of the examples that these teachers devised to measure what their students mastered and to reveal the dispositional and cognitive barriers students encountered to their understanding of critical concepts. Furthermore, this chapter reveals some of the challenges teachers encountered in having their students apply what they were taught in a variety of settings or in different scenarios.

DIRECT INSTRUCTION

Klahr, Zimmerman, and Jirout (2011) contrasted three teaching styles: direct instruction, Socratic instruction, and discovery processes. They reported that direct instruction (explicit teaching) was most effective in the short and long term. They reported that "children can learn scientific knowledge and thinking from less directed instruction, given extensive scaffolding, guided instruction and discovery, however, they take much longer to reach mastery and are no better at transferring knowledge" (p. 974).

In addition, they presented a summary of research that indicated preschool children could be trained to improve control of some mental processes that were widely agreed to be important for learning and understanding science (and mathematics): self-regulation, cognitive flexibility, and inhibitory control.

Teachers at all grade levels have to adopt certain common classroom management practices and support for learning before any process of formative assessment will help them to increase their students' mastery of subjects. Teachers have to establish classroom routines for self-management and personal responsibility.

Students must be taught how to work together, how to help one another, and under what conditions to seek teacher help. Teachers must provide direct and explicit instruction in the fundamental constructs and understandings of a subject. They must set the sequence and the building blocks that help students to learn how to construct knowledge from information or data, and these skills must be taught explicitly.

Teachers should design formative assessments upon a foundation of sequential building blocks within a curriculum. Well-designed assessments enable teachers to identify what students have mastered, what students do not know or understand, what they cannot transfer, and specific variations among students that reveal who require careful one-to-one or small-group instruction.

Often, in small groups of students, teachers can discover the misconceptions students have about a topic and the facts or procedures they have confused. In small groups and tutorials, students and teachers discover previously learned ideas that are wrong and that have become barriers to future learning. Direct instruction takes on many variations in a single classroom as students reveal what they do not know. Expert teachers are sensitive to all of their students and expect mastery from each one. They know in what stage of development each of their students is. They know how to develop empathetic dispositions and leadership skills among those who mastered a curriculum by assigning the task of being a peer instructor.

The formative assessments that expert teachers employ are related to deep understandings of the curriculum (what is to be mastered in the subject), knowledge of how to motivate and reduce student stress (care and support for learning), and a shared vision of how to design student assessments to verify what students have learned.

Formative assessments can improve indefinitely because they reflect the goals of the curriculum, the dispositions and skills of the students, and the changing landscape of national and state measurements of mastery. Expert teachers recognize that their local assessments are imperfect and that even the large-group tests administered by state and federal or international agencies have estimated errors of measurement. They see all tests as tools to reveal important information much like CAT scans. They use the results from formative and summative assessments to inform their instructional practice and to initiate preliminary inquiries with specific students who show weaknesses in a particular area. They do not view test results as indicators of student capacity or ability. They refuse to permit a test to set a cap on student learning.

X-ray, CAT, and PET scans do not devalue the judgment or the skills of physicians. Physicians use such digital tests to diagnose and prescribe and to evaluate the effects of interventions. The skillful diagnostic process that physicians employ helps them to select interventions that may bring patients back to health. Physicians must seek success with every patient. Teachers do the same. In schools, standardized and formative tests should serve the same purpose that digital scans serve in hospitals. All tests merely produce information. Test results should guide professional choice in the selection of interventions. Summative and standardized tests in schools attempt to measure the long-term health of students and the effects of teacher interventions. As such, they become tools to measure effective teaching. They should not be the only tool nor the dominant tool. Principals have to be accountable for the quality of learning occurring in their schools. They have to intervene in multiple and effective ways when they encounter teachers who are not successful.

By and large, standardized test results arrive at a particular school toward the end of the school year and rarely influence how teachers should adjust instruction for the students in front of them that year. The previous year's standardized tests can inform teachers about particular weaknesses and strengths members of a particular class possesses and even skills or themes that are undervalued within the district curriculum. Such information can sensitize teachers to the needs of particular students. In addition, teachers can reframe their curriculum to address more deeply important themes and skills embedded within the new CCSS. Finally, standardized test results can identify which students demonstrated poor mastery in a previous year. Only formative assessments help teachers change instructional strategies for the children in front of them.

Principals can use class observations, formative assessment results, summative test results, and professional interventions to help and to evaluate teachers. A series of scores on a single standard test should not be used as a measurement of effective teaching.

THE POWER OF FORMATIVE ASSESSMENTS

The kinds of assessments that can make the greatest difference to students and teachers are formative assessments that are designed to assess important skills and understandings related to a particular building block in the curriculum. Such assessments are administered to students during the period that the skills and understandings are being taught.

Teachers should create frequent short and focused formative assessments in their classes. Such assessments should offer at least three to five opportunities for students to demonstrate appropriate knowledge in a particular curriculum objective. For instance, Florida State Standards for Grade 3–5 social studies require that a student knows significant people and their contributions in the field of communications and technology.

After providing appropriate direct instruction, a few discovery and reporting activities by small groups of students, and perhaps some visualization from YouTube or another digital format, teachers could require students to respond to five tasks for their formative assessment:

1. Match the names of five inventors to their contributions in communications.

2. Compare a laptop and an iPad as communicative tools.

3. Compare the contributions of Steve Jobs and Bill Gates to communications.

4. Contrast the contributions of Benjamin Franklin and Thomas Edison to understandings about electricity and its relationship to communications.

5. Compare the contributions of Alexander Graham Bell and Samuel B. Morse in the field of communications.

The formative assessment could take place in one class period or several depending on the learning needs of the students.

For a student to achieve a determination of mastery about this topic, teachers would develop a rubric that describes inadequate, barely adequate, proficient, and expert responses. In order for a student to receive a score equivalent to mastery, a student would have to achieve expert responses three out of five times and at least one proficient or greater score. If teachers think of a four-scale rubric as holding 2.5 points in each level of potential response, an expert response would represent 10 points. The entire formative assessment would represent 50 points, and 40 points would be required for mastery with 30 points for proficiency.

A simpler scoring rubric that might appeal to teachers and that we witnessed working very efficiently is a single point or zero for each of the five responses. If students provide a correct and mostly complete answer, they receive 1 point. On a formative assessment with five items, teachers can easily see who achieved mastery with scores of 4 and 5 and for which items students need attention that is more personal.

For eighth grade students studying social studies and particularly the Reconstruction Period and Immigration from 1830 to 1900, teachers might agree to use the following five formative assessments:

1. Please explain why immigrants came to the United States between 1830 and 1900. Distinguish between *pull* and *push* factors and incentives that motivated these immigrants.

2. Please describe the difficulties that immigrants faced in the United States between 1830 and 1900.

3. Compare and contrast immigrant groups to the United States from Eastern and Western Europe between 1830 and 1900.

4. Compare and contrast groups of people coming to the United States from Europe and non-European countries between 1830 and 1900.

5. Please describe how immigrant groups entering the United States between 1830 and 1900 contributed to the future of the United States.

Once these eighth grade teachers agree to a rubric that described the level of comprehension that would reflect less-than-adequate,

adequate, proficient, and expert responses, they have a powerful tool to assess the level of mastery for each student in the class. The power of this rubric's quantitative aspect is that teachers can report and contrast a whole class within itself and simultaneously compare students across other classes that they teach.

For example, in Table 6.1 we present a simple spreadsheet that would allow teachers to contrast the performance of their students in a single class or several classes by representing the four categories of student performance on five formative assessment items within one test.

Table 6.1   Class Rubric Performance Report for Immigration 1830–1900

Class: Period 1

Name	Q1	Q2	Q3	Q4	Q5	Total Score	Interpretation
J. Jones	2.5	5	7.5	7.5	10	32.5	Proficient in topic. Needs tutorial Q1. Conference on Q2
R. Smith	5	5	7.5	2.5	7.5	27.5	Not Proficient yet. Tutor Q1, Q2, Q4

Rubric Score: 2.5 or less = inadequate, 5 = adequate, 7.5 = proficient, 10 = expert.

The rubric process is very popular with many state education officials. Teachers may prefer a rubric system or something less complex that allows them more autonomy. Table 6.2 presents the holistic process of yes, this is correct, or no, this is not correct. Yes equals one point, and no is blank and equals zero points. In this system, teachers count successes and address the areas where students have not demonstrated success.

Table 6.2   Class Item Correct Performance Report for Immigration 1830–1900

Class: Period 1

Name	Q1	Q2	Q3	Q4	Q5	Total Score	Interpretation
J. Jones	1		1	1		3	Proficient in topic. Needs tutorial Q2 and Q5.
R. Smith	1				1	2	Not Proficient yet. Tutor Q2, Q3, Q4

Score range: 1 to 2 = less than adequate, 3 = proficient, 4 to 5 = mastery.

Within a single Excel spreadsheet, most teachers could contrast and compare their entire classes. Teachers working on a single common theme could examine their collective results and determine if one or more teachers had an unusual number of students whose performance on the topic was less than proficient. In such cases, the teachers might have authorization from the principal or subject department chairperson to meet and share academic intervention resources so that students failing to show proficiency in a topic would have immediate remediation with appropriate time and attention to their personal needs.

In some schools, we witnessed teachers rearranging their academic tutorial schedules or their academic intervention assignments so that they could reduce the burden on a colleague and share their total resources of time, materials, and prior experience. They created a more equitable distribution of students in need of individual help by co-teaching in their tutorial sessions. In another school, teachers used the Castle Learning Systems (2001) software to identify disparities among students and to design learning tutorials.

In these effective schools, teachers helped colleagues have greater success with their students. They shared the responsibility to have all children approach mastery because they believed they were working on the same team. In addition, school leaders ensured that they had the autonomy to work together for the benefit of their students.

Specifically, in one school we witnessed fourth grade teachers identify one colleague with 11 non-proficient students while the other three teachers had between 2 and 4 struggling students in each class. The four teachers at the grade level decided to pool their students for the next two weeks in afterschool tutorial sessions. Each of them addressed the learning needs of five students, knowing full well where each student struggled. After many weeks of shared responsibility, they were successful in moving all children in fourth grade to proficiency levels.

Teacher collaboration at a grade level is a powerful tool to intervene in the failing learning patterns that their students exhibit. Students in such schools quickly recognize that teachers are working together to make them more successful. Students know almost intuitively that their teachers care about their success.

Shonkoff (2011) noted that new preschool curricula with a focus on science, numeracy, and executive functioning skills that include training in attention and impulse control make a difference in student performance. Also, interventions such as caring and motivational exchanges with students and parents can reduce the disruptive effects of toxic stress in the child's home. The combination of these efforts by trained teachers in preschools shrinks the socioeconomic disparities in educational achievement that one finds in American schools, especially in cities where a majority of public school students live in poverty.

Shonkoff (2011) noted the power of training in executive function:

> Vulnerable children who do well in school often have well developed capacities in executive function and emotional regulation which help them manage adversity more effectively and provide a solid foundation for academic achievement and social competence. (p. 982)

Teachers, at every grade level, should be encouraged to professionalize their dialogues with each other. School leaders should structure the teaching day so that teachers will have time to converse about their students' performance on formative assessments, their learning needs, and the planned interventions they will employ. Teachers need to discuss how to motivate students to engage in learning events. They have to have time to assure students that they are in a safe environment where it is OK to make errors. They must believe themselves that their own errors are the origin of how they learn too. Teachers need to be able to schedule expert support staff to intervene in their classes and not suffer multiple interruptions throughout the day as children are pulled out of their classes. Students need to know that their classroom is a place where they can experiment as they learn, find their errors, and achieve at a masterful level.

FORMATIVE ASSESSMENT EXAMPLES FROM REAL SCHOOLS

In Grade 9, we witnessed a group of committed teachers whose most precious goal was to have every child find success in their mathematical pursuits of algebra. They created a strong collaborative process to design formative assessments for every major theme in their ninth grade curriculum.

They learned how to summarize the results of the formative assessments using a rubric reporting system for each class. Then, they compared and contrasted results by discussing the individual performances of their students and the patterns of success that they found in each class. They identified alternative instructional strategies, technology, and software tools they could use to help students visualize or draw understandings about new themes in the curriculum. Their students who failed to demonstrate proficiency in a topic quickly learned that they would have their teacher's full attention and persistence. Their teachers were determined to help them be successful.

This high school had cut back department supervisors, and in the face of less state aid, the central administration provided a math and a literacy coach to the school. The literacy coach worked diligently to help teachers in social studies, science, and English use thinking maps and formative assessments to identify gaps in learning. The math coach organized her math department colleagues to restructure a new scope and sequence in the math curriculum aligned with the Common Core State Math Standards (CCSMS). Grade 9 and 10 math teachers set a precise sequence of instruction accompanied by collaborative formative assessments for each chapter in the math text. Some teachers immediately used the formative assessments to verify mastery learning by students and to identify precisely which students needed more individualized attention for a particular topic. These teachers changed the pace of instruction and created team-learning groups within the class to differentiate instruction. One example of a formative assessment developed for an algebra topic asked students to solve for an unknown. See Table 6.3.

One of the most interesting elements of the work that the math coach did with her colleagues in the high school was the collaborative thinking and decision making that her team did. Lead teachers can influence the thinking of colleagues in profound ways. Working with her, the ninth grade math team raised their teaching performance from technicians following a manual and teaching to a test to professionals designing a scope and sequence for learning. They created collaborative and content-valid formative and summative assessments. They used student results to guide changes in their instructional strategies. They paced their instruction according to formative assessments, personal diagnoses, and their own prescriptions for interventions.

More than half of their students are English language learners (ELLs) and second-generation Latino students. A majority of these teachers made significant improvements in their students' mastery

Table 6.3   Ninth Grade Formative Assessment for a Curriculum Theme

Related to a Chapter in the Algebra Text: Solving for an Unknown

1. Expressed in terms of d, the number of weeks in d days is
   a. $d/7$
   b. $7/d$
   c. $7d$
   d. $7 + d$

2. Which expression represents the number of eggs in x dozen?
   a. $x/12$
   b. $12/x$
   c. $12 + x$
   d. $12x$

3. The sum of Scott's age and Greg's age is 33 years. If Greg's age is represented by g, Scott's age is represented by
   a. $33 - g$
   b. $g - 33$
   c. $g + 33$
   d. $33g$

4. Which expression represents "5 less than the product of 7 and x"?
   a. $7(x - 5)$
   b. $7x - 5$
   c. $7 + x - 5$
   d. $5 - 7x$

5. Which is the correct verbal expression for the mathematical expression $3n + 2$?
   a. Two more than three times a number
   b. Two less than three times a number
   c. Two more than a number, times three
   d. Three times two plus some number

Source: Castle Learning Systems (2001).

of the subject. These teachers learned to use the formative assessments to diagnose student needs, plan and implement appropriate interventions for their students, and evaluate how well their interventions work. Such teachers expect that they will find ways to have their students master what they are required to know in ninth grade. Effective formative assessments are one of the first interventions teachers must design to accelerate learning.

Homework and grading systems must be reexamined. Summative tests should align to the actual teaching that occurred in the class and not to a canned set of software with easy-to-use tests. Teachers who devise frequent systems to identify what their students know and do not know raise their own efficacy and capacity to help students learn.

Effective math teachers have their students master all of the CCSS in mathematics for Grade 9. In the case of this high school, the ninth grade teachers increased passing rates by 17 percent in mathematics between 2009 and 2011. They continue to work on ways to improve instruction, assessments, and learning. A small majority of these teachers changed from identifying the deficits and failures students had to using formative assessments to calculate the grades students received after reteaching and reevaluating students. In June 2012, one teacher had 100 percent of her students pass the New York State (NYS) Algebra Regents examination. All of her students were in the general Regents track.

Deborah Stone (2002) wrote in her book, *Policy Paradox*, that we get what we count, meaning if we count mastery among students, we will get more mastery, and if we count failure, we will get more students who fail. The math teachers who measure successful use of math concepts to solve problems and who diversify their instructional strategies according to student needs have more students passing.

James Popham (2008) in his book *Transformative Assessment* makes a strong case that formative assessment should be "a planned process in which assessment-elicited evidence of students' status is used by teachers to adjust their ongoing instructional procedures or by students to adjust their current learning tactics" (p. 112). Popham chose his words very carefully. He was determined to warn teachers and administrators that formative assessment was not a non-verbal, spur-of-the-moment reaction to a student gesture or facial expression. Rather, he forcefully notes that formative assessment is a planned process that produces evidence of student learning or lack of learning. The evidence comes from opportunities students have in multiple expressions (three to five) to demonstrate they know how to apply what has been taught.

Both the teacher and the student, in a review of results in a formative assessment, can see the strengths and weaknesses that the student's responses reveal. Popham (2008) suggests that five opportunities to show mastery of a topic should be sufficient for a student or a teacher to determine the level of mastery that the student exhibits in those responses.

Popham (2008) notes that formative assessment "arises when teachers or students or both use assessment evidence to make decisions first about whether to make improvement-aimed adjustments and then about what sort of adjustments to make" (p. 113). He goes on to explain that teachers should supply students with assessment-based, descriptive feedback indicating what students can do currently and what they need to do to achieve a targeted curricular aim. He reaffirms that descriptive feedback based on empirical evidence in formative assessment is much more effective in the improvement of learning than comparative feedback that results in a grade or a rank in class (p. 114).

Black and Wiliam (2009), in their effort to develop a theory of formative assessment beyond their earlier work in 1998, observed that teacher feedback to the learner functioned formatively only if the information given to the learner was used by the learner to improve performance (p. 13). They chose self-regulated learning (SRL) processes as underlying motivators or barriers to student improvement that all teachers had to consider.

Black and Wiliam (2009) make a strong case for several stages of thinking that students must adopt to facilitate their learning:

1. a desire to grow so as to increase resources, knowledge, and social skills

2. well-being in which students seek to hold onto social status, sense of belonging, or feelings

3. volitional strategies and autonomy that make them aware of ways to interpret strategy failure

4. how to discipline themselves to work effectively alone and with others.

In each response that a teacher receives from a student, the teacher "has to decide how a student came to make a response" (Black & Wiliam, 2009, p. 16). Black and Wiliam point out that students continuously self-assess, sometimes erroneously, and that teachers must first interpret the student's thinking and motivation embedded in the response. Then, an effective teacher would diagnose what the student desires, needs, or lacks and choose an optimum response.

Black and Wiliam (2009) observe that learning is described best in terms of dynamic assessments or cognitive acceleration programs. They agree with Vygotsky (1978), who stated that good learning is that which supports the acquisition of new psychological functions by creating cognitive conflict. In this scenario, teachers instruct and then challenge students to reflect on their own thinking, to make their thinking public, and to reveal how they are dealing with seriation, causality, classification, proportionality, probability, and other contexts in which their knowledge and thinking process applies.

Dynamic assessments cause teachers to address a learner's capacity to sustain new learning about a topic. These approaches include the sensitive elements of teacher formative feedback that all teachers must learn to address. "There is not, from the evidence, a clear indication of choosing between positive and negative feedback: the former can enhance motivation, whilst the latter may, depending on the recipient's self-belief, be accepted as a challenge which helps trigger self-regulation" (Black & Wiliam, 2009, p. 24).

In every classroom, teachers must interpret students' contributions to discussions and their responses to assessments in terms of how each student's response reveals the student's thinking and motivation. This is the diagnostic challenge that all teachers face. On the other hand, the prognostic choices teachers have to make involve complex decisions about the optimum responses teachers must offer their students (Black & Wiliam, 2009, p. 27).

Teaching students at any age is a complex endeavor. Formative assessments that teachers design collectively provide them with data they can analyze collegially. Their shared dialogue and inquiry about student results reduces the complexity of teaching and the difficulties one encounters alone to a shared practice where teachers implement collective wisdom that should help each child grow as a learner. Black and Wiliam (2009) remind us that expert teachers differ from novice teachers in several important ways:

a. novice teachers tend to treat individual questions as coming from an individual learner
b. expert teachers use individual questions to formulate responses to a collective student
c. expert teachers draw out implications for the learning of the whole class. (p. 21)

Essentially, Black and Wiliam (2009) offer five key strategies to conceptualize formative assessments:

1. Clarifying and sharing learning intentions and criteria for success;

2. Engineering effective classroom discussions and other learning tasks that elicit evidence of student understanding;

3. Providing feedback that move learners forward;

4. Activating students as instructional resources for one another; and

5. Activating students as owners of their own learning. (p. 8)

In another learning event, science teachers in Grade 9 provided their students with 3 questions and 14 opportunities to demonstrate knowledge of the scientific method (see Table 6.4).

Table 6.4   Ninth Grade Formative Assessment for the Scientific Method

1. Advertisers claim that a certain brand of cough drop reduces coughing for eight hours. Describe an investigation that could be used to determine if this claim is valid. In your answer, describe
   a. what treatment is given to an experimental group
   b. what treatment is given to a control group
   c. data that should be collected
   d. when data should be collected
   e. how data analysis would demonstrate a null hypothesis

2. A speaker claims that people who exercise vigorously for 15 minutes or more every day are able to solve math problems more rapidly than those who do no vigorous exercise daily. Describe an experiment to test this claim.
   a. State the purpose of this experiment.
   b. Give a rationale for the size of the population in the experiment.
   c. Describe treatment of experimental and control groups.
   d. State the method and data to be collected.
   e. State how to analyze the data to draw a conclusion.

3. Some people claim that large doses of vitamin C introduced into a vein speed up the healing of surgical wounds. Describe how to test this hypothesis.
   a. Explain how the control and experimental groups are similar or different.
   b. What are two conditions that must be kept constant in both groups?
   c. What data must be collected?
   d. What experimental results would support this claim?
   e. What permissions would be required to conduct this experiment?

This example of a formative assessment in science is a bit more complex in that the teachers devised several similar processes across multiple experiments and offered some unique scaffolding to assess the student's knowledge of the scientific method. In addition, the teachers developed a rubric to describe several levels of student responses from inadequate, barely adequate, and proficient to masterful. These four categories represent distinctive levels of performance that the teachers agreed that they could assess.

A teacher or a group of teachers with student responses to these questions can determine easily how well the students understand the scientific method using the comparative rubric descriptions. It is less clear how well students may comprehend the necessary protections that human subjects are entitled to in any scientific experiment. In this formative analysis, the teachers offered only one opportunity for students to address this question of protection of human subjects. Why would they do this?

They reported that Question 3e was placed in the formative process to guide the teachers' lesson planning for the next lesson on the protection of human subjects in scientific experiments. These teachers wanted to know as much as they could about the current thinking of the students on the next topic before they began to build new lesson aims and structures for the next series of classes. Still, one item offers a very small assessment of what students know about a topic. In every formative assessment and test, there is room for improvement.

For the other items in this formative assessment, these science teachers analyzed and assigned a value to each student response from the rubric and scale system: inadequate = 2.5; barely adequate = 5; proficient = 7.5; and masterful = 10. Their summative assessment table looked something like Table 6.5.

Table 6.5   Sample of Comparative Scores for Ninth Grade Formative Assessment: Scientific Method

Student Score	Q1a	Q1b	Q1c	Q1d	Q1e	Q2a	Q2b	Q2c	Q2d	Q2e	Q3a	Q3b	Q3c	Q3d	Total
J. Jones	2.5	5	7.5	7.5	7.5	5	5	7.5	10	10	5	7.5	7.5	7.5	95
R. Smith	5	5	5	10	10	7.5	2.5	7.5	7.5	10	7.5	5	10	10	102.5

A perfect score would be 14 × 10, so these teachers want their students to achieve at least 112 points in their total score analysis to move forward on their own without additional interventions. If a student has a score below 7.5 on any individual item in the formative assessment, the student's teacher will address the content of the question and the responses individually or in small groups with students. For each item deemed less than proficient for a student, teachers will seek feedback from students and will adjust their responses to what they diagnose as needs for self-concept support, self-regulation strategies, and improved content understandings.

Margaret Heritage (2010) in her position paper for the Council of Chief State School Officers (CCSSO) offered this insight about teacher feedback: "Feedback designed to improve learning is more effective when it is focused on the task and provides the student with suggestions, hints, or cues, rather than offered in the form of praise or comments about performance" (p. 5). She endorses Sadler's (1989) ideas about students having a need to know the goal and standard for learning, being able to compare current level of performance to the standard, and engaging in appropriate action to close the gap between current performance and the standard.

Heritage (2010) writes, in agreement with Sadler, that

> the teacher's role in formative assessment is not simply to use feedback to promote content learning, but also to help students understand the goal being aimed for, assist them to develop skills to make judgments about their learning in relation to the standard, and establish a repertoire of operational strategies to regulate their own learning. (p. 6)

At the outset of formative work, Heritage (2010) reminds teachers and school leaders that formative assessment is about teaching and learning and not testing. She reiterates that Vygotsky's zone of proximal development is the focus of formative assessment and the area "where learning takes place through a process of scaffolding" (p. 8) in which more expert others provide interactions that guide and help the learner acquire expert knowledge.

Heritage (2010) wants teachers to recognize that learning is a reciprocal activity in which students and teachers respond to evidence about learning. In the best of teaching practices, teachers and students assume the roles of partners in the learning process. The norms in the classroom that drive inquiry and direct instruction are "mutual support, trust, respect, and collaboration" (p. 9).

Teachers can implement a number of formative assessment strategies during class, such as informal observations, conversations, brainstorming, and multiple questions designed to elicit student thinking about a topic. All formative assessments seek information about the learner and the instruction to help the instructor decide where the learner is in the process of learning, where the learner needs to go, and how to move forward.

Teachers should use formative assessments as a resource for continuous development in planning assessments, collective inquiry about design and result analysis, and interpretation of evidence regarding learning. Teachers should share assessment results with learners to provide feedback and help them acquire self-assessment and self-regulating skills to manage their own learning (Heritage, 2010, p. 12). Peer review and evaluation about each other's work can be good evidence of "how well they understand the learning goals and success criteria, and the depth of their thinking about the task at hand" (p. 14).

Heritage (2010) points out the distinctive differences in classrooms where teachers use formative assessments to inform instruction, not as a measurement tool per se but rather as a tool to redirect teaching and learning. She provides a contrast between what teachers used to do and the desired current reality for what teachers should do (see Table 6.6).

Table 6.6   Contrast Between Former Practice and Modified, Current Practice

Teacher	Former Practice	Current Practice
Shawn	Explaining	Questioning
	A lot of talking	A lot of listening
	Thinking about curriculum	Thinking about the student (Heritage, 2010, p. 17)

BUILDING SUCCESSFUL SCHOOLS

In many affluent suburban schools, highly effective rural schools, and urban magnet schools, teachers are working at instructional and assessment levels that exceed the criteria of the CCSS. Such schools, their teachers, school leaders, and students deserve commendations. The students do exceedingly well on national assessments and devote many hours to community service.

The parents of these students, their community leaders, and residents should be recognized for their investments in education and their constant vigilance about the quality of education under construction in their schools. Such schools need less help and no federal or state interventions. They represent a majority of schools in the United States but not a vast majority of students. In 2011, within the United States, many more poor-performing students gather in urban environments where the community is low in resources and high in family poverty.

The alignment of local curriculum and CCSS in Grades K–12 can help successful schools verify that their expectations for learning are deep and comprehensive. An overemphasis on standardized testing can delimit curriculum to what is tested, narrow learning objectives, and demoralize students and teachers. Sadly, in the United States, only the wealthy school districts seem immune to the national fervor for testing. Parents in these wealthy communities and their representatives seem to have acquired in their professions a deep understanding of the limits of tests. They value the interactions they have with their children's teachers and school leaders more than they do test results. In many cases, they approach school personnel the way most people in top-performing countries like Finland do—with respect. They want evidence of success, and they are willing to look beyond a single test for affirmation of the quality of instruction at their schools.

Essentially, these parents, school leaders, and teachers in high-performing schools agree about what they want for education in the public schools, and they get it. Their students excel at research, critical thinking, writing, and creative expressions of what they know and wish to explore. The parents celebrate these high-level expressions of knowledge, courage, and commitment to learning and service. Many beautiful examples of student commitment to learning are evident in science fairs, performing groups, athletic teams, and community service clubs.

On the other hand, schools with high levels of student poverty have greater challenges. Their teachers almost never try nor are they expected to exceed the state standards. School leaders in these districts insist that teachers have students achieve proficiency and pass tests. Testing is more important than learning. These teachers need to adopt the CCSS and commit to new teaching and learning models that will change student performance from ritualistic practice to inventive and creative learning. Teachers in schools with struggling students must initiate collaborative formative assessments across subjects and grades to take control of the learning process at their schools. They need to see beyond the state tests to the child as a learner.

Teachers need to see students as Howard Gardner (2011) explains in his book, *Frames of Mind: The Theory of Multiple Intelligences,* where he notes seven aspects of intelligence and describes children as young people who have multiple assets that are not measured in school. Tests in the United States should be the background and not the foreground of our portraits of children. The state tests have taken over the foreground, and the child has moved to the background in current educational portraits.

Teachers must align their summative tests with their own formative tests so that they can redesign the learning experience and ensure that students master what they teach. State and standardized tests will never help teachers reform their teaching practice day after day. An effective use of formative tests changes the tone of the school from a *deficit center,* where students are classified by what they did not score on a test, to a *learning center,* where students are rewarded for what they master and how they apply knowledge in multiple ways.

In communities with high levels of poverty, parents struggle to make ends meet and to pay bills. Their daily living requirements engender stress within their homes. Often, students have more work to do at home than they do at school. The school day in many of these poor communities is too brief and too unfocused to redress what students have not learned in relationship to what they have yet to learn. In these communities, teachers have to slow down and seek mastery knowledge for their students. They have to assess what prior knowledge is necessary for new learning to occur. Their students have to be prepared to learn, and students have to feel that their teachers expect them to be successful.

What can school district and school leaders, teachers, parents, and students do in this age of testing and false accountability? What can those in poor communities do to ensure their students learn? All community stakeholders must come together. They must demand clear curriculum goals, learning aims, and formative assessments that drive instruction and academic interventions.

School leaders can create greater transparency at school by posting the curriculum on the school website. They can support highly structured teacher development programs that address learning theory, literacy, math and science skills, and especially assessment skills. They can design teacher-training programs to meet the identified needs of teachers and students. They can have teachers post summative understandings from training they received so that their colleagues can learn from them. School leaders can have teachers describe and explain technology applications that promote learning and creativity on the school website. School principals can lead and not manage just school operations and safety issues.

Finally, school leaders in poor communities must find ways to help teachers identify students who need help every week. They must be creative in their efforts to extend the learning day for these students. They must build a partnership with students, teachers, and parents that guarantees sufficient support for each child to master as much of the curriculum as possible (Steele, 2012).

SPECIAL EDUCATION AND GENERAL EDUCATION

Individualized Educational Plans (IEPs) for students with learning disabilities (LDs) are mandated and necessary to guide instruction for these children. IEPs are necessary for all children who are not mastering the curriculum. They do not have to be elaborate plans. They should be practical plans based on formative assessments that give evidence that desired learning has or has not taken place. The individual academic intervention plan for a student should address a formative need. All children classified as special learners with disabilities, ELLs, and general education learners require individual support for their learning. Even the most gifted require special attention to their cognitive and social-emotional needs.

Principals have to initiate inquiry and training that make it possible for teachers to transform their practice from one bound by regulations and testing to one driven by creative decision making. The principal has to lead the inquiry into how well teachers are meeting the needs of each child in their classes.

Challenged schools require extensive teacher and school leader knowledge of formative assessments. In these schools, teachers need more structured time to engage in collaborative dialogue and inquiry about their students' learning needs. School leaders must ensure that the collaborative dialogue among teachers is productive and that teachers' discussions focus on helping children master curriculum. A clear vision about what the school needs to become to change student outcomes must be the foundational conversation among teachers, students, parents, and school leaders.

In our next chapter, we will discuss school leaders and their roles, skills, dispositions, and partnerships with students, teachers, and parents that will change the quality of learning in any school.

CHAPTER 7

The Leadership Challenge

*Creating Common Understandings of
the Common Core State Standards*

The stakes for education in America have never been higher. The very core of the United States of America's future economic well-being has never been more dependent on education and educators. The quality of our system of education seen through an international lens reveals results that are mediocre in comparison to other nations. Frankly, that is a generous assessment. Within school-age populations, children of poverty and those who are African American and Latino, and increasingly male, are systematically destined to a poor education and therefore a low quality of life. Our school leaders frequently hold low expectations for all of these groups and accept bare proficiency as a primary goal. Unfortunately for us, as Friedman and Mandelbaum (2011) put it, "average is over" (p. 133).

Whether the international comparisons are fair or not, it is hard to argue with the overwhelming and increasingly mounting data that the quality of education in the United States has to get better for all children—and fast! The role of educational leaders needs to be on center stage during this critical juncture in our nation's history. Now, more than ever before, a visionary and courageous leader matters.

THE ROLE OF SCHOOL LEADERS

As Thomas Friedman pointed out in 2005, the world is indeed flat. The end of the Cold War coupled with rapid globalization, the Internet, and other digital technological innovations have combined to level the world's playing field. The economic dominance the United States has enjoyed worldwide is not sustainable in a global economy. What is sustainable is a highly educated citizenry and its capacity to create new work for themselves. Geography and an abundance of natural resources are diminishing as the most dominant factor ensuring prominence in the global economy. Now, anyone with an education, a computer, and an Internet connection can become an entrepreneur from anywhere in the world (Friedman & Mandelbaum, 2011).

Aside from our relatively poor showing on international measures of achievement, one of the biggest problems we face is that we do not have enough top-performing engineering and science students to compete with those in China or India. In fact, we simply do not have enough students. In China and India, "they have more honor students then we have kids" (pketco, 2010). We can no longer waste any child's mind or fail to nurture a child's capacity to learn deeply in a very demanding academic and work environment.

In their latest book, *That Used to Be Us*, Friedman and Mandelbaum (2011) recount the story of Grinnell College, a rural Midwestern college wherein nearly one of every 10 applicants for admission in the class of 2015 came from China. The question Friedman and Mandelbaum pose is "How do they choose perhaps 15 students from the more than 200 applicants from China? . . . Consider, for example, that half of Grinnell's applicants from China this year have perfect scores of 800 on the Math portion of the SAT . . . ?" (Friedman & Mandelbaum, 2011, p. 134). A sobering reflection is that this is a college in Iowa, not Los Angeles, Boston, Princeton, or New York. All educators and all students must recognize that education is a global enterprise. Competition for education is worldwide.

As leaders, we should not fight the constant comparisons to successful educational systems worldwide. By focusing upon and refining all of the attendant and legitimate arguments about why we cannot be like Finland, or any other high-performing nation, we miss all of the ways in which we can. The fact is that many educational leaders know what it takes to leave no child behind, yet expressing it aloud is akin to entering a political and corporate minefield.

We will not address our difficulties until we face our fears and recognize that there is no panacea for "sick" schools. Failing schools are a problem in the United States. Policy makers must identify failing schools and treat them as sick institutions that need immediate and intensive care. Successful schools must charge ahead with their own innovative and particularistic efforts unencumbered by public policy.

Our future as a country and our children's quality of life depend on school and community leaders who stand up and are willing to be among those who demand that government reward successful schools. We need to redirect the conversation about the quality of our schools to one about what it will take to transform failing schools into successful schools. We must avoid defending the indefensible and start using facts to support our story—a story that redirects our nation into a plan that actually has a chance of success. Educational leaders must become vocal about what does not work and tireless advocates for what does work.

Educators and children in the United States can no longer compare their performance to their peers in neighboring schools—even those that are considered high performing by current U.S standards. Our children are clearly competing with students from around the world for seats in the best colleges and for the best jobs upon graduation. This is not a time to tinker with reforms in education. We must literally transform our education system completely to ensure our competitiveness on the world's stage. All schools must become learning communities where teachers and school leaders focus on creating successful learners. Teachers should be able to demonstrate that their students are mastering the curriculum with results from formative assessments that they design cooperatively. Student performance on state outcome exams should inform this analysis too.

Envisioning Excellence

Our major competitors on the world stage have convinced their major stakeholders of the role education plays in both national security and a viable economy. They get it. For the most part, Americans have to learn what these more intellectually mature countries know.

Despite the rhetoric heard from the White House and state houses across the land about the importance of education, our vision, policies, and resources simply do not align with the theories we espouse. Our teachers and administrators have been demonized and, in some states, stripped of their right to bargain collectively for their wages and conditions of employment. Teaching for the test has been guaranteed by the national preoccupation with output with little regard to input.

Because of the emphasis on testing, our children are getting narrower curricula. Proficiency, which is actually the most common denominator of permissible error that our students can make on a test, depresses the creative edge that our children have always possessed when compared with international peers. Ken Robinson (2010) cites research that divergent thinking skills exist in 98 percent of youngsters tested prior to entering school, and this percentage diminishes the longer they experience formal education. This is frightening because Robinson states that divergent thinking is a prerequisite to creativity.

Our standardized tests have helped to disguise our educational flaws and ensure the poor quality of American schools nationwide. For instance, if we examine our fixation on high-stakes, standardized tests, data show that the only thing these tests raised is anxiety among educators, parents, and students. Like most states, New York legislators and policy makers have never met a child they did not want to test. Teachers and administrators do not design these tests, nor do they have input into what is tested or what passing scores are. The entire testing process originates in a state education department that contracts with private testing companies, often associated with publishing companies, capable of influencing state legislatures, mayors, and governors. This is a formula that promotes cronyism as opposed to altruism and virtually assures systemic regression to the mean in ways that guarantee mediocrity for American children.

Teachers and administrators have little voice about how their children are tested or on what content. Complicating matters further, the advent of private corporations hired by states to design standardized tests has limited the transparency that once was part of the tests and no longer allows teachers and school leaders to conduct timely item analyses of student scores. Test design, as well as validity and reliability of data, are now closely guarded secrets. The testing companies are private; therefore, most information concerning the test design is considered proprietary. Despite the mystery and intrigue surrounding these tests and the tendency for them to avoid testing 21st-century skills, most teachers dutifully try to teach to these tests and the standards they espouse.

In New York State (NYS), all state-sanctioned standardized tests generate score results that fall within four levels. Level 1 is the lowest, and Level 4 is the highest. Level 3 is classified as proficient.

A score of "proficient" on the NYS's standardized tests falls within an equivalent grade range of 65 percent to 84 percent using traditional 0 through 100 score ranges. In other words, NYS, which is allegedly among those states with the so-called highest standards nationally, proclaims children "proficient" in reading, writing, math, social studies, and science with equivalent test scores as low as a 65, which is equal to a letter grade of D. Large numbers of students with proficient scores leave elementary school and enter a more content-driven secondary school with a 65 percent average in all core subjects in elementary school, and we wonder why middle school failure rates and high school dropout rates are climbing nationwide?

In 2009, there was an epiphany in NYS. What most educators and parents failed to understand (or ignored) until recently is that a child who qualifies on all NYS-designed and U.S. Department of Education (DOE)-approved measures as "proficient" more often than not is scoring at the low end of the grading range. This was demonstrated elegantly by the NYS Education Department itself when a new commissioner with a background in academia was appropriately appalled at the current reality. With little notice, and armed with an in-depth study designed to assess college and workplace readiness, he moved the passing score for proficiency to an equivalent of 75 percent—unfortunately, with little warning and after the test was already taken. A cascade of new "failures" ensued. Students, teachers, and parents were confused and in some cases outraged. In the end, the commissioner "voluntarily" resigned shortly afterward to "pursue other interests."

The politicization of our educational system has been disastrous. The list of failed, uninformed, and misguided policies is endless. Our high-stakes tests are manipulated politically to ensure that mayors and governors can give speeches that proclaim how they have vastly improved our educational systems and at a lower cost to the taxpayers than ever before. Taken as a whole, the lack of alignment between what we currently do and what we need to do to compete on the global stage will ultimately assure the demise of our country and the middle-class standard of living many enjoy (Friedman & Mandlebaum, 2011).

We Get the Results We Design Schools to Achieve

W. Edwards Deming, widely acknowledged as the deceased father of the continuous improvement movement, is probably viewing the U.S. system of education and shaking his head in disgust and frustration. When one views Deming's *Fourteen Points* and *Seven Deadly Sins* (Walton, 1986), it is hard to find a point that our politicians and their corporate benefactors implement well or a "sin" that they did not commit. Ironically, many of the international educational systems that routinely outperform most American students seem to get Deming's guidance right. As Deming elegantly counseled, if you design quality into a system at the start and continuously listen to and train those implementing the system, you do not have to rely on inspecting quality at the end (Deming, 1986).

Just think of all the highly effective teachers we could employ and train with the money saved from eliminating or minimizing high-stakes tests. The evidence supporting Deming's wisdom is overwhelming.

According to Friedman and Mandelbaum (2011), in the private sector, more and more companies are becoming increasingly dependent on the worker for innovation. Concerned about losing our innovative edge, some perspicacious U.S. companies are actually bringing manufacturing back from overseas. Bottom-up innovation is becoming far more prevalent than that generated from the top down. Of course, this trend requires a highly educated and skilled workforce. Given an educated workforce, those closest to the work have a view of what is happening in real time and therefore have valuable insights into how to improve productivity and invent new, better, and often more cost-effective ways to accomplish a goal or to produce a product.

The ability and responsibility to innovate are expectations for continued employment in multiple sectors of our economy—except education. In the United States, teachers rarely are consulted on improving the learning environment or curriculum. They are not expected (and, in some cases, allowed) to innovate. No wonder, except for a few computers and some other useless tech toys, schools look and function like 19th-century schools (albeit sometimes with better heat).

Educational leaders and their faculties in high-quality school systems across the globe focus on designing 21st-century schools. In Finland, best is not good enough. They are pushing the innovation envelope even further. Aside from teaching entrepreneurship, they are in the midst of a national discussion to define and design the steps necessary toward readying their children for even greater success in the 21st century (Compton, 2011). Their focus is not on high-stakes tests, blame, or judging teachers. Finland and other quality schools systems throughout the globe create a laser-like focus on the teaching and learning process. They select high performers into the teaching profession and train and develop them relentlessly.

Our international competitors tend to provide their students with highly educated and well-trained teachers who teach rigorous curricula and who hold students to high expectations. Their professional development is continuous and aligned to the needs of their children. Educators follow a guaranteed, rigorous, relevant curriculum. In Finland, curriculum is developed mostly at the local level with minimalist yet concrete guidance from the national government. Teachers teach in an environment that promotes dignity for all, and school leaders invite and encourage creativity and risk taking among students and professionals.

In Finland, student assessments tend to be authentic, and they focus on learning and growth, not judgment and grades. Students have access to and use the latest technology to enhance learning. A teacher's primary means of determining quality is through authentic formative assessments that lead to occasional relevant, rigorous, and authentic summative assessments. It is easy to see why people in Finland hold their teachers in high esteem and why their students do so well on many given measures of success. Their teachers are professionals.

Politicians, parents, and communities in countries with highly effective schools understand what is at stake nationally, and they support the educational standards and designs that have propelled them past the United States in virtually every category on every significant international measure of educational progress and achievement. They treat the human brain and the children who own them as their most vital national resource. What is holding us back in the United States from behaving accordingly?

Vision or Nightmare?

Aside from our current financial woes, what we in the United States suffer from most is a lack of vision about the role and importance of education in America. Regrettably, our lack of vision is quickly becoming a nightmare. Our national dialogue on education tends toward blame: cost, tenure, and taxes. We have not engaged in an intellectual inquiry into the new, flattened world we face in the 21st century. We are not discussing how we must transform all of our institutions accordingly. Transformation is no longer optional. It must be a national priority.

It is time for visionary educational leaders who have the courage to buck the political trends to do what is best for our children's education and, therefore, what is best for our nation. Yet, leaders often fail to see the big picture. As Peter Senge (1990) said, a system is bigger and more complex than the sum of its parts. One needs to see the big picture in order to understand how each part connects, interconnects, and affects all of the others.

Senge (1990) uses a three-legged stool as a metaphor for the disciplines necessary for the optimal performance of any system. When one leg breaks, the entire stool tumbles. To be sure, our educational system is complex. The variables are numerous. If education were a three-legged stool, one leg would be missing, and the other two would be cracked and in danger of collapse.

There are no easy answers to complicated problems. Yet, in America's quest for quick solutions to complicated issues, we tend to overcomplicate the original issue by layering symptomatic fixes and their unintended consequences on the initial problem. Soon, the problem becomes unrecognizable. Quick fixes that temporarily relieve the symptom of a problem are applied repeatedly. The root cause of the disease is ignored. Eventually, so many complications from the symptomatic fixes and the multitude of unintended consequences occur that the enterprise dies, much as mistreated patients eventually die. We have to examine current reality with new lenses such as the Common Core State Standards (CCSS) offer. We have to transform ourselves from judges of student work to responsible developers of student work.

ENTER THE COMMON CORE STATE STANDARDS

The CCSS are a response to the global competition we face as a nation. They prompt us to raise the bar in every core academic subject. The CCSS also provide some well-considered guidance to the educational field on what needs to be done to restore America's competitive edge. They also provide guidance on *when* certain topics should be taught developmentally as well as suggestions about what indicators might look like if students were to meet the standards.

The CCSS give us a window into the knowledge and skills that are required for our children to become competitive on the world stage. The window we are looking through to get a glimpse of reality is on a high-speed train moving at 200 miles per hour. The view, in our flattened world, is ever changing. The CCSS are not enough. Like the state standards before them, the CCSS will not assure any significant change in the performance of our students in the United States without strong, well-informed leaders.

It is incumbent on educational leaders everywhere to ensure that the CCSS become a way that literally and figuratively enables our youth to use the knowledge, skills, and dispositions required for life where change is constant and technology is ubiquitous. We live in a world where brainpower and social-emotional literacy equal economic security. It is a world for which we are ill prepared.

Leaders must use the CCSS as a catalyst for a national dialogue that filters through every school and community. All stakeholders must have a deep awareness about the need to transform our nation's schools. It is the role and responsibility of school leaders everywhere to create this dialogue about America's children and the academic, emotional, and social skills necessary for them to perform successfully within a global economy.

We believe that the CCSS present a grand opportunity for educational leaders to engage in a powerful discussion about how to make America's educational system once again rise to prominence on the world stage. All stakeholders need to know what other countries are doing differently than the United States and the results of their efforts relative to ours. Every citizen must come to understand that the global economy and digital communications have affected our economy negatively by flattening the world. The game has changed while we slept. It is time to awaken America's pride and creative spirit. It is urgent that we transform our schools and our children's experiences at school from memorization centers to conversation and demonstration centers of student learning. Every school should be a school of fine and performing arts, math, science, and technology.

Change on the magnitude that is required for our schools demands marathon runners and not sprinters. Because it seems the race has begun without us, there will be a tendency to jump right in and catch up with the front-runners. This would be a mistake. The runner who employs this strategy often experiences fatigue and frequently fails to finish the race. We, as a nation, cannot afford to lose this race.

In our experience, the transformation of a high school or middle school can take two to four years of constant dialogue, inquiry, and data analysis with monthly check-ins to achieve break-through conversation between teachers in a department and school leaders. The ensuing three years that follow make or break the school spirit to reform. Reform has to emanate from the changes in belief that teachers and school leaders make. Often, an external voice is necessary to shine a light on what is and what might be.

The CCSS are a well-intended attempt to address directly the lack of rigor and coherence within our academic curricula and programs nationally. The CCSS present a platform on which we can influence our economic challenges internationally. The CCSS provide guidance, both in content and process, about what our children should know and be able to do to be intellectually competitive and economically viable in the 21st century.

However, the fact is that, unless we seriously reenvision and transform our entire national system of education, it will fail entirely. We must move away from debilitating assumptions that student achievement reflects a normal curve to a new commitment that all children will master the necessary dispositions, skills, and knowledge to regulate their own learning at masterful levels. As education goes, so goes our country. The roles and responsibilities for educational leaders have never been clearer.

Effective leaders spark a sense of urgency within their local communities by creating awareness around the risks and challenges we face nationally in the 21st century. Remember, through deep dialogue about the issues and challenges we face globally, common understanding emerges. Once there is common understanding, a shared vision of the rationale for the new CCSS and their intended effect is within reach of each school community. Highly successful districts are not exempt from critical changes when their reputations are based upon high percentages of children who are proficient with few who qualify as mastering the curriculum.

The CCSS, with their focus on both content and process, represent an opportunity to begin a dialogue with the American public about the future of our nation's children without the political rhetoric and polemic positions. What we are advocating is that the public we serve understand the challenges our children face and the ramifications if we fail to help them compete in a new reality—a global economy. Educational leaders need to expose all internal and external stakeholders in communities from coast to coast to the challenges our children and our nation face. It needs to happen now.

CHAPTER 8

Dialogue

Providing Opportunity
So Facts Influence Opinions

In the movie *A Few Good Men,* there is a famous scene where Tom Cruise is grilling Jack Nicholson. Cruise, who plays the role of Naval Judge Advocate General Officer Dan Kaffee, is deposing Nicholson, a tough, old-school marine, Colonel Jessup. Kaffee is trying to reveal the truth about a suspected cover-up of the death of a marine in Colonel Jessup's command. As their tempers flare, Cruise relentlessly pushes and pushes Nicholson to tell the truth. Finally, in a fit of rage, Nicholson screams, "You want the truth? You can't handle the truth!"

Well, unlike the opinion held by Colonel Jessup, we think American stakeholders can handle the truth, and they have the capacity to understand it and its implications. The real question is this: "Who will help stakeholders process the truth and its implications"? This is a job for educational leaders, especially the 50 state commissioners of education and the leaders of national associations of education in administration, supervision, science, math, social studies, and English. Research associations like the American Educational Research Association and the Association for Supervision and Curriculum Development and the American Association of School Administrators must also play significant roles. They must come together in a summit sponsored by the federal department of education and hammer out a new American Creed for Education.

Our state and national association leaders have important roles to play in presenting the story of the Common Core State Standards (CCSS). On their national and state websites, they can invite their communities to engage in conversations about the CCSS, their value, and methods to implement higher standards for mastery. They should sponsor open dialogues about national implications if we fail to have almost all students master the common core standards in math, science, social studies, and English. Such conversations in an open and digital forum that permit interested citizens and educators an opportunity to participate in a national summit where ideas are carefully examined and evaluated lead to a better-informed citizenry. Transparent data and open dialogue will lead to great ideas about the implementation of the CCSS and make them operable in every school community.

In the meantime, school district leaders, trustees on boards of education, school leaders, teachers, parents, and students cannot wait for new directives and guidance, nor should they wait. Every local community has it within its own power to transform itself and its schools into world-class institutions of learning. The major change required is that they design the school day and all activities to implement the CCSS.

We advocate the use of a dialogic process to build common understanding among all stakeholders. Another major benefit of the process is that it builds trust and transparency with constituents. The information developed at a local school district summit should appear on an open blog, and all papers and presentations should be available on the summit's website. The transmission of such information will be valuable to all stakeholders. The information that summit participants receive back will be priceless and invaluable to the design and implementation phase of the CCSS.

If school leaders want the CCSS to realize their potential in the design of 21st-century schools, we must break with the patterns of the past, which too often relegate new innovations into a stream of buzzwords that have little or no meaning to those responsible for implementing them or to those upon whom they are implemented. We do not want to happen in many schools and communities what has happened to good ideas in the past. We do not want the CCSS to be the latest fad relegated to the long list of things tried and subsequently abandoned.

The stakes are too high, and educational leaders simply cannot allow the CCSS to fall to the wayside. There must be greater awareness and sensitivity among all stakeholders about the whys. You know some of them:

- Why do we need to do this?
- Why now? Can't this wait? I'm too busy as it is.
- Why can't we continue doing what we are doing? It works just fine.
- We seem successful. Why must everything change?

The list is endless—and that is the point. By engaging stakeholders to discuss the facts, the why questions are answered before the design phase of transforming our schools commences. Ultimately, by going slowly at the start, we ensure we will go much faster during implementation.

Dialogue is the first step in the change process. Its initial role is to set the stage and create common understanding about the need for change. The dialogic process, one in which data and inquiry drive discussion, should be used at every step in the change process to continually refine and clarify issues that arise. To create awareness and sensitivity to the challenges we face, leaders must present key information and data to all stakeholders and facilitate a discussion of the materials presented.

We believe data should be presented as a story that outlines the challenges we face in educating our youth in the 21st century. It should also depict the realities our students face for sustainable employment in the 21st century. Using a constructivist model, the story, if compelling, allows stakeholders to examine the current reality and compare and contrast it with a new worldview that incorporates what changes are necessary for our educational system. This exploratory process leads to further dialogue about the CCSS as one of the structures that could assist educators and communities in the development of new schooling experiences that guarantee continued prosperity for children into their adulthood.

Nevertheless, even though we know that open dialogue leads to an expansion of ideas and creativity, we also recognize that the work of improving teaching and learning takes place one school at a time. The school leader sets the tone and provides the forum for quality dialogue, valuable inquiry, and professional training to guide change and support innovation.

In dialogue, the leader's primary role is to tell the story, facilitate dialogue, listen, encourage clarity, and keep participants on task. In *Designing School Systems for All Students* (Manley & Hawkins, 2010), we discuss the concept of dialogue in depth and its use in creating trust as well as its capacity to promote understanding of complex issues among stakeholders. For our purposes here, it is critical that we as leaders understand that dialogue is different from our usual discussions that, more often than not, are politicized debates where new learning does not take place. In dialogue, each party contributes to a transformation of one's original position, and members achieve a new understanding that may be a synthesis of previous knowledge or a leap forward into an untested realm.

William Issacs (1999) once described our typical conversation as a repetitive process of "loading and reloading." Issacs believed that, if deep listening fails to take place, no learning takes place.

In contrast, dialogue promotes listening and common understanding, encourages clarifications, and creates new awareness. There are no winners or losers in a dialogue. Dialogue is process wherein leaders prompt and facilitate a conversation among stakeholders to process information and to clarify the issues one faces. Leaders can lead through inquiry and build trust and common ground with their constituents (Manley & Hawkins, 2010).

The goal we pursue through dialogue is to create new knowledge and a sense of urgency (not fear) and awareness about the challenges students face in a global economy. The implications for the future education of our children and our economic survival as a country need examination and dialogue in an open forum. The last thing we want to do is rush to conclusions and action. Ultimately, the decisions about how to transform today's schools into 21st-century schools are left mostly, although not exclusively, to the educators at local schools.

Through an open dialogic process, stakeholders can share in developing the rationale and the reasons for the changes that will be forthcoming. Normally, many of the necessary changes for consideration in our transformative design emerge from the participants, and over time, participants in an open forum come to broaden their thinking, create new insights, and cement commitment to changes that they must enact.

Interestingly, we, the people, must create this dialogue everywhere—from ice cream parlors to iPhones to interstate truck stops and blogs. The high-stakes arena in which we must play before we can transform our educational institutions into 21st-century learning centers requires a national, well-informed dialogue about our schools. It is critical that we create the context or schema among all stakeholders so that they understand why the CCSS are so important for our country's future.

CREATING CONTEXT FOR THE COMMON CORE STATE STANDARDS

With the adoption of the CCSS in 45 states, school leaders have a grand opportunity to engage community stakeholders and school personnel in a powerful examination of the current reality at their schools in contrast to international school realities and desired realities for our children. To have this conversation, stakeholders need to know what other countries are doing differently than the United States and the results of their efforts relative to those in our schools. Unfortunately, the process used in schools nationwide, particularly in urban areas where command-and-control leadership is often the norm, safety and good behavior are prized more than masterful learning.

We have witnessed too many ineffective leaders hand out the CCSS to their faculty, with little or no conversation or explanation, and demand their implementation immediately. In one case, a leader asked that teachers write a new pacing guide to use the CCSS. Here again, without a conversation (or a curriculum), one wonders what we are pacing.

Apparently, for this school leader, the CCSS were the new curriculum. This is simply unacceptable and borders on malpractice. The CCSS are not a curriculum, nor are they intended to be one. They are designed to generate curriculum and assessments locally. Ultimately, the local assessments that teachers use to indicate their students' levels of mastery for the building blocks to common core standards are critically important. The transformation of teaching from adults telling a story to teachers enabling students to tell well-documented stories is the progression that the CCSS seek to emulate.

Implementing the CCSS effectively requires planning and execution, monitoring and replanning (Deming, 1986; Drucker, 1999; Senge et al., 2000). The larger the required change, the more that context must be discussed with internal and external stakeholders, and implementation must include continuous feedback strategies.

Through dialogue, we attempt to answer the why questions about how the CCSS came into being in the first place. Answering the question why change is required makes leaders show how the big picture affects their organizations locally. In our experiences, the best way to accomplish this is by telling a story and inviting all stakeholders to process the story collaboratively. In other words, move from the motivation for the CCSS toward allowing everyone to discover their impact locally. Next, when stakeholders are ready to plan for implementation and actually implement action plans, double-loop feedback keeps the change process authentic and sufficiently flexible to accommodate the pressures of reality.

TEACHERS NEED DEEP UNDERSTANDING OF THE COMMON CORE STATE STANDARDS

Most leaders and many teachers have some level of awareness that the CCSS increase the curriculum rigor and its relevance to a digital information age so that our students will be successful in the global economy. School leaders and teachers actually have few details or data to understand deeply the problems and challenges we face. School leaders have to present pictures and graphs that show the data and tell the story of failed mastery in our schools in the same manner that medieval artists presented critical behavioral stories in their icons.

We recommend telling the story to all stakeholders and set context, or schema, for the changes the schools face. School leaders should describe the shift in teaching and learning embedded within the new CCSS. Setting the context enables leaders to begin developing common understanding among stakeholders, the antecedent for any successful change initiative. In a collaborative dialogic process, it is better that data tell the story and that the stakeholders process their significant learning in cooperation with school leaders. One failing many school leaders have is to allow a new and important story to become the leader's story and not the community's belief.

There is no shortage of information regarding globalization and communication technology. Educators face unique challenges preparing students for success in this digital environment. In our leadership classes, we often turn to technology and media to construct an important story. We frequently use YouTube to create awareness and discussion. Information technology makes data ubiquitous. However, teachers and students must learn together how to evaluate the quality and veracity, the validity and reliability, of much of the digital data they collect. In the same vein, all stakeholders engaged in a change effort must share the same data and information.

The *Shift Happens* series on YouTube, updated annually, provides great information about our changing world internationally and the implications for our educational systems locally. Sir Ken Robinson's (2010) video *Changing Education Paradigms* and other similar analyses of creativity are sure to spark conversation. A quick YouTube or Google search reveals a veritable treasure trove of items that could promote stakeholder discussions on many topics.

Friedman and Mandelbaum (2011), in their book *That Used to Be Us: How America Fell Behind in the World It Invented and How We Can Come Back*, provide great insight into the competition we face internationally and why the economic future and security of the United States relies on the education sector more than any other enterprise in our economy. It is sure to generate conversation and some dynamic tension that will stimulate faculty discussions. Tony Wagner's video about *The Finland Phenomenon* (Compton, 2011) or his book *The Global Achievement Gap* (Wagner, 2010) provide great source material for school leaders to share with faculty and parents.

Look into the 2millionminutes.com videos (Compton, 2011), a series comparing education in America with China and India. Do you want more quantitative data? Try the McKinsey (2009) and Company report titled *The Economic Impact of the Achievement Gap in America's Schools*. The point is, no matter what materials you select, school leaders must start educating their communities about the real high stakes facing education and their children.

After a presentation using the types of materials discussed above, open the floor to questions and comments. The leader's role here is one of facilitator. Generate conversation by asking questions like, "What did you learn from this presentation, and what do you see as the impact on our children and schools?" As these discussions advance, the leader's role is to continue facilitating discussion among stakeholders. When people share their thoughts and concerns, leaders must verify that they heard them accurately and use inquiry to clarify what they heard. People love to know that they have been heard and that their points of view are valued. Leaders do not have to agree with every point of view. If they listen carefully, they will gain the respect of participants, and they may find themselves learning too. School leaders must be builders of learning communities.

Many stakeholders can serve as facilitators of dialogue if they deepen the query by asking follow-up questions. For instance, in many cases when using materials that show school life in other countries, parents may bristle at the length of the school day or year. Ask their reactions to what they saw, and inquire into their feelings about how they see what happens in Finland applied at home. Listen for patterns and trends that emerge.

If things are moving in the "wrong" direction, do not engage in advocacy or attempt to correct the stakeholders "mistakes." Deepen the query to understand why they feel as they do. Another technique is reframing. For instance, let us suppose that some in a group take exception to schooling in India; acknowledge their concern, and follow up with, "I heard your concern about the considerable time children spend in school compared to our kids. That aside, what does India do that is feasible for our consideration here? Do we have anything to learn from them?"

Allow space for different opinions and, as no decisions are required, present the audience with opportunities to further investigate the area of disagreement at the next meeting. Leaders should accept responsibility to find additional data that could create greater understanding. Invite stakeholders to do the same. Summarize all patterns and trends, whether about consensus or open issues. Consider posting your presentations and meeting notes electronically, meeting by meeting, so that nonattendees can follow the conversation and post their insights and comments.

Leaders must be cognizant that, the more important the issue, the more protracted the dialogue. The more diverse the composition of stakeholder groups, the more productive and challenging their concerns will be. Essentially, diversity is the mother of creativity, and leaders must embrace different points of view and connect them to data, pilot projects, and actions that will improve understanding for the stakeholders and, ultimately, student performance at their schools. Almost all schools can improve mastery-level performance among their students.

It is easy to see how discussing the future of education in the 21st century could easily lead to continually refining common understandings about the CCSS. The process of inquiry, data analysis, and dialogue should lead to a consensus about the potential of the CCSS to be the foundation for a new school experience. Dialogue can be a time-consuming process, so plan accordingly. As we are fond of stating, sometimes you simply must go slowly to go fast. In other words, the more time you put into planning and creating common understanding among all stakeholders, the faster the implementation phase of your initiative to transform your school will gain support and momentum (Manley & Hawkins, 2010).

As stated earlier, the dialogic process itself is what builds understanding and common insights. Another major benefit of the collaborative process is the building of trust and transparency among all participants. It is the smoothest means possible for school leaders to create the context for the change that they anticipate and yet do not fully know. The information school leaders exchange with all stakeholders will be invaluable for planning and designing the implementation phase of the CCSS.

In our scenario, the ultimate goal is to create common understanding among all stakeholders surrounding the issues facing their community and its children as the world becomes increasingly flat (Friedman, 2005). Most importantly, we seek to answer the whys behind the CCSS before audience opposition coalesces around a few opponents.

Once the whys have been explored thoroughly behind the CCSS, we focus on the data we have organized into new knowledge through the dialogic process. We will use the data to describe where we are today in contrast to where we need to be tomorrow. The gaps between current reality and our desired future for our students present the building blocks for a new future.

IDENTIFYING GAPS: CURRENT VERSUS DESIRED REALITY

The dialogic process builds new insights into why change is needed. It also gives stakeholders a glimpse into the practices and policies that may need to shift if they are to realize a goal of providing children with an excellent education. Here again, leaders should minimize their opinions, and data should be maximized. Patterns in participant commentaries, whether the leader agrees with them or not, signal the level of understanding held by constituents. Understanding is what the leader seeks for him- or herself and the audience.

If there is a gap between what stakeholders view as issues and the leader's view, this means a leader needs to go back to the designing board. Further data and dialogue may be required in those areas before actions are considered. Leaders should start by focusing on the areas of agreement then address the gaps in agreement so that everyone can begin moving from inquiry, dialogue, and consensus to action plans. Leaders must be open to changing their own views and improving their own visions and guiding principles if the dialogue is to be authentic.

Once a school community has examined the backdrop of education worldwide, the school stakeholders must assess how the school measures up organizationally to world-class educational standards. Fortunately, the CCSS have provided us with much of the information about what we need to compare current reality with desired future reality. An informed view of organizational culture is imperative in designing change. In our example, we have spent a great deal of time setting context, so we can assume that there is awareness and sensitivity about the challenges we face.

We thus avoid the complications created by leaders who start offering solutions to problems that the members of the organization do not know exist and have not had an opportunity to examine collectively, much less collaboratively. Assume for the moment that you have gotten stakeholders excited to become like Finland. Drilling further into the organization, we would also want to compare and contrast:

- Performance data
- Stakeholders and their relationship to the change
- Practices
- Technology and usage
- Curriculum
- Teacher training (initial and ongoing)
- Attitudes, beliefs, biases, and assumptions toward teaching, children, and learning
- Supervision

There are numerous ways to excavate this data. Whatever the choice, make sure it is a collaborative process that engages representation from every stakeholder. You might even consider guiding ideas (GIs) to focus the discussion.

When the New York State (NYS) Standards were introduced in 1996, the district that Rich led developed the William Floyd Standards Project. It was a two-pronged approach. The first part of the project compared and contrasted existing teaching expectations and practices with those espoused by the new standards. The second part was to examine every curriculum for its relevance with the standards and to visit classrooms to see if the teaching was in alignment with the existing curriculum. These two data sets provided a wealth of information on what was happening in the classrooms and where teachers needed to change or improve their practices.

Teachers, administrators, and department chairs examined the new standards and the teacher practices that supported, avoided, or ignored them. The state standards-based practices were merged into a new lesson observation form with other generic practices that were valued in the existing teacher evaluation process. School district officials and union leaders devised a separate class observation form for every department and grade level. The business departments' form contained the generic behaviors from the district's evaluation process and the behaviors associated with the new business standards. The math departments' form included the generic behaviors from the district's evaluation process and those associated with the new math standards.

On the elementary level, the lesson observation forms aligned to the content taught and the state standards. There was a different elementary form for English language arts (ELA), math, science, and social studies. Local school systems have to develop their own supportive observational and supervisory processes and forms that conform with the vision the stakeholders have adopted for a school implementing the CCSS.

In the process Rich used to develop supportive practices to institute new standards, after discussion with the administrative cabinet, the new forms were marked *draft* and shared with the formal union leadership. Union leaders participated in the early discussions, and they could validate that they had been part of the design. The superintendent suspended formal observations for five months so that administrators and supervisors could conduct 10-minute visits to multiple classrooms daily. Their only role was to check off whether the listed behaviors in the new teaching and learning forms were observable within the period of the visit or not. No other judgments were offered. Data were collected to identify teacher needs for training in the new standard instructional system.

After agreement, the union and administration copresented the project to every school faculty. Every principal or chairperson followed up, "taught" the new format for observations, and answered all of the why-change-the-system questions—something they could do because they were partners in the process from its inception.

The second component of the William Floyd Standards Project contracted out to our local Board of Cooperative Educational Services and coordinated a review of our curricula. Organized experts in their subject fields visited our classrooms to see if our espoused curriculum matched the curriculum in use. Their report added more data to the discussion about our readiness to initiate the new state standards.

At the end of approximately four and a half months, we had data from thousands of classroom snapshots about our readiness to address the new state standards. The superintendent shared the data from Phases 1 and 2 with the faculty. Ultimately, with assistance from administrators, chairs, and other specially trained teacher–facilitators, those data were discussed, and the implications for future revisions in curriculum and practice were identified in each department and school. The patterns that emerged also gave us valuable insight about our next steps in teacher training and curriculum development.

Rich's biggest discovery was that the collaborative process used to acquire a sense of readiness to make the necessary changes in practice required authentic data, careful analysis, and shared conclusions. Another realization was that the process itself *was* professional development. Data and even a lack of data informed every next step that we tried to create. Second, everyone owned and processed the data because they were available for all to see. Transparency was essential to achieving common understanding and building trust. Systemic and lasting changes require trust among school leaders, teachers, and parents. Transformative change begins with changes in beliefs and in mental models that are the most difficult barriers to improvement that any learning community has to tackle. In every case, dialogue and data should inform the content and process necessary for the transformation teachers and principals seek.

SECTION IV

Creating Systems That Accelerate Learning for All

Multicultural Issues That Teachers and School Leaders Must Face Beyond the Common Core State Standards

At the beginning of the 21st century, the population of the United States is undergoing a new wave of immigration and an expansion of second- and third-generations of students whose parents and grandparents immigrated to the United States from lands other than those speaking English as a primary language. Many of these students remain language-minority students who share some demographic similarities with some native English-speaking peers, including low socioeconomic status and struggles with reading comprehension (Lesaux & Kieffer, 2010).

Immigration status, language-minority dominant use, or shared use of English at home have been associated with other sociological issues, such as race, ethnicity, and poverty, to excuse students' failure to comprehend essential school texts. A more profound understanding of immigration and how America deals with nondominant cultures is required if school leaders and teachers are to find new ways to help struggling readers and avoid assigning their struggles to the "deficits" they have at home, within their culture, or within themselves.

Educators who wish to have a more profound historical perspective regarding immigrants should reflect on an essay by Randolph Bourne (1916) in which he wrote how quickly our national rhetoric turned to fear of loss in the face of independent thinking that newcomers offered as they entered the political dialogue about the future of our country. Bourne wrote:

> To face the fact that our aliens are already strong enough to take a share in the direction of their own destiny, and that the strong cultural movements represented by the foreign press, schools, and colonies are a challenge to our facile attempts, is not, however, to admit the failure of Americanization. It is not to fear the failure of democracy. It is rather to urge us to an investigation of what Americanism may rightly mean. It is to ask ourselves whether our ideal has been broad or narrow—whether perhaps the time has not come to assert a higher ideal than the "melting-pot." Surely we cannot be certain of our spiritual democracy when, claiming to melt the nations within us to a comprehension of our free and democratic institutions, we fly into panic at the first sign of their own will and tendency. We act as if we wanted Americanization to take place only on our own terms, and not by the consent of the governed. All our elaborate machinery of settlement and school and union, of social and political naturalization, however, will move with friction just in so far as it neglects to take into account this strong and virile insistence that America shall be what the immigrant will have a hand in making it, and not what a ruling class, descendant of those British stocks which were the first permanent immigrants, decide that America shall be made. This is the condition which confronts us, and which demands a clear and general readjustment of our attitude and our ideal. (p. 86)

Bourne saw America as a democracy first and a land of competing forces secondly. He recognized the virtues of Americans as those of a free people who cherished liberty, equality, and the rule of law where all people were presumed to be innocent until proven guilty. The American historian, Samuel Huntington (2004), describes America's past as one of a successful melting pot wherein diverse people were acculturated into a Protestant ethic of hard work and individualism. According to Huntington, "Americans, it is often said, are a people defined by and united by their commitment to the political principles of liberty, equality, democracy, individualism, human rights, the rule of law, and private property embodied in the American Creed" (p. 47).

Huntington (2004) notes that the "American Creed" as a descriptor of a people was first expressed by Gunnar Myrdal in 1944, when he argued that Americans have a common social ethos and political creed that values human dignity, political equality for all, and inalienable rights of freedom, justice, and fair opportunity. Individualism and hard work are the visible manifestations of a belief in the American Creed (Huntington, 2004).

The civil rights movement led by black Americans, which took full-bodied expression in the 1960s, was totally engaged in holding America's policies, laws, and judiciary to the test of its avowed values of freedom, justice, fair opportunity, individualism, and hard work. Martin Luther King, Jr. held America's Constitution before the public and demanded that American legislators and judges live by its tenets.

Huntington (2004) argues that cultural assimilation of immigrants, although never complete, has been the underlying story of America's success. Cultural assimilation, he wrote, "enabled America to expand its population, occupy a continent, and develop its economy with millions of dedicated, energetic, ambitious, and talented people, who became overwhelmingly committed to America's Anglo-Protestant culture and the values of the American Creed, and who helped make America a major force in global affairs" (p. 183).

Huntington (2004) argues that, after 1965, assimilation of immigrant groups underwent a radical change as a spirit of multiculturalism took over the political arena of the United States. Huntington does not see the 1960s and what follows as an expression of individualism and a desire for freedom. He sees a decline in the Protestant ethic and the spread of diverse beliefs, values, races, ethnicities, and conflicting interests across the face of America.

Almost 90 years before Huntington published his views about multiculturalism, Bourne (1916) noted that we were not dealing with static factors and that contrasting the older and the newer immigrants as one "motivated by love of liberty, and the other by mere money-getting, is not to illuminate the future. To think of earlier nationalities as culturally assimilated to America, while we picture the latter as sodden and resistive masses, makes only for bitterness and misunderstanding" (p. 87).

Bourne (1916) observed that the early Anglo-Saxon class were tenacious in their cultural allegiance to the mother country and that foreign cultures had not been "melted down or run together, made into some homogeneous Americanism, but have remained distinct but cooperating to the greater glory and benefit, not only of themselves but of all the native Americanism around them" (p. 89).

Jorge Ramos (2006), in his book *La Otra Cara de America (The Other Face of America)*, presents an essay by Carlos Fuentes, who notes, "In 2003 only 11 percent of the population of the United States was born outside of the country; in 1910, on the other hand, almost 15 percent of the inhabitants of the United States were foreigners" (p. 194, Manley, Trans.).

Fuentes takes issue with Huntington's thesis presented in his essay, "The Hispanic Challenge" (2004), published in *Foreign Policy* and examined in Ramos (2006). In the essay, Huntington observed, "The persistent inflow of Hispanic immigrants threatens to divide the United States into two peoples, two cultures, and two languages" (in Ramos, 2006, p. 195). Fuentes believes that many members of white culture in America cannot "see themselves in the mirror and recognize that they are a mixture of many colors and not white or black" (p. 196, Manley, Trans.).

Ramos (2006) uses statistics from Fuentes's essay to illustrate the contributions of Hispanics to the body politic of the United States.

- In 2004, 4 million Hispanics were in the process of becoming citizens of the United States.
- More than 500,000 Hispanics in the United States are doctors or lawyers or have earned master's or doctoral degrees.
- There are 1.2 million businesses in the United States owned by Latinos.
- More than 30 thousand Hispanic soldiers fought for the U.S. military in the Iraq war. (in Ramos, 2006, p. 196, Manley, Trans.)

Ramos (2006) observes,

What unites the United States is not English. No. What unifies the United States are the concepts that comprise the North

American creed—equality, liberty, social justice—and the basic principles that hold together the American society: tolerance of diversity, acceptance of immigrants, and the constant search for the new and the innovative. These elements made the United States a prosperous and powerful nation. Not English. (p. 198, Manley, Trans.)

In spite of the differences between the Latinos Ramos and Fuentes and the conservative historian Huntington, they agree on the principles that hold America together: equality, liberty, and social justice.

COMMON CORE STATE STANDARDS LIFT US BEYOND DIFFERENCE

The politics of multiculturalism and the metaphors for *them* and *us* are barriers to learning in schools. Teachers and school leaders must lead students beyond cultural and racial differences by celebrating diversity, engaging in cooperative learning practices, and focusing all of their attention on helping each child master the curriculum (Slavin, 1988; Johnson & Johnson, 2002).

Teachers are the guardians of our democracy, and in one sense, they lead in the development of democratic mental models within the minds of the young. School leaders and teachers must deal with current reality and remove the barriers that create enclaves of preposterous and separatist ideals. Cooperative learning is a tried method that reduces barriers among students when teachers know how to implement its tenets.

Children of the 21st century encounter diversity in their digital and global learning communities. In their daily school experiences, they can enjoy ever-changing mixtures of peers who vary in culture and beliefs more than peers whom their parents or grandparents encountered in any of their school days. The youth of the world, not just America, connect digitally, and their minds are open to an ever-expanding cultural world. Our schools must be open portals to diverse ideas, creative and cultural thinking, and new definitions of problems and innovative solutions.

Schools, teachers, and students need supportive structures and positive relations with one another and a strong focus on effective teaching and mastery learning (Strong, Gargani, & Hacifazlioglu, 2011). Multicultural instruction and grouping students by English language skills will not expand their mastery of math, science, social studies, and English. Patricia Gandara (2010) notes the isolation of English languages learners (ELLs) in schools where there are "few opportunities for students—even English speaking students—to come in contact with mainstream English, especially as it is used in academic contexts" (p. 62).

Gandara (2010) recommends good bilingual immersion programs that give "English speakers and English learners ample opportunities to interact in and out of the classroom. Successful programs share a respect for students' native languages. When students are more culturally comfortable in a classroom, they are more able to link their cultural knowledge to the classroom work" (p. 63).

Gandara (2010) supports the belief that bilingual education should be an opportunity for English speakers and English learners to grow together by citing the results of the 2008 study by Suarez-Orozco, Suarez-Orozco, & Todorova in which they identified the best predictor of an "immigrant student gaining a firm mastery of English was whether the student had a good friend who was a native speaker of English" (in Gandara, 2010, p. 63).

Boykin and Noguera (2011) identify the most critical issues in schools that contribute to students with special needs failing to make yearly academic progress.

First, schools use special education and English as a second language (ESL) classes as a place to put children who require additional support, but they often do not monitor the performance of these students to ensure that they receive high-quality instruction and are making academic progress. (p. 187)

They note that programs designed for students with special needs can become "dumping grounds" where students who are needy and the lowest academic performers are housed and often punished disproportionately because they act out against their isolation.

Instead of examining the underlying causes of their behaviors and changing their relationships to school personnel and their peers, school leaders punish them and restrict their movements throughout their day. In order to change this negative relationship with special need and ESL students, schools must be open "to using alternative forms of punishment that focus on developing character" (Boykin &

Noguera, 2011, p. 188). If a school staff wants students to change, Boykin and Noguera note, then, that school leader and teachers must promote social values, ethics, essential character virtues, and opportunities for students to work together in solving problems and serving their community.

Children with special learning needs and formal Individual Education Plans (IEPs) have the same social and emotional developmental needs that every other child has. All of the programs for the learning disabled and English language learners (ELLs) should be highly integrated into the regular class space of the school. These students receive no benefit from isolation and segregation within the school space.

The time has come for teachers to engage all youth, and especially our children who are poor and those who are middle class, in shared learning opportunities so that they interact with one another. Children and adolescents need individual attention. Secondary school students choose to stay in school and to work at learning because of the relationships they have with teachers and peers (Lesaux & Kieffer, 2010). Teachers must accept a higher order of responsibilities and orchestrate positive relationships and shared learning responsibilities in their classes.

All of our children must be engaged in dialogues about our democracy and its weaknesses and strengths. Our schools are the best place to have this conversation. In our schools, trained educators, political, community leaders, our youth, and their parents can construct an American Creed for the 21st century. School leaders have the responsibility to prepare the staff for multicultural learning by championing and celebrating diversity of culture, ethnicity, language, and talents and disabilities.

Multicultural acceptance should be part of the culture and the climate of the school and every classroom. The climate of the school must be healthy for learning to take place, a healthy climate that is safe for students. It promotes many opportunities in which they can share, explore, and discover how to apply knowledge. A healthy school climate is a prerequisite for learning (Hoy & Miskel, 1996). School climate can be a barrier to learning and yet, when the climate is open and inviting, it is not the masterstroke that guarantees children will learn.

Children learn when teachers include pauses in the pace of curriculum and instruction to ensure that everyone is mastering the application of the vocabulary, concepts, understandings, process, and procedures necessary to use what was taught. In the most effective schools, teachers use brief to-do assignments at the outset of classes or instructional periods to verify that students have the prior knowledge to begin a new lesson.

In one high school with very diverse children, a teacher reported that she used her formative assessments to identify several concepts that many students in her class failed to grasp. She devised different ways to reteach the concepts and helped her students master their applications. She stated that, on the retest, her students "unexpectedly achieved 80 percent correct or better across the entire class. Only, now I am behind in my curriculum by one week."

She was struggling to resolve the cognitive dissonance between the state testing pressures to cover every topic that might be on the state exam and her desire to ensure that her students learned what she had taught. She had to resolve whether covering less of the curriculum was actually more learning. She and her colleagues have to determine what is the best instruction and how much of the CCSS the students in front of them shall master this year. They have to adopt the guiding principle that all of their students learning at mastery levels must be the only prerogative that drives instruction if they are to raise student achievement for all of their students.

The number of chapters in the text should not drive the pace of instruction. Learning has to be the guiding principle. Teaching should respond to shared expectations for student mastery of critical themes, skills, applied knowledge, and the quality of the exchanges that students exhibit in their use of knowledge. Teachers have to feel empowered to alter the pace of curriculum and instruction while not defaulting on their responsibilities to hold students accountable for the CCSS.

Teaching is an art that requires a delicate balance among many competing forces and expectations. A guiding principle that can help teachers adjust the pace of curriculum should be their commitment that "every child will master what I teach." This guiding principle applies to every diverse learner, every special needs child, and every struggling learner.

WHAT ALL TEACHERS AND SCHOOL LEADERS NEED TO KNOW ABOUT MULTICULTURALISM

Multiculturalism cannot be an excuse for school failure. Understanding, accepting, and celebrating cultural differences at school does not take the place of a sincere and caring teacher with an open disposition toward children who differ from the teacher by race, ethnicity, or citizenship. A supportive multicultural climate may be necessary for learning and, yet, it will not create quality teaching or higher student achievement. Teaching and learning intertwine like DNA with school climate and supportive multicultural structures. One of the most powerful teacher behaviors related to student learning is a teacher who uses self-reflection to identify what is working and what is not working with particular children and then adjusts his or her teaching to better meet the needs of the child (Dalley, 2012).

Study after study of immigrant and poor children in public schools illustrate the importance of teacher relationships with students (Cantor, 2010; Lesaux & Kieffer, 2010; Velasquez, 2011). Student–teacher relationships can be positive or negative. In both cases, they are highly related to the academic success of all students, especially poor children who come to school less prepared for the practice of school (Dalley, 2012; Velasquez, 2011). When teacher adaptations to multiculturalism include being sensitive and seeking to understand and, moreover, capture the prior knowledge that students bring to school, teachers tend to have more growth in learning among their students.

Stronge, Ward, and Grant (2011) in their study of highly effective and ineffective teachers observed that effective teachers "have some particular set of attitudes, approaches, strategies, or connections with students that manifest themselves in non-academic ways (positive relationships, encouragement of responsibility, classroom management and organization) that lead to higher achievement" (p. 348).

One of the difficulties that instructors in teacher preparation programs, school leaders, school-based instructional coaches, and teachers encounter is how to determine what works with so many diverse students. The identification of teaching behaviors and dispositions that contribute to growth in the achievement of students in a particular setting is extremely difficult to discern and nearly impossible to transfer to a new and distinctive setting. The complex combinations of variables that come together within an effective classroom always include a successful teacher orchestrating unique relationships, stories, reflections, and writings. Teaching is much more of an art than a science, more like the conducting of a symphonic orchestra than playing a compact disk with great music.

Lesson observers see the outcomes of instruction in what children can do and how they perform. In an excellent sixth grade choral performance, the audience witnesses the outcomes of months of intricate work and motivation. Few teachers or school leaders can identify a teacher who will have great success with her or his students by observing one or two classes.

Strong and colleagues (2011) report their findings on whether judges can correctly rate teachers as effective or not when their ability to raise student achievement is unknown to the judges. In their study, these researchers had judges view film clips of the teachers who had been categorized previously and confidentially as effective or ineffective based on their students' growth scores in mathematics. The effective teachers had growth scores that were .5 of one standard deviation or greater above the mean, while ineffective teachers had growth scores below the mean.

Judges did not know how the teachers had been categorized. The film clips showed the teachers providing instruction and interacting with students. Judges varied from math educators, mentors, college educators in teacher preparation programs, school administrators, parents, and college students. In the first experimental group, judges tended to cite certain teaching strategies more frequently as important in their judgments about who appeared to be an effective teacher (see Table 9.1).

Table 9.1   Percent of Teaching Strategies Observed (Experimental)

Strategy	% of judges making cite
Accesses students' prior knowledge	67
Has active interaction with students	36
Moves around classroom	34
Enables students to generate ideas	23
Creates stimulating class environment	23
Uses visuals and manipulatives	23
Checks for student understanding	18
Has clear objectives	14
Presents concepts clearly	11
Exhibits equity	8
Differentiates instruction	7

Source: Strong et al. (2011, p. 374).

The first experiment was repeated a second and a third time with more stringent requirements for participant judges' knowledge and experience as teachers and supervisors. Finally, trained administrators were asked to evaluate teachers using the Classroom Assessment Scoring System (CLASS) observational tool with its 11 dimensions that cover four domains: emotional support, classroom organization, instructional support, and student engagement. Only a small subset of scores on teacher behaviors accurately identified teachers as either above or below average for student growth in achievement. All of these items that judges scored to distinguish effective from ineffective teachers were in the instructional domain.

Table 9.2 presents seven instructional behaviors that judges identified as predictive of effective teaching.

In order for teachers to be able to operate autonomously and creatively as they retrieve feedback from their students within a class lecture, they need a profound understanding of the CCSS, of their local curriculum, of the teaching principles and theories that are the foundation of their discipline, and of the multicultural strengths of their students. Teachers in ESL programs or those in bilingual programs must address the CCSS in English and in the native language of the students.

Too often, we find in our visits to ESL and bilingual classes that the rich curriculum of the CCSS are not addressed and, in fact, are deliberately avoided, and the students' English-language deficits are used to excuse teachers and students from the difficult work of mastering a challenging curriculum.

Darling-Hammond and Youngs (2002) observed that teaching is a very complex endeavor and difficult to measure because it entails what the teacher is doing, thinking, and feeling and what

Table 9.2   Items Judges Identified as Related to Effective Teachers

1. Clearly expressing the lesson objective
2. Integrating students' prior knowledge
3. Using opportunities to go beyond the current lesson
4. Using more than one delivery mechanism or modality
5. Using multiple examples
6. Giving feedback about process
7. Asking how and why questions

Source: Strong et al. (2011, p. 378).

the students do, think, and feel in their interactions with the teacher and the curriculum.

In a high school where 61 percent of the students are Hispanic, 30 percent are African American, and 9 percent are white, Asian, or mixed, we observed more than 60 teachers in English, math, science, social studies, and special education classrooms. We developed a practical class observation tool that identified teachers whose students presented evidence of strong academic growth on formative and summative class exams and state exams. Student growth was not related to their socioeconomic status, ethnicity, or race. Student growth was related directly to the quality of teaching and student interactions with peers and teachers. The proper use of formative assessments was associated with quality teaching and greater student success. When teachers performed at their peak, socioeconomic and racial differences did not predict performance.

Ainsworth, Prain, and Tyler (2011) make a strong case for multiple forms of formative assessments. They write: "Scientists do not use words only but rely on diagrams, graphs, videos, photographs and other images to make discoveries, explain findings, and excite public interests" (p. 1096). They note that students in science classes rarely are asked to draw or "create their own visual forms to develop and show understandings" (p. 1096). They offer five reasons why students' drawings should be recognized as a key element in science education:

1. When students draw to explore, justify and communicate science understandings, they are more motivated to learn

2. Generating their own representations can deepen students' understandings

3. Selecting different features to represent helps students to align drawings with observations

4. Visual representations require students to generate new inferences and organize their knowledge

5. Drawing helps students make their knowledge explicit, specific and ready for dialogue, inquiry and an exchange of ideas with peers. (pp. 1096–1097)

Ainsworth and colleagues (2011) conclude that student drawings (including digital depictions) serve as windows into student thinking and offer diagnostic, formative, and summative assessments of student learning. Thinking maps are pictorial drawings that help students connect related ideas. Ainsworth and colleagues suggest that drawing can be a way that learners interact with a scientific system, problem, or experiment. New technologies offer broad opportunities for students to create animations, for example, using digital cameras and clay models or making stop-frame movies, to illustrate a process they wish to communicate to their peers.

In a school district committed to learning with technology that we visited, we met students who began Grade 3 with their own laptops. One eighth grade student stands out in our minds. He entered this school in Grade 6 as a non-English speaker. We spoke with him about his computer project. He was developing a film to explain photosynthesis to his classmates. He employed a digital dictionary to help them understand technical and unique vocabulary. He had completed the visualizations for his film, and his teacher adjudicated that the scientific presentation was accurate. He was pleased with the selection of music, and he was placing his own voice on the sound track to describe for his classmates what they were seeing. He told us that his biggest challenge was to pose interesting and motivating questions to his peers to get them to think about what they were seeing. He said, "I am trying to tell the story like it was a mystery tale."

How does one evaluate the lesson this teacher is delivering? Students are in every corner of the room working to visualize a scientific principle, and some are in the library. Multicultural constraints and conflicts have been absorbed by the technology and the autonomy that the teacher invested in her students.

We believe that school leaders must be more autonomous and better prepared. They need a brief guideline to scan the landscape of teacher–student exchanges so that they can assess effective lessons. We know that checklists remove thoughtful reflection, inquiry, and dialogue among teachers, their students, and school leaders. Such paper-driven processes serve as barriers to improving instruction and prevent greater mastery among students. Much of the rubric-driven teacher evaluation models are laden with excessive data points that describe 50 to 100 behaviors teachers share with students and that supervisors or school leaders are asked to verify as occurring at an exemplary level.

Stop the madness. Schools are not McDonalds. No simple practices exist in teaching that can be broken down into 100 parts to verify good teaching, especially in multicultural schools using digital software to individuate learning. Effective school leaders have to be given the autonomy to lead and to evaluate teaching and learning within a collaborative process that professional teachers endorse and enjoy. Professional evaluation means dialogue, experimentation, planning, execution, and analysis of outcomes. To improve learning for students in multicultural settings or in any setting, for that matter, school leaders need to focus on behaviors that are highly associated with learning in schools. They need to examine interactions within the class, talk to students, have teachers verify growth in student learning with comparative products produced by the students, and find the courage to make authentic judgments about the quality of every teacher under their supervision.

To help school leaders in their observations of classes, we devised a brief observational guideline of important instruction and learning dimensions that school leaders could use to evaluate how well learning was delivered in a particular classroom (see Table 9.3). We have used the same items in visits to 60 classrooms within two multicultural schools and found that they help reveal the strengths and weaknesses in the teaching and learning we observed in those classrooms. We shared those observations with teachers in department meetings and found that teachers focused immediately on the things that they could change.

"Addressing the effectiveness of teachers must be an essential part of education reform" (Boykin & Noguera, 2011, p. 189). Boykin and Noguera note that an undue emphasis on state test and standardized test results has altered teaching to narrow curricula with less opportunities for students to engage in higher-order thinking and discovery or inventive analysis of facts, events, or processes.

What can school leaders and teachers do in the face of multicultural challenges or state and standardized exams that are used to measure value-added achievement for students? Will a new national recognition take hold that our high school graduates must compete on a world stage where higher-order and creative thinking are more valuable than ever and required for new jobs? Friedman and Mandelbaum (2011) in their book, *That Used to Be Us,* quoted General Martin Dempsey, chairman of the Joint Chiefs of Staff and former commander of the First Armored Division in Iraq, who stated:

> We need a member, who wants to belong to a values-based group . . . who can communicate, who is inquisitive, and who has an instinct to collaborate. . . . You need people who can constantly adapt and innovate . . . respond to the unpredictable experiences. (pp. 188–189)

Friedman and Mandelbaum (2011) observe that these thinking and communicative skills are the same for private industry and the military because these are the virtues and skills that new technology allows and the marketplace demands. The CCSS call for this new public servant and citizen to be developed in our public schools.

Recently, we presented a synthesis of this book about how to make the CCSS work in schools to student and practicing teachers who were members of Phi Delta Kappa, a national honor society of educators, and several experienced teachers derided our emphasis on collaboration and cooperation to make schools work for children. They said, "Don't you know what Professional Performance Assessments are doing to schools? Student scores rank teachers. Teachers compete with peers for effective and highly effective rankings. No one wants to share successful methods. Teachers are reluctant to have struggling learners in their classes because they are fearful they will get a low ranking on state exams."

We know the negative outcomes of public policy gone astray. Our reply to this audience and to all teachers is the same: See yourself as a member of a profession. Collaborate with others who have dedicated their lives to learning and mastering the art of teaching. Help the young teachers master what you know. Be a lifelong learner. Be a teacher. Be part of the solution and not a contributor to the problem. Work with your school leader, with parents, and with your students to enrich the learning process at your school. Work above and beyond your state tests. You will always be a valued member of your school. You will always be more than a developing professional. You will be a teacher, and there will be a place in a school for you always.

To improve teaching and learning, school leaders and teachers need a common set of instructional and learning standards that any observer spending several days with a teacher could witness or fail to see. The elaborate state rubrics, student gain score analyses, and sundry other cumbersome mandates from state education departments and the federal government will not improve instruction for students in failing schools. At best, they may record accurately where large numbers of students fall along a continuum of learning, and at the worst, they may actually harm instructional and supervisory practices in highly effective schools.

Federal and state governments should focus on broad educational issues, such as the graduation rates among poor and ELLs in our schools. In most states, less than 20 percent of the high schools have large portions of their students failing to graduate. Those schools that have one fifth or more of their students failing to graduate need special interventions.

States must begin with schools that have 20 percent or more of the ninth grade entering class failing to graduate within four years. States need to initiate teams of educational experts to visit and work with the schools where students have high failure rates and to close them if they fail to improve within three years.

Most schools with challenged ELLs and competent principals need structural support and a simple and elegant classroom observation system similar to the simple and elegant process that Steve Jobs brought to digital communication tools. Classroom observations can make a difference for all learners if they focus upon important teaching and learning behaviors and if they lead to dialogue, inquiry, new directions, and creative results for teachers. Table 9.3 presents the variables that we used to identify quality teaching.

Lesson observations of teachers and students that include multiple sessions where observers, teachers, and students have time to dialogue are more helpful than one-visit, summative assessments or value-added measures of accountability to determine effective teaching and learning. Harris (2011) reports, "Even if the value added measures contained no bias or imprecision, there is no guarantee that incentives based upon them would improve performance" (p. 827). He goes on to state: "Teacher value-added measures should therefore be combined with more direct measures of classroom practice when making overall performance judgments" (p. 827). He concludes that "it is only possible to say with statistical confidence that teachers at the extremes of the performance distribution can be distinguished from one another" (p. 827).

Teachers should not permit their expectations for student mastery to be marginalized by grouping labels assigned to students. A school philosophy that assumes all children must master set curriculum and high standards leads to teachers ensuring that students in "life skill"

Table 9.3 Classroom Visitation Worksheet

School _____ Subject _____

Observer _____ Grade _____

Number of students registered _____ Number of students in class _____

Note: A classroom observer should place an X under evident or not evident for each item and write a comment to explain the judgment.

Teaching Behaviors	Evident	Not Evident	Comments
Teacher aligns instructional goals to the curriculum			
Teacher varies instructional strategies			
Pacing and sequence of instruction is appropriate for learning			
Transitions within the lesson and among students occur smoothly			
Teacher addresses the diverse learning needs of their students			
Teacher uses ongoing formative assessments to evaluate individual learning			
Teacher verifies student mastery of the curriculum goals or lesson objective			

Student Behaviors	Evident	Not Evident	Comments
Students express how instructional activities are meaningful to them in their actions, attitudes, or comments			
Students feel free to include their cultures, families, and natural history into constructive instructional activities			
Students are actively engaged in learning			
Students understand the goals of the lesson			
Students display quality academic work in the class			
Students express higher-order thinking in their exchanges with peers and their teacher			
Students solve problems posed by peers and their teacher			

classes with severe learning disabilities learn to use adult technologies, make decisions, develop civic virtues, and gain employment or, at least, contributory volunteer positions in the community. The learning goals for these students reflect the most admirable guidelines in the CCSS that require all students to receive an education that helps them to become productive and participatory citizens in our great democracy.

Teachers must become advocates of professional evaluation systems and conduct research to justify their own evaluation systems. They must reject self-serving manipulations of current evaluation systems and the associative competition for successful students placed in their classes. They have to seek comprehensive and authentic evaluation systems for their work that require multiple observations of their exchanges with students and the gains their students exhibit.

GROUPING AND LABELING STUDENTS

Lesaux and Kieffer (2010) designed a study to "explore the nature of reading difficulties in a sample of adolescent language minority learners (LM) and native English speakers as they begin middle school in an urban district" (p. 601). They wanted to determine if LM and native English-speaking Grade 6 students who struggled with reading comprehension showed "the same variation in types of comprehension difficulty" (p. 601) when the demographic and instructional contexts were held constant. They found that struggling readers exhibit similar difficulties with underdeveloped general vocabulary and word recognition skills across the two groups of LM and native English speakers.

Lesaux and Kieffer (2010) observed, "a student with very low decoding, word reading, and fluency abilities, who performed well below average on a silent reading comprehension measure, in fact employed many strategies that good comprehenders do when the text was read to her" (p. 621). For the majority of students who share low socioeconomic home environments and LM status and who struggle with reading comprehension, classroom-based vocabulary instruction is necessary.

Many teachers fail to realize that words must possess images and invoke feelings to have meaning. For special needs children and ELLs, many academic words are devoid of meaning. Vocabulary development is an art that many teachers ignore with struggling readers. Effective teachers verify that students can provide visual descriptions for terms, definitions, and key concepts as well as connect words to experience and prior knowledge.

Many of the commonly used grade-level texts will prove challenging, especially without extensive vocabulary development efforts and multiple activities to improve vocabulary within classrooms (Lesaux & Kieffer, 2010). In fact, struggling readers "would benefit from explicit, systematic vocabulary and reading comprehension instruction as part of the core classroom curriculum" (p. 622).

Explicit attention should be given to academic language and content area knowledge in addition to a focus on high-utility words, multiple meanings of words, and strategies for students to learn words independently. Finally, Lesaux and Kieffer (2010) caution that "identifying similar skill profiles among Language Minority learners and their Native English-speaking peers does not mean that these two populations of students will respond similarly to intervention" (p. 625.)

One basic understanding that we must draw from Lesaux and Kieffer (2010) is that grouping students according to their LM status rather than their reader skill profiles will not improve their academic performance. Reading comprehension must be the principal criterion for selection of instructional strategies, and all teachers must learn to investigate the prior knowledge, misinformation and misunderstandings, and vocabulary needs of their students before and during instruction.

BUILDING A MULTICULTURAL LEARNING COMMUNITY

School leaders set the tone for the school. They model the values, beliefs, and culture of the school. They embody the level of cultural awareness and acceptance that students will encounter among their teachers and the school staff (Sergiovanni, 1994). What school leaders see inside the classrooms of their schools will be mirror images of who they are in the eyes of their students and staff. The school leader presents the metaphor for learning and multicultural celebrations and successes at the school. Effective school leaders inspire all members of the school to adopt the metaphor of a learning community and infuse it with a living spirit. The spirit is open to questions: Who needs help? Who can help someone else here?

In this chapter, we tried to address a broad picture of multicultural issues in the United States to give school leaders and teachers deeper understandings of where they stand in the historical development of the diversity within the people of the country. We showed school leaders how diversity and multicultural issues in schools do not have to be barriers to learning if we choose to champion diversity.

In addition, we hope that school leaders and teachers gained a deeper understanding of how struggling readers fail to learn whether they are immigrants, LM students, native English speakers, or students with disabilities. The CCSS are helpful roadways toward success, but students have to be able to read and comprehend the highway signs. The CCSS are pathways for success that all students can follow. How far they will follow the trail and how long it will take, they and their teachers will determine with dedication, commitment, inventiveness, and proper support.

Teachers can use the CCSS as road maps to academic understandings that their students must comprehend. At every grade along the highway to employment or higher education, students must master the skills required in the 21st-century CCSS. The CCSS serve as mile markers along the highway of knowledge.

No curriculum guide can take the place of a persistent and patient teacher whose students know she or he cares deeply about how they feel and how well they are learning. We strongly favor clear and demanding curricula for students, highly prepared teachers, and even more so, teacher-developed, frequent formative assessments to guide instruction.

We have witnessed the power of formative assessments to change how teachers converse with students about their learning, how they see students' strengths and weaknesses, and how they reframe their teaching to meet the needs of students. Just as important, we have seen students examine with their teachers and peers, in small groups, what they did not understand about a question and then gain the insight to apply their new knowledge. We saw students look at their teacher with more curiosity and more respect, knowing how she or he had helped them learn. We saw the teacher and the learner build a partnership to begin new learning, and we saw teachers transform their schools into learning communities as formative assessments and a heightened sense of their own professional efficacy permeated the classrooms.

We know school leaders, teachers, central administrators, and school boards want and need help to make their schools more effective. Even the most successful schools in the United States can improve. Almost all schools can improve the percent of students achieving mastery on state exams. In our next chapter, we will explore ways that schools can find appropriate help to improve. Testing is not improvement (Deming, 1986). Differentiated teaching and mastery learning are the hallmarks of improving schools. Many school leaders and teachers need consistent professional guidance to transform their schools into learning communities. In order to help school leaders implement transformative plans for their schools, we will present a school intervention plan in our next chapter that makes sense for the 21st century.

CHAPTER 10

An Effective Intervention in Schools That Improves Instruction and Learning

There are very few simple and uncomplicated systems available to assess schools that actually help school personnel to improve teaching and learning at a particular school. Some school improvement systems are so cumbersome that they distract school leaders and personnel from the necessary work required to improve schools, such as a focus on teaching, curriculum, formative assessments, learning, multiple classroom observations, and the evaluation of teachers.

School improvement systems that do not work require large investments of time and teacher training in the applications of product-driven processes that achieve small changes in student outcomes. For example, a new textbook with software applications or, even worse, a statewide change in testing will not improve teaching and learning. Often, these large-scale endeavors touch on so many variables that elements of change in one section of the school system are in opposition to efforts to improve in another section (Deming, 1994).

Under No Child Left Behind and Race to the Top policies, efforts that are more draconian are underway to improve student achievement. They will create more drastic disruptions for everyone at the school—the good, the bad, and the beautiful. In the most disruptive models, a school is closed, a new school is opened, and school employees and the principal are replaced in many cases, while the new school is charged to achieve some small gains in student performance on state exams.

Any changes in performance a reorganized school achieves will be more highly related to the shifting of students into smaller schools with new teachers who spend a bit more time with individual students. Little improvement in the quality of teaching and assessment will occur because the former leader and the new leader were not prepared to lead this struggling staff and students.

Are there schools that should close? Of course there are. Can test scores identify those schools? No. Test scores can identify schools with children having difficulty meeting state test standards as measured by standardized assessments. Only teams of highly trained educational specialists who visit a school and its classrooms for several days can diagnose critical barriers to quality instruction. Such expert teams can provide guidance for structural changes and professional development for teachers. If they work with school leaders and teachers for 24 months or more, they can assess effective improvements in learning and the potential of the school to change. School change is difficult to initiate and even more difficult to sustain. Schools that cannot demonstrate significant student learning improvements after 24 months of guidance and professional development should have one year of probation with additional help, monitoring, and analysis. After 36 months, a school should be able to demonstrate significant improvements equivalent to .5 effect size change, or the school should close, and new staff should be hired.

CREATING SUSTAINABLE CHANGE IN STRUGGLING SCHOOLS

A school in need of restructuring requires extensive guidance, classroom visitations, leadership improvements, and teacher training along with a shared vision and mission to change how employees and stakeholders view the school. Such school communities, their leaders, staff, and parents need consistent and supportive guidance in the restructuring and monitoring of their school improvements. Certainly, the teachers and school leaders need deeper knowledge of the Common Core State Standards (CCSS) and the scope and sequence for structured assessments that identify valuable learning.

A highly unionized secondary school that we worked with required a full semester for a team of educational specialists to identify critical barriers to better teaching and to convince teachers to try substantive changes in their instructional practices. Before the school leader and teachers could envision any changes, they had to create a new vision of the school that included adoption of the CCSS. Not all of the teachers accepted a need to change or the CCSS. In most cases, change has to begin with the few who will venture out into new frontiers. In this school, two departments took the lead.

In this case, the joint intervention educational team (JIT) identified Grade 9 as the point in the child's high school experience where instructional changes had to take place first. Almost 40 percent of the freshman at the school failed three or more subjects annually. Teachers accepted the evidence that the ninth grade failure rates contributed to excessive dropout rates. Cohort failure to achieve competitive graduation rates started with ninth graders failing three or more subjects.

Teachers in the four core subjects were asked to identify six major themes that every ninth grade student had to master in their curriculum. After the teachers identified the learning themes in the curriculum, they were asked to align them with the CCSS and their local state standards.

Following this effort to create a scope and sequence for the curriculum that teachers agreed to, they received guidance from members of the JIT in developing formative assessments. They learned to design formative assessments with five opportunities in each set for students to demonstrate mastery of the building blocks that comprised a major theme in the curriculum.

In addition, teachers were asked to set the scope and sequence of these collaboratively designed formative assessments so that students were assessed each month between October and April. In the first year, teachers used the six cooperative formative assessments as benchmarks to identify student mastery, and then, they incorporated into their daily practice multiple forms of formative assessments, such as a series of class-opening to-do assignments that collectively represented a formative assessment after several days.

Examples of two large themes that a social studies team selected were the Migration of People in the Classical World and the Recurring Causes of Wars Between Nations in the Classical Period.

In every department, teachers found the identification and sequencing of themes a familiar task. They had to learn about and adopt a deeper understanding of the difference between short quizzes with a great deal of recall work and more formative assessments that challenged students to use textual references to justify their answers.

Typically, teachers employed five questions of varying cognitive operations in each formative assessment to evaluate multiple levels of knowledge within a theme. Teachers came to see who had little, moderate, and strong mastery in their lessons. The only teachers who made a difference in their students' learning curves were those who redirected their teaching to help those with moderate and little success on their formative assessments.

Teachers had to learn how to organize their student results on formative assessments in simple and easy-to-read spreadsheets so that they could compare how well their own students performed on each item. Then, they could contrast student performance in one class with several classes they taught and with students that their colleagues taught.

Part of the resistance that we encountered at the outset seemed motivated by fear of the unknown, especially the unknown quality demanded by the CCSS and fear that the design of more demanding measurements of mastery in the formative assessment style would expose teachers to higher levels of criticism. Once teachers learned that innovative, inventive, and experimental responses to formative assessment results helped them win accolades from peers and supervisors, they moved quickly to improve their assessments and focus on student mastery of their lessons.

Many teachers developed multiple forms of formative assessments to elicit brief and quick responses from students that would reveal what they knew and did not know. After two group practice sessions and several periods of working together, teachers adopted their first formative assessment in the four core subjects at Grade 9. They shared results, noted some different patterns of success among colleagues, and asked their peers to describe what they did to address a building block where most of the students showed mastery. Teachers began to focus on what worked. We recognized quite quickly they were learning from each other how to help their students achieve higher mastery levels.

The school leader initiated thoughtful dialogue and inquiry into how this variation in performance with similar children occurred.

Teachers began to experiment with each others' techniques and strategies. They created multiple ways to help their students master a major theme and the skills embedded within the theme.

We are three years into the transformative process, and we see the teacher dialogue with school leaders changing from defensive and directive comments to thoughtful exchanges about what is known and not known about students. Teachers are offering descriptions of multiple experiments throughout the school that they initiated to make a difference in their students' achievement. Teachers are taking leadership roles in helping innovative experiments that work take hold in most classrooms.

In this high school, they increased Grade 9 successes for an additional 13 percent of the ninth grade from 57 percent to 70 percent. Triple subject failures for grade nine students fell below 20 percent of the class. We expect more than 80 percent of the students will graduate after four to six years of targeted and persistent interventions. More and more teachers are changing their beliefs about what works for struggling students. Students who are not well prepared for school need many innovative approaches. One tool that teachers learned to employ effectively was cooperative learning, where students were taught how to work together, how to reach a common goal in a lesson, and how to be personally responsible for specific tasks. Students were held accountable for their group and their personal achievement (Slavin, 1988, 1991).

The formative assessment data indicate that teachers continue to have students master the curriculum in larger and larger numbers. Yet, each year brings a new crop of students with a new set of challenges. Some teachers seem to tire of the extensive effort that they have to make in the face of small amounts of student improvement. They struggled with the desire to keep the old ways with their low levels of student mastery and they feared the unknown where they would have to meet much higher expectations. Effective leadership, support, and celebrations of success helped to motivate almost everyone to renew their efforts.

LEADERS CREATE THE CONTEXT AND DESIGN FOR CHANGE TO SUCCEED

School leaders are most important to teachers who are suffering the emotional turmoil that change brings. They can calm the waters, build efficacy, and motivate greater effort by keeping their focus on the goal of more learning, by using the inquiry process that everyone enjoys, and by sustaining respectful dialogue. School leaders who rely on diverse teachers to take on leadership roles such as peer coaches achieve the best results.

Can almost all schools improve? Yes, they can if school leaders and teachers change their focus from who is failing to who is mastering the curriculum. Then, their question becomes how to help those who are struggling to master the curriculum. All of their efforts focus on enabling their students to exceed the CCSS and other highly respected national standards that many national subject associations provide.

Change begins with the school leader believing that he or she can find help to make better school learning opportunities for students. For schools that have unacceptable levels of students failing state exams, there is a better way to intervene than charter schools, school vouchers, or closing school. Accomplished educational experts can be found to intervene in the schools and work with school leaders. In the exceptional case where school leaders and teachers refuse to change and continue to support a pattern wherein large numbers of children fail to learn, the school should close. For most schools with struggling learners, an empowered JIT should be able to work with competent school leaders who are willing to examine data about teaching and learning, and together, they can create a new learning culture that teachers help to design.

In 2009–2010, New York State (NYS) adopted a JIT approach modeled on the English Inspector General System, in which a team of outside experts engaged a school leader, assistants if available, faculty, staff, students, and parents in an evaluative system that required dialogue and inquiry. In NYS, if schools had more than 20 percent of their students failing to meet state standards or had 20 percent or more of subgroups within the student body failing to meet growth standards, they were placed under review. A team of expert educators and specialists were employed to visit the school, examine every aspect of the school, and make recommendations for change based upon their findings.

Much of the school reform literature concludes that the individual school is the point at which school improvement efforts must focus. The JIT is designed to have a state education department representative as a consultant to the team. The team itself has a chairperson who is an experienced school leader who has demonstrated the capacity to *turn around,* or improve, a school previously. The chair of the JIT is the educational expert for the team and the designated writer for the JIT report.

The educational expert, serving as the JIT chairperson, selects a central administrator approved by the district as a member of the JIT and two to three specialists who will help to evaluate structural designs, practices, policies, the quality of teaching and learning, and school interventions within specific areas of concern, such as Individual Education Plans (IEPs) and their implementations at the school, mathematical curriculum, and other specialties that the JIT chair has identified from the school data analysis.

Before the JIT members interview stakeholders at the school, the members must become familiar with the critical data trends at the school for the last three years, including core curriculum and state test passing rates for the school population and subgroups. With the academic data, JIT members must examine quarterly and period-by-period attendance reports, violent and disruptive behavior reports, suspension reports, and student activities and sports participation reports.

The members of the JIT interview the school administrators, the teacher union representatives, a sample of the teaching staff, counselors and social workers, support staff, students, and parents. Some interviews are conducted in focus groups with an opportunity for individuals to have time to address members of the JIT more privately within a one-to-one conversation at the end of each session.

A series of open-ended questions that NYS education officials developed to guide the focus groups were well intentioned and helpful to identify major constructs in successful schools. On the other hand, questions often were too numerous, too generic, and too cumbersome to be applied effectively in a focus group. Fortunately, the state education officials permitted the JIT chair to adapt guiding questions for the focus groups and individual interviews.

In this chapter, we will present guiding questions that we recommend to elicit important information for JIT members to consider. JIT members may need training in the basic qualitative processes of theme analysis, pattern recognition, and similarity and discrepancy analysis that focus groups and interviews frequently provide. Any school principal seeking to improve teaching and learning at his or her school can use a JIT without waiting for the state to act. All one needs are the guidelines and interview questions contained in this chapter, a clear understanding of the CCSS, the right members for the JIT, and school district support for the endeavor.

It is important that JIT members examine trend data for the school by percent of cohort grade level and subgroup members achieving success in required subjects and state exams. Cohort data should be analyzed by the year the cohort members entered the school and their expected normative departure date (transition or graduation). JIT members should expect to spend three to five days at the school depending on the number and severity of student issues that the data reveal. In addition, the neediest schools may require extensive and regular professional development, classroom visitations, regularly planned assistance, support, and helpful data analysis for principals and teachers.

Once the JIT arrives on site, JIT members should meet together for one hour to debrief at the end of each school day. They should examine their findings, discuss recommendations, and come to a consensus on both. In some instances, the afternoon session leads to a more precise focus for the next day's activities assigned to each member. The JIT chair serves as the facilitator to coordinate summative reports.

After the JIT daily debriefing meeting, the school principal should meet with the team to discuss preliminary observations and to verify data. This is an opportunity for the JIT members and the principal to seek additional insight into conditions at the school and to inform their decision making with concrete knowledge of practices at the school.

JIT members should visit at least six classes each day. The JIT chair should assign class visitations. The protocol for JIT classroom visitations emphasized the quality of thinking that teacher and student exchanges should achieve in the classroom (see Table 9.2).

Classroom observers should focus on teacher and student behaviors and dispositions related to instruction and learning. In classroom observations, JIT members try to identify patterns of teacher or student behavior that promote or interfere with mastery learning. Frequently, positive patterns are behaviors that teachers and students control, change, or make more pervasive for every student in the class. Behaviors that are desirable because they clearly reveal evidence of student mastery should be encouraged, and those that are highly related to students' failure to learn should be identified and sanctioned. JIT observers can identify helpful and harmful patterns in classes across a school. The JIT chair must reveal the patterns to the entire faculty if they are to begin a dialogue and inquiry into how they need to improve. The JIT chair should publish the positive and negative patterns for the faculty so that teachers who receive new visits to their classes will have had appropriate information and dialogue to improve.

Classroom visitations should occur for two to three days depending on the school size. Because observers are trying to identify recurring patterns, two or more observers who work together with the same observation protocol in the same or different classrooms can accurately discern patterns of instruction and learning within a department or grade level at a particular school.

In our experience, during three days of classroom visitations at a low-student-wealth high school, we observed a full period for each of 42 lessons. Each of us visited four to five classrooms in each of the core subjects and several special education and inclusion classrooms daily. We noted a series of strengths and weaknesses that teachers in all departments exhibited and needed to address at the school (see Tables 10.1 and 10.2).

Interestingly, we noted that, in certain subjects, classroom patterns of strengths were more prevalent than in other disciplines. After interviewing the teachers, we learned that the department with more common strengths across multiple lessons had the highest level of teacher collaboration about curriculum and instruction. Had we continued to observe all core subject classes, we would have observed approximately 280 lessons.

The power of JIT classroom visitations is that, with 42 lessons spread across four disciplines and three grade levels, the members of the JIT were able to discern similar patterns, strengths, and weaknesses in the lessons. Table 10.2 presents the patterns of instructional weaknesses identified across multiple classes.

Effective supervisory support and teacher dialogue and inquiry could remediate many of the weaknesses that we observed in the lessons. One of the common weaknesses that we observed was the inconsistent and somewhat detrimental use of homework that actually harmed students by penalizing their quarterly grade for missing homework assignments.

Table 10.1   Patterns of Teaching Strengths

Teaching Strengths

- Students have assigned seats and a regular routine for the opening of each class.
- Teachers have management control over the classroom space.
- Classroom is orderly and neat.
- Current individual work from students is displayed on bulletin boards.
- The purpose of group work is clearly stated.
- Teacher presents a question, pauses, and then calls on a student.
- Teachers scaffold questions and use analysis and evaluation to guide students.
- Homework is checked and is used as a tool to reward students for extra work.
- Cooperative learning lessons are well organized; each student has an assignment; the learning objective is clear, and each student is held individually accountable to show mastery of the required learning and the application of new knowledge.
- Formative assessments are used to verify student mastery of lesson goals.
- Individual students are required to participate and contribute to each lesson.
- Each student in a group has a clear role.
- Each student in a group is responsible for a quality product.
- Every student has to be prepared to answer.
- Students share multiple reactions to a text.
- Students know they must raise hands and wait to be called upon for a response.

HOMEWORK

A major weakness in classes where high percentages of students failed each quarter was the use of homework to determine grades. In many of these classes, teachers assigned 25 percent or more of the quarterly grade to homework or even more harmfully reduced a student's grade point average by a single point for each homework missed during a quarter. Essentially, these penalty programs were justified by teachers as real-world events that should prepare their students for the world of work. What work?

Table 10.2   Patterns of Teaching Weaknesses

Teaching Weaknesses

- Students are permitted to call out answers to teacher questions.
- No individual accountability for learning is evident in the class.
- The teacher does not pose broad questions, and not every student has to reflect upon what will be learned in the lesson.
- The majority of teacher questions require students to recall answers from the text.
- Less than one third of the students participate in the lesson.
- Students take over the classroom space and separate themselves from the teacher.
- Group work is haphazard and poorly defined, and individual contributions and knowledge are not evaluated.
- No real cooperative learning is taking place in the group work.
- Homework frequently results in an academic punishment for failure to complete.
- Little student writing is evident.
- Discussion centers on feelings and opinions.
- No justification for an opinion is required.
- Students do not have to justify their answers.
- Students do not have to use textual references to explain their thinking or to show how they arrived at an answer, nor do they address a higher-order level of inquiry.
- Teachers do not scaffold their questions or lead students to think critically.
- Students are passive, listening, and watching.
- Teachers are doing most of the work.
- There is very little engagement in learning for everyone in the class.

The homework system clearly contributed to the high failure rates that motivated almost 15 percent of the students to leave school by the end of 10th grade and another 25 percent who failed three subjects to consider leaving as soon as they could. What career employment will they ever get? Shouldn't homework help the teacher assess who learned to apply a previously taught curriculum skill or concept? Shouldn't homework lead to rewards like overtime at work?

Students who come from homes with high levels of poverty may need a homework system that is flexible and motivating, that allows them school time to complete, and that involves the application of what was taught to new scenarios. In other words, homework should ask students to apply what they have learned in an important or meaningful way, and it need not be done at home. Homework should be an assessment tool. A few well-chosen questions can be more informative to a teacher than a long list of repetitive questions.

STUDENT WORK AND DEFICIT ASSUMPTIONS

In two high schools that we visited for several days, we found many teachers used homework as a deficit measurement system and reduced their students' average scores on tests if the students failed to complete homework. Many students failed to do homework and lost points on their average grades for the quarter and failed courses because 20 percent of the average or more was related to homework completion.

One telling example occurred in science. Teachers assigned laboratory class reports to be completed at home. Students failed to complete the labs at home and failed the course. A large portion of the high level of failure for students was the result of this homework system. Even worse, teachers reported that student patterns of failure to do homework had been operating for a long time. No one thought that changing the system might change the repetitive and annual failure results.

Why did no one question the system and its recurring failure rates? Human beings acculturate to systems and learn to operate within systems. Few question or ever think they might change systems. Edwards Deming (1986) noted that, once a system is stable, it will produce similar results year in and year out. To obtain different results, teachers must design new systems. However, Deming noted that leaders design systems, reinforce them, and sustain them.

School leaders, department leaders, union leaders, and informal leaders in a school sustain the design. We suggest that teachers rethink what they are doing when their student results do not meet a desired reality or vision for the school. For example, when a homework system produces this negative pattern of student failure year after year, teachers should discard the old homework system and institute a new system.

We would like teachers in the schools that are similar to the ones we described to examine the afterschool lives of many of their high school students. Many work at home or outside the home after school. They do not have much time outside of school for homework. By getting to know their students and what they can do, teachers can invent new homework systems that reward students for applications of classroom learning and instruction.

We ask that teachers consider homework as a multiday task. An example of a new homework system in this high school might include 20 or 15 homework assignments for each marking period of 45 class days. Notice homework can occur every two or three days and be an effective learning tool. Homework should engage students in discussion, discovery, or application of knowledge that they gained in the classroom. Homework should help them practice a skill. Homework should produce an immediate benefit for the student. For example:

> Students who complete 20 homework assignments would receive 5 points added to their average grade.
>
> Students with more than 15 assignments completed would receive 4 points.
>
> Students with more than 12 assignments completed would receive 3 points.
>
> Students with more than 9 assignments completed would receive 2 points.
>
> Students with more than 6 assignments completed would receive 1 point.

In this new design for homework, teachers would change their penalty-driven system that produced high rates of student failures into a bonus system for completed homework. In science, all required laboratory reports would be completed during the instructional time assigned to science as there are seven instructional periods for each science course each week with two full laboratory periods.

A bonus system for homework enables teachers to use their academic intervention sessions at the school to differentiate instruction according to student needs revealed within homework assignments.

Even those who fail to do a quality homework assignment reveal a potential gap in learning that needs attention. Other formative assessments in class reveal important opportunities for teachers to explore mental models and misinformation that students hold that may be barriers to mastering what is taught in class.

Cooperative learning assignments took the place of daily homework and became motivational processes that induced students to appreciate their own diversity, strengths, and talents as well as their teacher's inventiveness (Johnson & Johnson, 2002a,b).

In other words, homework can be another option that teachers use to assess how to help children master a lesson. A few applications are more than sufficient to assess how well a student can apply knowledge. If teachers adjust instruction according to formative assessment principles, and used homework analysis and student responses in their classes or cooperative-group academic interventions to differentiate instruction, they would have much higher passing rates for their students.

When teachers observe that their student results do not meet a desired reality or vision for the school, they should rethink what they have been doing. One way to begin the rethinking process is to describe the system one uses as accurately as possible. Then, ask what is it about this system that contributes to so many students failing.

For example, when a homework system produces this negative pattern of failure year after year, a thoughtful analysis would precisely describe how students lose credits for missing homework and the degree to which their grades are reduced. Sometimes, reversing an element within a system transforms the whole system. For instance, transforming homework from a deficit to a bonus system changes the impact and use of homework from a sanction to a reward.

Interestingly, a math teacher at one of these high schools told us she would prove us wrong, and she set up an experiment with two of her classes. One class had the old system—minus one point for every homework assignment missed—and the other class received the bonus option. To her credit, she announced her results at a meeting of her peers. The class with the bonus system completed more homework and had higher grades at the end of 10 weeks.

We worry about science instruction for struggling learners. If teachers insist that all required laboratory reports be completed during the instructional time assigned to science, student failure would decline significantly. In NYS, students have to complete 33 laboratory reports to sit for the required regents' examination. As the school year has approximately 40 weeks and 75 laboratory sessions, students have to complete a laboratory report almost every week. Some inventive teachers open class on every Monday or the first day of the week with a 20-minute session for laboratory report completions. They start the week with almost every student ready for new learning. We wonder why some teachers see opportunities to change and others accept so much failure to learn among their students.

In addition, at one school we visited, science teachers reserved the third Thursday of each month for a discussion of a scientific myth or common belief that students were required to defend or debunk. Students received their myth on the first Friday afternoon of the month and had 15 days to explore the facts with their teammates. Ninth and tenth grade students worked in small and large teams to crack the mysteries that these teachers posed. The rest of the week, they worked with their teachers to acquire the scientific and engineering skills that their curriculum required and their future learning made necessary. Much of what they were learning in class had to be mastered in order for them to solve the myth or common belief.

Students were enthralled with science at this urban high school. Students who encountered learning difficulties had tutorial opportunities available to them also. Teachers had designed the entire science program to deliver successful students.

In these effective classrooms, teachers presented tutorials in their academic intervention sessions to help students master a subject. They offered differentiated instructional activities and individual tutoring. They used formative assessments from the students' classes to formulate questions that helped each student reveal what he or she did not understand. Teachers adjusted instruction according to formative assessments. They listened carefully to student responses to identify what the students did and did not know, and their sensible reward system led to many more students that were successful.

Focus Groups

Beyond the classroom visitations, the JIT process employs focus groups to elicit the mental models and assumptions that participants hold about the school, about teaching and learning, and about other practices that make the school what it is. Mental models, Peter Senge and colleagues (2000) observe, often represent barriers to new learning and to change.

The JIT questions for teachers help interviewers discover how teachers use the curriculum in terms of the CCSS and the expectations that they have for all students in their classes. In addition, these six questions that we designed explore how teachers assess students, how they work with peers to analyze and verify their interpretation of student results, and how creative they are in designing responses to students who need help.

In the focus group, one JIT member has to take notes, serves as the recorder of the meeting, and later, becomes the one who summarizes what was said in terms of repetitive patterns, discrepancies among respondents, and any unique responses pertinent to one individual. The commentaries in the focus groups reveal a valuable insight into the school and how or why things are done the way they are (Schön, 1983).

Members of the JIT have to feel free to follow up on a comment from a member of the focus group with an additional probing question that helps the respondent to clarify the meaning or information he or she shared. JIT members must examine the commentary together to identify patterns, discrepancies, and unique themes that respondents reveal about any topic

Table 10.3 presents questions that we suggest JIT members use for the teacher focus group.

School Leaders

Each focus group is conducted with a protocol of interview questions that have been designed to help the respondents reveal their thinking, assumptions, mental models, and the steps or elements that comprise the school's instruction and assessment systems.

The school leader questions are designed to elicit information about how the principal works with teachers, conducts lesson observations, leads collaborative analyses of student data, and creates a shared vision

Table 10.3   JIT Questions for Teacher Focus Group

Team member/recorder: _____ Date: _____

Question	Response
How do you know what you are expected to teach?	
How do you ensure that your scope and sequence for the curriculum align with CCSS and local state standards?	
What is the school policy regarding grading and student assessments? How do you implement the policy?	
How do you use student assessments to monitor student progress?	
Who helps you to assess student progress?	
How do you intervene with students who are struggling to make progress in your class?	

and inquiry system to continuously support the improvements that the school needs to make. Table 10.4 presents the school leader questions.

Table 10.4   Questions for School Leader Focus Group

Question	Response
How is the curriculum designed and monitored at this school?	
How do teachers and administrators monitor student achievement at this school?	
How do you assure that English language learners and special need students are making appropriate progress?	
How do you evaluate teachers at this school?	
Describe how you and your faculty use data to determine strategies for academic intervention services at this school?	
Describe how you and your faculty identify and develop professional development and training programs annually at this school?	

Parent Involvement

For the parent focus group, we recommend a few ground rules.

- This focus group is a *no ridicule* zone.
- We must listen to one another, learn, and offer helpful suggestions.
- We must not be afraid to report problems as long as we do not use the names of children, parents, or teachers in the discussions at the open forum.

The purpose of the parent forum is to assess what parents like, do not like, and wish for at the school. Secondly, the support parents are willing to give to the vision and academic expectations that the school holds for all students should be analyzed from the parent perspective. Also, the comfort that parents feel coming to the school should be evaluated. Table 10.5 presents the parent interview questions.

Table 10.5 Questions for Parent Focus Group

Question	Response
What do you like about this school?	
What do you dislike about this school?	
What do you wish this school offered?	
What do you think the principal and teachers are trying to do for students here?	
How safe are children in this school?	
How welcome are parents at this school? Please explain.	

Students

Student focus groups should have the same guidelines that parents receive. In order to get a good cross section of students, we recommend that the students in the student association or student government comprise one focus group. In addition, we recommend that a sample of upper-grade students in performing arts or athletic teams comprise a second focus group. Lastly, we recommend that students from several intermediate grades or, in secondary schools, several English classes be invited to have lunch with the JIT in a small conference room. When dealing with students, the JIT should try to get a broad spectrum of students who attend the school. A guidance counselor who is well known to the students should attend all meetings with students in case a follow-up interview is required. Table 10.6 presents the questions for the students.

No one can predict what important information these forums will reveal about a particular school. Schools are unique communities or social systems with defined cultures that reflect the expectations and dispositions of the school leader, teachers and staff, students, and parents. JITs, whose members have proper training and skills, can identify the barriers to greater learning among students and suggest strategies and methodologies to achieve desired outcomes.

Table 10.6   Questions for Student Focus Group

Questions	Response
What do you like about your school?	
What do you dislike about your school?	
Why do you think some of your peers are successful in school and others are not?	
If you need help understanding something your teacher taught, what do you do?	
Why are some teachers able to get all students in their classes to be successful?	
What would you change to assure that all students would be successful?	

School improvement efforts fail because of a lack of follow-up that occurs after JITs visit the school and deliver recommendations. Weak follow-up is a substantive error in many organizations (Drucker, 1999). When the JIT process fails to provide powerful follow-up, no real change will occur at the school. To effect deep and profound change, the JIT leader and one or two support specialists will have to continue to work with the school leader and teachers to guide the development of planned changes and to monitor their effects on students and teachers.

Change, especially profound and meaningful innovation, comes slowly as teachers, school leaders, and support staff at a school change their beliefs, dispositions, and practices. Jose Ortega y Gasset (2005) wrote at the turn of the 20th century that the greatest revolution a people can undergo is a change in belief. Lasting change requires careful monitoring, celebrating of successes, human resource development that alters beliefs and mental models, supportive structures, analysis of student performance on multiple measures, and constant vigilance (Passi, 2010). These school elements are the descriptors of a true learning community.

Changing Public Mental Models About School Reform

In our last chapter of this book, we offer several challenges to federal, state, and local legislators to abandon 40 years of failed school reform efforts by giving up the dream that legislators can demand testing programs that will improve schools. Testing is like one MRI exam; it reveals the present condition. Dr. Laura Esserman (2011), director of the breast care center at the University of California, San Francisco, summed up the basic power of screening (testing):

> Screening is not prevention. We are not going to screen our way to a cure. . . . The treatments that we have actually make up for a good deal of the benefits of screening. (pp. D1, D6)

To improve the patient's condition, one must offer expert care, time, medicines, experimentation, innovative thinking, and a series of treatments and exams to verify the effects of the physician's decisions and efforts. Schools are like patients. They improve one school at a time with elaborate care and constant vigilance. Children improve their learning in much the same way.

Teachers know that public testing policies will not improve schools nor increase how many students make gains in their learning. Teachers do not oppose all schools having their pulse taken annually but not in every grade. Most successful schools can be identified with achievement tests administered in Grades 3, 5, 7, 9, and 11.

The United States has to target federal funds at failing schools and communities that states recognize as *critically needy schools.* Some of these funds should be assigned to JITs led by experts who have proven their capacity to improve the mastery rates of students in other schools. Needy schools require intensive care units. They cannot cure themselves. Personnel in those schools need high doses of professional development and coaching and monitoring.

Healthy schools need national rewards that celebrate student achievement at excellent levels. The residents of communities with highly effective schools need to be acclaimed for their commitment to excellence within their communities and their schools. These fortunate citizens should be praised for the commitment they have made to invest large portions of their wealth into their communities and their schools. It is an essential role of government to promote the education of its citizens and to recognize successful communities. One of the best recognitions that government can bestow on highly effective schools is to free them from government reporting and monitoring procedures. Schools with more than 90 percent of their students proficient on state measurements and more than 60 percent of their students performing at mastery levels should be free of state monitoring systems and state regulations on teacher and principal evaluations using student scores. Targeted and necessary state interventions should be the norm for schools that do not meet expectations. A focused approach to school improvement will free limited resources so that schools in need of help will receive them.

Unhealthy schools require intense investments, support, and scrutiny because they do not have sufficient resources to provide corrective action for themselves. State governments and their education departments are the proper vehicles to deliver these services. State governments require fair-share portions of the nation's wealth to turn around these failing schools and communities. If we are to have highly productive citizens in all of our communities, we must invest in the resources that make a difference.

Our urban school systems need help now. We need to recognize that most failing schools have large numbers of students in poverty. Federal dollars should place state-approved intervention personnel with sufficient funds in failing schools to enable them and the JITs to make a difference in the learning process of every student. All failing schools in any part of our country need similar intervention help. School interventions should be managed by the states. State departments of education and governors will respond to federal incentives to improve schools in poor communities. The federal government must require states to develop monitoring and reporting systems that give clear evidence of student progress. To motivate states to improve their urban schools, sufficient funds and empowered JITs should be required for federal aid to make an impact on the target schools.

The JIT process and the CCSS are two public policies that can make a difference in how many of our students master important knowledge, such as preengineering math, text interpretation, writing, and graphing for communication in the arts and sciences, and innovative uses of technology related to opportunities for learning and employment. All we need is the belief that we can improve our schools, the will to do it, and the drive to execute plans that work (Friedman & Mandelbaum, 2011).

State legislators must rethink their criteria for school success. When state tests identify healthy and unhealthy schools, state policy should provide rewards for outstanding performance by students at healthy schools. In addition, state policy should support JITs at unhealthy schools. These JITs should provide an evaluation of the schools and guide school leaders and teachers to devise a plan for continuous improvement. The JIT should assess progress at the school and be required to give evidence to the state education commissioner that a school is making progress. Schools that do not make progress within three years should close.

Local school boards concerned about student performance at their schools should examine the portion of students achieving mastery results on state tests. Frequently, school boards are surprised by how few students in a grade achieve mastery-level performance. In schools with excellent performance, more than 60 percent of the students achieve mastery performance and 85 percent of their responses on tests are correct.

School boards should provide recognition for excellent performance at each school in their districts. They should not wait for the state to provide JITs for their failing schools when they have the authority to intervene.

When school performance lacks the desired results, school boards should consider and use the tried and proven JIT process described thoroughly in this book. Local school district officials and school boards should take action and improve the health of their schools without waiting for others to force them to act.

Citizens, teachers, and school principals should band together to demand JITs for their failing schools. It is a moral failure on the part of every stakeholder in a school district to permit failing schools to continue unchecked in the 21st century.

Essentially, ignoring known and effective interventions for failing schools is like knowing there is an inoculation for a contagious disease and choosing not to invest the funds because a cost-benefit analysis does not indicate immediate payback. If small percentages of our country's citizens had a disease and all of us would have to make sacrifices to save them, we know we would sacrifice because ultimately we would be saving ourselves. In the case of our schoolchildren, ignorance is a disease we cannot afford to ignore. Unattended, a growing plague of ignorance will destroy a democracy.

CHAPTER 11

Public Policy

Helpful and Harmful

Will the United States improve school performance for all children in the first quarter of the 21st century? Most likely, federal, state, and local legislators will continue to tinker with the public education system and attempt large-scale reform for all schools where failing schools are identifiable and well known in every state. Senators Harkin and Enzi (in Dillon, 2011a, b) cosponsored the 2012 Elementary and Secondary Education (ESEA) Reauthorization Act that added a dramatic change in focus and that could potentially reduce the excessive testing required in No Child Left Behind. Their legislation directs the states to focus improvement efforts on the bottom 5 percent of the schools. Schools that would graduate less than 80 percent of their students or those that have less than 80 percent achieve proficiency on state exams represent between 10 and 20 percent of the schools in most states.

Senators Harkin and Enzi have the right idea. Give the states the resources to change how their poor-performing schools function. Focus America's energies on the sick schools where so many students suffer with school leaders and teachers who need the inoculation of new experts to work with them and help them change how things are done. Federal and state legislative committees should focus their efforts on monitoring interventions at failed schools and celebrate excellent schools where large portions of the students achieve mastery on standardized and national exams.

gh schools do not graduate large portions of their
priate students annually, and more than 30 percent of the
rade population who entered 9th grade four years earlier never
duate. These patterns can change with targeted and persistent
intervention by educational experts who have the authorization to
close the school if school personnel fail to cooperate and redesign
what they do.

Schools that are under review for high failure rates among their
students need at least 36 months to show improvements in student
performance results. The power of joint intervention teams (JITs) is
their capacity to monitor changes in structure, process, and results.
JITs need sufficient time to influence schools. School leaders and
teachers need sufficient exposure to their current reality and time to
develop a more desirable reality for their school. They need extensive staff development, patience, prudence, and persistence. At the
end of 36 months, if a JIT cannot motivate and help teachers and the
school leader to change the learning curve for students at the school,
the JIT leader should recommend that the school close and reopen
as a new school with substantially new staff.

The 2010 PEW Charitable Trusts reports clearly document that
most of the students who fail to graduate in the United States live in
urban areas where there is high unemployment and poor health care
and the children are in homes where parents cannot find employment. Many of these children are English language learners (ELL)
or children of color who have been isolated within these schools and
neighborhoods because they reside with families or friends with high
levels of poverty in their homes. Many parents and child-care provid-
ers would benefit from and want programs with effective personnel
to help them and their children be successful learners and citizens.

Many schools with student populations that reflect high levels
of poverty need to redesign the typical day so that teachers and
students experience new relationships. School leaders with students
living with high levels of poverty cannot use the same techniques
that school leaders and teachers use with large middle-class student
populations. The school day cannot be the same. The supports cannot
be the same. Expectations have to move from safety and caring concerns to highly engaged learning activities that drive the development
of leadership, critical thinking, and creativity among the students.

Students in high-poverty communities need to write about what
they know, to create and to draw, to think deeply, and to perform

from their strengths. They need to be free of workbooks and photocopies and fill-in-the-blank questions. They need the enriched curriculum of their highly successful peers in more wealthy communities, and they need to experience, in diverse and appropriate ways, teachers and school leaders who respect them as individual learners.

There are rural and suburban communities that reflect the same high levels of poverty and unemployment, poor health care services, and frequent turnover of teachers at their schools. All of these failing schools have one thing in common: high poverty rates among the students. Poverty is an environment in which failed learning thrives. It is a precondition and not a cause for failure. Like any precondition, it can be treated and neutralized with appropriate care.

Is a new testing program likely to change these conditions? Can testing alter the weak structural support patterns in these schools? Can new federal legislation requiring that teachers and principals be judged and ranked partly by growth in student scores change teaching and learning practices in these schools? No.

The legislative efforts are backward. Failing schools need targeted funds to extend the school day for children. They need to employ JIT members to work regularly with school personnel on necessary changes, improved teaching and formative assessments that inform teaching.

In every state in the United States, there are many outstanding schools where community members, parents, and grandparents offer enriched opportunities to the children. Teachers build upon these enriched environments and celebrate their successful learners. These schools and communities do not need No Child Left Behind and Race to the Top legislations. They are going to have many successful children in their schools. Their real need is to change from proficiency (65 to 75 percent accurate work) to mastery achievement for all of their students. In many cases, these wealthy schools have students performing much better than students in neighboring schools do, and yet, these students with enriched support systems at home and rich learning environments in school are underperforming. Expectations for proficiency are too low for these students.

All schools need incentives to raise the bar and have more children excel and exceed Common Core State Standards (CCSS). The entire structure of U.S. public schools focuses on the normal curve and learning, and the learners have been relegated to the background. Children are permitted to pass through the gates from grade to grade without requisite skills because we have been acculturated to accept mediocrity in our students and ourselves as educators.

The time has come for educators to stop excusing failure and to do something to increase the number of students who master what we teach daily. As educators, school leaders, and teachers, we have to collaborate with all of the resources, material and human, to increase learning and mastery among all of the students we serve.

Federal and state legislators should establish policies that reward outstanding schools and communities by recognizing the great efforts they make to increase excellent academic performance. Intel Scholars, National Merit Award and Nominated students, and students who excel on advanced placement exams with scores of 4 or 5 in math, computer science, living and physical science, statistics, the fine arts, languages other than English, history and global studies, and English literature and writing should feel as highly valued as school athletes do. The excellent schools in the United States will increase if legislators provide recognition and rewards for outstanding accomplishments.

In addition, communities that produce student scholars who score a perfect 800 on SAT subject exams should be rewarded as nation builders. Why not reward those achievements with matching grants to the student and the school for $2,500? The whole nation benefits from what these gifted scholars do.

Once federal and state legislative committees focus public policy on rewards for students and schools that have high-achieving students, policy makers can turn their attention to the remaining 20 percent of the schools in the United States that house more than half of the high school dropouts in the nation. What can federal and state policy makers do?

First, federal lawmakers must understand that, to make a difference, they must distribute tax dollars to where the greatest needs are in ways that require local interventions that work. One of the tried and effective intervention systems in New York State (NYS) and one that other states should employ is the JIT of educational experts. Federal legislation should offer incentives to states that identify failing schools if they establish duties and responsibilities for JITs and monitor the effects of the funded interventions. Too much of what we do in public policy is measure inputs into a failed system rather than verify desired effects.

As the United States makes a slow and hopefully steady climb out of the Great Recession of 2008, the states will need federal funds to ensure that school visitations result in continuous planning, execution of appropriate actions, and better achievement. Governors must be held responsible to prove that trend data from their schools after 24 months of federally funded interventions show improvement, or the state will lose its federal funding for JITs.

Continuous improvement should be the goal. If schools with histories of large numbers of students failing show progress of five to six percentage points of student growth, their funds should continue. Small gains in troubled schools indicate larger successes will follow. Nothing motivates a teaching force to change better than external evaluators who continuously visit the classrooms and monitor the planned changes in teaching.

By bearing witness to how well teachers describe and verify how students engage in learning and demonstrate mastery of lesson content, JIT members continue to influence changes in teacher and school leader beliefs and practices at the school.

The federal government has to focus a two-pronged attack on ignorance in our communities and schools. First, reward excellence, and second, support targeted interventions. In the same vein as the federal government targets funds toward national health interventions to prevent the spread of disease or to reward research, experimentation, and discoveries, schools must be monitored and rewarded. Foundations could easily support federal and state efforts to improve schools and recognize highly successful schools if states would initiate partnerships.

State governments must focus on similar endeavors: rewards for high performance in local schools, targeted interventions for failing schools, and early childhood interventions with highly trained teachers who know how to change the learning trajectories of struggling learners. Simple and direct systems to monitor the outcomes produced by these planned interventions have to be initiated at the state level.

Local school boards, school officials, and local community leaders must convene community summits to establish a renewed vision for the schools that reflects the CCSS and international demands for graduates who can compete in a global economy and marketplace. The school system vision must address the learning expectations and opportunities that the school will offer using technology, challenging curriculum, character development, and service learning.

The quality of support that teachers and students receive will determine how well they master the new and highly competitive demands that the global economy requires. The new global economy does not pay off on effort; it pays off on results (Friedman & Mandelbaum, 2011).

Before American schoolchildren graduate high school, they have to master mathematical skills that reflect preengineering mathematical knowledge. They need living science, earth science, and biology knowledge to be informed voters and consumers. They need a thorough knowledge of their heritage as Americans and of their ancestors to comprehend that the responsibilities they carry were passed onto them from the generations who preceded them. They need to acquire a sense of themselves in history if this democracy is to prevail. In order to achieve these goals, they must be able to read and comprehend, to think and write, to be creative and innovative, and to solve unexpected problems.

How will they learn to do these things? Who is responsible to make this future a reality? We, the local voters, are responsible. We need to hold annual summits to address our future in every school community. There, in individual communities, we capture the diversity and strength of America, and we gain innovation and productivity from our diversity (Page, 2008).

To serve our nation and ourselves, we must ask our school boards: Where is the vision for our schoolchildren that describes what we expect they will be able to do when they graduate from high school? Where is the curriculum aligned with the CCSS? Where is the professional development plan for our teachers and school leaders with the evidence that the plan addresses their needs to help our children? Where are aggregate formative and summative assessment results for our children? What are we doing to improve? Where are our school district goals and strategies? Where are the trend data that demonstrate how we are progressing? What more do we need to do?

Instead of having a tea party or occupying Wall Street, we need to do the local work in our local schools that will make a great difference in our future. As far as politicians and legislators are concerned, we need to hold their feet to the fire of public opinion by sharing broadly their claims and their actions and by requiring them to do what we expect our children to do in school: Learn to solve problems.

Politicians are quick to create legislation to close schools and eliminate teachers and principals if schools have large numbers of failing students who come from families where parents are unemployed. When community health care is poor, infrastructure is weak, and criminals have learned how to move across the landscape and avoid serious harm, punishing teachers and principals with the loss of their jobs will not improve learning in poor communities or the threat to personal safety experienced on a daily basis.

The politicians who cannot get together and solve problems should be removed. Watch the development of the 2012 ESEA in the Senate and the House to determine who should stay and who should leave those hallowed halls. In every state capital, there are politicians who will not or cannot find solutions to our problems because they are not ready for the 21st century and its global economic demands.

They live in the past with assumptions rooted in an America that does not exist. The world economy needs us to solve our debt and revenue problems. Anyone who manages a budget knows that one cannot borrow more than one can pay back in time; a household cannot be sustained if the owners make commitments to buy things on credit and they cannot afford to pay the principal and the interest on the loan. State legislators need to rein in pension and health care benefit costs in a planned and prudent manner and not drive schools into fitful economic crises with state aid cuts (Friedman & Mandelbaum, 2011).

All state and municipal employees should contribute to their pension funds throughout their entire careers. They should become accustomed to employing municipalities agreeing to four-year contracts that freeze the level of municipal investment in health care at a flat dollar amount. In return for fixed costs, the state management team should continue defined pension benefit plans and not include options for 401k plans with all of their internal risks.

At the most local of representative levels in the United States, school boards must build long-term plans for compensation, benefits, and investments in personnel. They have an obligation to examine the needs of students, their current preparation and performance, and the future skills they will need as citizens. School boards with narrow agendas and short-term goals will drag their schools back to the 20th century. No one who attends those schools will thank them in 10 years when they cannot find work.

Vision determines the future. School boards would do themselves and their communities a favor if they were to seek consultants from local colleges to help them build a vision for their students and their community. The vision they hold should serve the needs of the children in the second and third decade of the 21st century.

Our national and state associations of school boards, school administrators, school teachers, and parents and teachers must build new alliances greater than any previous cooperative and more focused than ever before on two critical issues. First, these grand educational promoters must require legislators to reward successful schools and their students for excellent achievements in national and international assessments. Second, they must demand that legislators focus interventional policies on failing schools and their communities. They must cause national policy to provide both financial and expert human resources to failing schools under the supervision of states. They must seek trained JITs, devise monitoring systems, and provide consequences for schools that fail to show improvements during a four-year cycle.

Our nation needs a new and profoundly different approach to schooling, much like Google's approach to information, an open forum for learning and, in a sense, a way to share who we are. Schools must depart from the common metaphor of being places where students take exams to centers of mastery learning, innovative thinking, and creative exploration.

Who will lead the way? In 2009, when Bob was in Mumbai, India, he presented a keynote address to educators at Shri M.D. Shah Mahila College. A member of the audience rose to ask him, "How can we innovate if our government is too slow to change, if we are stuck with an old curriculum and leaders who believe in the old ways?" Bob paused and thought of all the times people had told him to stay where he was—where he was safe and comfortable, where he appeared to know what he was doing. He realized that, if he had followed their advice, he would not be in India at that moment presenting a lecture to several hundred people. Therefore, he replied:

- Do not wait for government or for anyone else to do for you what you can do for yourself.
- Ask yourselves, "What do our students need to know?"
- How will they learn to apply that knowledge?
- How must I change to make their learning possible?

- What else must I change other than myself?
- Go and do it. Ask for forgiveness if you are wrong.
- Never ask for permission to do what is right for children.

American educators, are you willing to change? Will you adopt the CCSS and formative assessments to guarantee mastery of higher-order thinking skills among all of your students? Will you demand the preparation and training necessary to make it possible for students to excel in the CCSS? Are you committed to changing the focus within schools from standardized testing to mastery learning? Will you lead the transformation of American schools to world-class centers of learning? If not you, then who will?

We believe that American educators have the desire to have every child master the CCSS. Superintendents, principals, and teachers need to invest in one another to develop greater capacities to innovate and ensure that all adults and students continue to grow and improve as learners. It is critical that school leaders engage with their communities to discuss the context of education in the 21st century and to develop a shared vision of education in which the diversity among students is seen as a strength that nourishes and sustains our nation. This is the only way Americans can maintain our standard of living and influence in our rapidly changing global environment. The stakes are high. So are the rewards. We believe educators in America are up for the challenge.

References

Ainsworth, S., Prain, V., & Tyler, R. (2011). Drawing to learn in science. *Science, 333,* 1096–1097.

Black, P., & Wiliam, D. (2009, February). Developing the theory of formative assessment. In J. MacBeath & L. Moss (Eds.), *Education assessment, evaluation and accountability, Vol. 21* (pp. 5–31). London: Springer.

Bloom, B. S. (1981). *All our children learning.* New York: McGraw-Hill.

Bloom, B. S., & Krathwohl, D. R. (1956). *Taxonomy of educational objectives:The classification of educational goals by a committee of college and university examiners* (Handbook 1, Cognitive Domain, Ed.). New York: Longmans.

Bourne, R. (1916). Trans-national America. *Atlantic Monthly, 118,* 86–97.

Boykin, A. W., & Noguera, P. (2011). *Creating the opportunity to learn.* Alexandria, VA: Association for Supervision and Curriculum Development.

Briggs, C. L. (2007). Curriculum collaboration: A key to continuous program renewal. *Journal of Higher Education, 78*(6), 676–711. Retrieved December 22, 2008, from Galegroup.com

Cantor, M. (2010). Three economic regions of New York State, the fiscal adequacy of their high schools, and the financial practices of their school district superintendents, school board presidents and school district business officials. Unpublished doctoral dissertation, Dowling College, New York.

Castle Learning Online. (2001). Depew, NY: Castle Software Incorporated.

Chapter 126, Laws of New York. S8142 (2000).

Collins, J. (2001). *Good to great: Why some companies make the leap . . . and others don't.* New York: HarperCollins.

Common Core State Standards, I. (2010a). *About the standards.* Retrieved March 23, 2011, from http://www.corestandards.org/about-the-standards

Common Core State Standards, I. (2010b). *Introduction to math standards.* Retrieved March 23, 2011, from http://www.corestandards.org/about-the-standards

Compton, R. (Writer/Producer). (2011). *The Finland phenomenon.* [Internet video]. Retrieved from 2millionminutes.org

Condron, D. (2011). Egalitarianism and educational excellence: Compatible goals for affluent societies. *Educational Researcher, 40*(2), 47–55.

Cundell, D. R. (2006). Science as a borderless discipline. *The National Education Association Journal: Thought and Action, 22,* 41–48.

Dalley, C. (2012). *Teacher caring, deficit thinking, engagement of students, involvement of parents and the relationship with middle school achievement of at-risk students.* Unpublished dissertation. Dowling College, New York.

Darling-Hammond, L., & Youngs, P. (2002). Defining highly qualified teachers: What does scientifically-based research actually tell us? *Educational Researcher, 31*(9), 13–25.

Davis, B. (2011). Mathematics teachers' subtle, complex disciplinary knowledge. *Science, 332,* 506–507.

Deming, E. W. (1986). *Out of crisis.* Cambridge: MIT: Center for Advanced Engineering Study. (Original work published 1982)

Deming, E. W. (2000). *The new economics for industry, government, education* (2nd ed.). Cambridge: MIT.

Diamond, A., & Lee, K. (2011). Interventions shown to aid executive function development in children 4 to 12 years old. *Science, 333,* 959–963.

Dillon, S. (2011a, October 11). Bill will overhaul No Child Left Behind. *New York Times,* Education Section.

Dillon, S. (2011b, October 21). Senate panel approves bill that rewrites education law. *New York Times,* Education Section.

Domenech, D. (2011, April 2). *A diverse look at the current status of education in the United States.* Dowling College Research Symposium, Brookhaven, New York.

Drucker, P. (1999, March/April). Managing oneself. *Harvard Business Review, 77*(2), 64–74.

DuFour, R. (2011). Work together: But only if you want to. *The Kappan, 92*(5), 57–61.

Esserman, L. (2011, December 12). *New York Times,* pp. D1, D6.

Friedman, T. L. (2005). *The world is flat: A brief history of the twenty-first century.* New York: Farrar, Straus and Giroux.

Friedman, T. L., & Mandelbaum, M. (2011). *That used to be us: how America fell behind in the world it invented and how we can come back.* New York: Farrar, Straus and Giroux.

Fry, R. (2010, May 13). *Hispanics, high school dropouts and the GED.* Washington, DC: The Pew Hispanic Center.

Fu, A., Raizen, S. A., & Shavelson, R. (2009). The nation's report card: A vision of large-scale science assessment. *Science, 326,* 1637–1638.

Fullan, M. (2001). *Leading in a culture of change.* San Francisco: Jossey-Bass.

Gandara, P. (2010). Overcoming triple segregation. *Educational Leadership, 68*(3), 60–64.

Gardner, H. (2011). *Frames of mind: The theory of multiple intelligences.* New York: Basic Books, Perseus Books Group. (Original work published 1983)

Glasser, W. (1990). *The quality school.* New York. Harper and Row.

Goleman, D. (1998). *Working with emotional intelligence.* New York: Bantam.

Harris, D. N. (August 12, 2011). Value-added measures and the future of educational accountability. *Science,* V. 333, 826–827.

Heritage, M. (2010). *Formative assessment and next-generation assessment systems: Are we losing an opportunity?* Washington, DC: Council of Chief State School Officers.

Hord, S. (1997). *Professional learning communities: Communities of continuous inquiry and improvement.* Austin, Texas: Southwest Educational Development Lab, United States Department of Education, Office of Education Research and Improvement.

Hoy, W. K., & Miskel, C. G. (1996). *Educational administration.* New York: McGraw-Hill.

Huntington, S. P. (March 1, 2004). The Hispanic Challenge. *Foreign Policy.* Retrieved October 1, 2012, from http://www.foreignpolicy.com

Huntington, S. P. (2004). *Who are we?* New York: Simon & Schuster.

Issacs, W. (1999). *Dialogue and the art of thinking together: A pioneering approach to communicating in business and in life.* New York: Currency.

Johnson, D. W., & Johnson, R. T. (2002a, Fall). Cooperative learning methods: A meta-analysis. *Journal of Educational Research, 12*(1), 5–24.

Johnson, R. T., & Johnson, D. W. (2002b, Fall). Teaching students to be peacemakers: A meta-analysis. *Journal of Research in Education, 12*(1), 25–39.

Klahr, D., Zimmerman, C., & Jirout, J. (2011). Educational interventions to advance children's scientific thinking. *Science, 333,* 971–975.

Kohn, A. (2006, September). The study of homework and other examples. *The Kappan, 88*(1), 8–22.

Lesaux, N. K., & Kieffer, M. J. (2010). Exploring sources of reading difficulties among language minority learners and their classmates in early adolescence. *American Educational Research Journal, 47*(3), 596–632.

Manley, R. J., & Hawkins, R. J. (2010). *Designing school systems for all students: A toolbox to fix America's schools.* Lanham, MD: Rowman and Littlefield.

Marzano, R. (2003). *What works in schools: Translating research into action.* Alexandria, VA: Association for Supervision and Curriculum Development.

Marzano, R., Waters, T., & McNulty, B. (2005). *School leadership that works.* Alexandria, VA: Association for Supervision and Curriculum Development.

McKinsey. (2009). *The economic impact of the achievement gap in America's schools.* Social Sector Office (Ed.). New York: Author.

Moore, S. (2011, April 1). We've become a nation of takers, not makers. *Wall Street Journal,* Opinion section.

Mullin, A. (2011). *Teacher knowledge of cognition, self regulated learning behaviors, instructional efficacy, and self regulated learning instructional practices in high, moderate and low ELA achieving and moderate need elementary schools.* Unpublished doctoral dissertation, Dowling College, New York.

National Governors Association, & Council of Chief State School Officers. (2010). *Common core state standards initiative.* Retrieved October 26, 2011, from http://www.corestandards.org/assets/CCSSI_ELA%20 Standards.pdf

Noddings, N. (2008). All our students thinking. *Educational Leadership, 85*(5), 9–13.

Ortega y Gasset, J. (2005). *La rebelion de las masas* (22nd ed.). Azcapotozal,Mexico: Alianza Editorial Mexicana. (Original work published in 1920 in Spain)

Otterman, S. (2011, August 9). City students slightly better on statewide exams. *New York Times,* p. A16.

Page, S. (2008). The power of diversity: A different way to think of differences that can benefit problem solving and predictive tasks in education. *The School Administrator, 9*(65), 32–35.

Paine, S. L. (2010). What the U.S. can learn from the world's most successful education reform efforts. In S. Payne and A. Schleicher (Eds.), *Policy paper: Lessons from PISA* (p. 16). New York: McGraw-Hill Research Foundation.

Parkay, F. W., Hass, G., & Anctil, E. J. (2006). *Curriculum leadership* (9th ed.). Boston: Allyn & Bacon.

Passi, G. (2010). *The dimensions of professional learning communities in high schools and student achievement in the New York State English language arts regents exam.* Unpublished dissertation, Dowling College, New York.

Pew Charitable Trusts. (2010, September 28). *Collateral costs: Incarceration's effect on economic mobility.* Washington, DC: Author.

pketco. (Producer). (2010). *Shift happens educational 2010.* [Internet video]. Retrieved October 17, 2011, from http://www.youtube.com/watch?v=SBwT_09boxE&feature=results_video&playnext=1&list=P LE7C810CD23321FB2

Popham, W. J. (2008). *Transformative assessment.* Alexandria, VA: Association for Supervision and Curriculum Development.

Porter, McMaken, Hwang, & Yang. (2011a). Assessing the common core standards: Opportunities for improving measures of instruction. *Educational Researcher, 40*(4), 186–189.

Porter, A., McMaken, J., Hwang, J., & Yang, R. (2011b). Common core standards: The new U.S. intended curriculum. *Educational Researcher, 40*(3), 103–116.

Ramos, J. (2006). *La otra cara de America.* New York: HarperCollins. (Original work published 2000)

Reeves, D. (2011). *The leadership and learning center.* Retrieved from http://www.leadandlearn.com/

Robinson, K. (Producer). (2010). *Ken Robinson: Changing education paradigms.* [Internet video]. Retrieved March 2, 2012, from http://www.ted.com/talks/ken_robinson_changing_education_paradigms.html

Rose, M. (2011). Something in common: AFT steps up efforts to keep common core state standards positive and on track. *American Teacher, 96*(1), 12–13.

Sadler, D. R. (1989). Formative assessment and the design of instructional systems. *Instructional Science, 18,* 119–140.

Schmidt, W. H., Houang, R., & Cogan, L. (2011, June 10). Preparing future math teachers. *Science, 332,* 1266–1267.

Schön, D. A. (1983). *The reflective practitioner: How professionals think in action.* London: Temple Smith.

Schön, D. A. (1987). *Educating the reflective practioner: Toward a new design for teaching and learning in the professions.* San Francisco: Jossey-Bass.

Senge, P. M. (1990). *The fifth discipline: The art and practice of a learning organization.* New York: Currency Doubleday.

Senge, P., Cambron-McCabe, N., Lucas, T., Smith, B., Dutton, J., & Kleiner, A. (2000). *Schools that learn: A fifth discipline fieldbook for educators, parents, and everyone who cares about education.* New York: Doubleday.

Senge, P., Ross, R., Smith, B., Roberts, C., & Kleiner, A. (1994). Moving forward. In *The fifth discipline field book* (pp. 15–47). New York: Currency Doubleday.

Sergiovanni, T. (1994). *Building community in schools.* San Francisco: Jossey-Bass.

Sharma, D., & Kamath, R. (2006). *Quality in education: The quality circle way.* Delhi, India: Kalpaz.

Shonkoff, J. P. (2011, August 19). Protecting brains, not simply stimulating minds. *Science, 333,* 982–983.

Slavin, R. (1988). Cooperative learning and educational achievement. *Educational Leadership, 46*(2), 31–33.

Slavin, R. (1991). Synthesis of research of cooperative learning. *Educational Leadership, 48*(5), 71–82.

Steele, G. (2012). *Teacher and principal perceptions of how transformational and instructional leadership behaviors relate to student achievement.* Unpublished dissertation. Dowling College, New York.

Stiglitz, J. (2010). *FreeFall.* New York: W.W. Norton.

Stone, D. (2002). *Policy paradox* (Rev. ed.). New York: W. W. Norton.

Strong, M., Gargani, J., & Hacifazlioglu, O. (2011). Do we know a successful teacher when we see one? Experiments in the identification of effective teachers. *Journal of Teacher Education, 62*(4), 367–382.

Stronge, J. H., Ward, T. J., & Grant, L. W. (2011). What makes good teachers good? A cross-case analysis of the connection between teacher effectiveness and student achievement. *Journal of Teacher Education, 62*(4), 339–355.

Velasquez, I. (2011). *Latino immigrant student attitudes of their high school experiences in Long Island, New York schools.* Unpublished dissertation. Dowling College, New York.

Vygotsky, L. S. (1978). *Mind and society: The development of higher mental processes.* Cambridge, MA: Harvard University Press.

Wagner, T. (2010). *The global achievement gap: Why even our best schools don't teach the new survival skills our children need—and what we can do about it* (2nd ed.). New York: Basic Books.

Walton, M. (1986). *The Deming management method.* New York: Putnam.

Wang, M., & Holcombe, R. (2010). Adolescents' perceptions of school environment, engagement, and academic achievement in middle school, *American Educational Research Journal, 47*(3), 633–662.

Wiggins, G. (2011, September 28). The common-core math standards: They don't add up. *Education Week,* 22–23.

Wiggins, G., & McTighe, J. (2005). *Understanding by design* (2nd ed.). Upper Saddle River, NJ: Prentice Hall.

Winerip, M. (2011, October 31). No Child Left Behind catches up with New Hampshire school: In a standardized era, a creative school is forced to be more so. *New York Times,* p. A11.

Wu, H-H. (2009). What's sophisticated about elementary mathematics? Plenty—that's why elementary schools need math teachers. *American Educator, 33*(3), 4–14.

Wu, H.-H. (2011). Phoenix rising: Bringing the common core state mathematics standards to life. *American Educator, 35*(3), 4–14.

Index

Porter, A., 88
Poverty:
   failing schools, 26, 157–159, 230
   homework system, 219–220
   public policy impact, 234–235
Preschool curriculum, 146–147
Professional development:
   CCSS implementation challenges,
     127, 128–131
   Common Core State Math
     Standards (CCSMS), 88–93
   for Common Core State Standards
     (CCSS), 21–23
   for formative assessment, 159
   for inquiry-based model, 47–51,
     52–54
   global educational assessment, 25
   leadership role, 166–167
   New York State (NYS), 53, 90
Protestant ethic:
   multicultural education, 188–189
   21st century education, 6
Public policy:
   achievement rewards, 236, 237, 240
   Common Core State Standards
     (CCSS), 123–126, 235–236,
     237–238, 241
   English language learners (ELL), 234
   failing schools, 233–234
   federal funding, 11, 236–237, 240
   instructional/learning interventions,
     229–231
   joint intervention educational team
     (JIT), 234, 237, 240
   leadership role, 240–241
   political support, 239
   poverty impact, 234–235
   school boards, 237–240
   standardized tests, 233, 235
   state policy, 237
   21st century education, 3–5, 8–13
   See also Legislative reform;
     specific legislation/policy
Quality in Education (Sharma and
   Kamath), 66
Quality School, The (Glasser), 80

Race to the Top, 209–210, 235
Ramos, J., 8, 190
Reading:
   Common Core State Standards
     (CCSS), 81–86
   curriculum, 81–86
   Grade 9, 82*t,* 83*t*
   Grade 10, 82*t,* 83*t*
   Grade 11, 83*t*
   Grade 12, 83*t*
Robinson, K., 179
Rubric assessment tool, 144–146, 148
Russian Federation, 22, 90, 91t

Scaffolding, 154, 155–156
School boards:
   instructional/learning
     interventions, 231
   public policy, 237–240
School identification:
   English language arts (ELA)
     curriculum, 63
   formative assessment and, 137
School participation:
   English language arts (ELA)
     curriculum, 63
   formative assessment and, 137
Science, 90
Science:
   formative assessment, 136, 153–155,
     198–199
   instructional/learning interventions,
     220, 221, 223
   student drawings, 198–199
"Science as a Borderless Discipline"
   (Cundell), 80–81
Self-reflective teachers, 13, 32, 42
Self-regulated learning (SRL):
   English language arts (ELA)
     curriculum, 62–64
   formative assessment and, 137, 151
Senge, P., 65
Shared leadership, 67–68
Shared vision, 65
Sharma, D., 66
Shift Happens, 179

CORWIN
A SAGE Company

The Corwin logo—a raven striding across an open book—represents the union of courage and learning. Corwin is committed to improving education for all learners by publishing books and other professional development resources for those serving the field of PreK–12 education. By providing practical, hands-on materials, Corwin continues to carry out the promise of its motto: **"Helping Educators Do Their Work Better."**